Advance Praise for
If Your Life Were a Business,
Would You Invest in It?

"*If Your Life Were a Business* . . . is a deeply reflective *and* practical guide. It has a significant ROI for you and all the stakeholders in your life!"

Charlotte Roberts, coauthor with Peter Senge of
The Fifth Dimension

"An easily digestible guide which affirms the messages of the heart, packaged in the language of the marketplace."

Peter Block, author of *The Answer to How Is Yes,
Stewardship, and the Empowered Manager*

"The Life Business metaphor is transformative. Thinking 'cash flow' rather than 'wealth creation' has changed our family's approach to our life, our money and our giving."

Peter Tavernise, Executive Director, Cisco
Systems Foundation

"Memo to leaders, managers, and business people: If you want to lead your life as consciously and creatively as you manage your business, you should read this book."

Jeffrey L. Moe, Ph.D., Director, Health Sector
Emerging Issues and Development, Fuqua
School of Business, Duke University

"Drs. Eckblad and Kiel's book teaches you how to take charge .of the most essential aspects of your life. It's practical tools and clear concepts will help you to align your behaviors with your values, and put your efforts where your heart wants you to go."

Wayne and Mary Sotile, coauthors of *The Resilient
Physician* and *Marriage Skills for Busy Couples*

"I have spent thirty years coaching physicians on how to balance their lives, yet felt some integrative money-value homework was missing. John and David's book is that super glue."

John-Henry Pfiffering, Ph.D., Director, Center
for Professional Well-Being

"We are seeking a comprehensive and engaing way of thinking through and acting on our future plans. Now, some nine years later, we find that the Life Business framework continues to give us a fresh and valuable way of ensuring that our decisions reflect our personal values and goals."

Sol and Diane Pelavin, President/CEO and
Senior Vice President for Education, respectively,
American Institutes for Research

"The author's insights about how to better the human condition through the business planning cycle will help readers unlock the passion and free up the financial resources required to live happier, more fulfilling lives."

Leigh Morgan, Global Project Leader, Culture and Change Management, GlaxoSmithKline

"The Life Business Program has been a solid base for my personal decision making for a decade. My wife and I have grown individually, and as a couple, knowing that our actions are congruent with our deepest values."

Jeffrey M. Levit, Senior Director, Investment Services Group, Advantis Real Estate Services Company

"The Life Business Program, discussed in this book, gave me a more holistic framework in which to view my life's work and purpose. I am so glad that John and David's new book will now make these ideas available to others who could benefit."

Mary Louise Cooper, Ph.D., Director of Human Resource Development, UNC Health Care

"Everywhere I turn in my work with executives, I see people wanting to establish a broader perspective on their lives. Life Business worked for me, and I am so glad this book is now available to guide others."

Vic Cocowitch, coauthor of *The Turnaround Imperative, the Leader's Guide for Survival in a Turbulent Health Care Environment*

"Today's world demands that we all see and feel our interdependency with the whole and that we all feel accountable for it. Having the courage to give voice to our values and to use our resources to help create the world we want to live in is essential to a life well lived. John and David's insights are a great support to achieving this goal."

Carolyn J. Lukensmeyer, President and Founder of AmericaSpeaks

If Your Life Were a Business, Would You Invest in It?

The 13-Step Program for Managing Your Life Like the Best CEOs Manage Their Companies

If Your Life Were a Business, Would You Invest in It?

The 13-Step Program for Managing Your Life Like the Best CEOs Manage Their Companies

John Eckblad, Ph.D., and David Kiel, D.P.H.

McGraw-Hill

New York   Chicago   San Francisco   Lisbon
London   Madrid   Mexico City   Milan   New Delhi
San Juan   Seoul   Singapore   Sydney   Toronto

LIFE BUSINESS™ is a registered trademark of the
Life Business Development Corporation
U.S. Trademark Registration number 2,887,690
References in the text using the term Life Business are
covered by this trademark registration.

1 2 3 4 5 6 7 8 9 0   DOC/DOC   0 9 8 7 6 5 4 3

ISBN 0-07-141039-2

McGraw-Hill books are available at special discounts to use as premiums and sales promotions, or for use in corporate training programs. For more information, please write
to the Director of Special Sales, Professional Publishing, McGraw-Hill, Two Penn Plaza,
New York, NY 10121-2298. Or contact your local bookstore.

 This book is printed on recycled, acid-free paper containing a minimum of 50%
recycled de-inked paper.

John: For Susie and all our children, Ben, Joshua, Vanina, Chris, Megan, Sarah, Ginny.

David: To Amey and Rachel, the primary customers and most important suppliers of my Life Enterprise. This book is also dedicated to David Hawkins, who continues to encourage me to practice what I preach.

Acknowledgments

The Life Business approach dates back to 1978. Those who have participated in the Program over the years are our essential stakeholders. Since day one, participants' experience and recommendations have led to numerous changes and modifications in our approach. The first people, then, whom we would like to thank are the 3500 plus men, women, and couples, from at least five countries, who have made our work and this book possible through their participation in our seminars and counseling programs. We particularly appreciate the real participants in the Life Business Program on whom the characters of Brad, Betty, Harry, Marc, Mary, Jena, Richard, Cy, Sandy, and Peter are based and through whom, hopefully, the Life Business Program will come alive for our readers.

Along the way many professionals have trained and/or sponsored Life Business initiatives. We particularly want to thank Dennis Bumstead, Wout de Leeuwerk, Stephen Merckx, Steve Targett, Garth Creswick, Susan Rosenthal, Jean Livermore, and Mike Thomas for their belief in this work and their commitment to continual improvement.

This book was made possible with the very valuable contributions of those who supported our project and benefited our work with their significant skills and efforts. From the book's early stages we have gotten help and encouragement from many more people than we can name here. Special thanks go to David Perry, Peggy Payne, Wayne Sotile, and Jeff Moe for their initial and continuing guidance; our agents, Gail Ross and Jenna Land for their consistently positive and insightful support; our sponsoring editor at McGraw-Hill, Mary Glenn, for tackling a challenging project; our editing supervisor at McGraw-Hill, Scott Kurtz, for helping to bring the project to completion; our supportive, yet critical reviewers, Susie Eckblad, Amey Miller, Susan Fowler, and Peter Tavernise; our "spin artist" Peter Guzzardi for helping us find the "hook"; our "art slave" Mark Dubowski; Nancy Tilly and Jill Ridkey for their understanding of the publishing business; our "print meister" Roger Growe; and our patient photographer, Louanne Watley.

John—On a personal level I would like to thank those who have been an abiding presence in my life as I've wrestled with these ideas and their presentation. These include but are certainly not limited to: Susie Eckblad, our children, Martine Eckblad, Thomas and Dorothy Bier, John Aram, Jim Clark, Marie Jose and Charles Profizi, Jean and Rene Klein, Eric and Turid Mongrolle, Jacques and Marie-Charlotte Lescault, Diane and Sol Pelavin, Jerry Levit, Kristine Kersey, Vic and Dawn Cocovitch.

Contents

Preface: Your Money AND Your Life

What successful businesses know that you should too

Of course you would invest in your life if it were a business. The real question is how—how exactly would you invest in your life if it were a business?

Think like a business thinks—put your dreams first.

We live in a paradoxical time—one of material abundance all around us, and, simultaneously, high anxiety about the future. We worry about the direction of the economy, the state of world affairs, and what will happen to our own dreams for a meaningful, satisfying, and financially secure life.

There is a need for another way of thinking about our personal and family dreams and how we can achieve them. This other way should be more in tune with our era of material abundance and personal concern. This way of thinking can be characterized by a simple but radical pair of propositions:

- You will be worse off if you "settle for" financial security as the primary basis of your life plan.
- You will be better off if you clarify and focus your dreams and develop a plan that helps you begin to realize those dreams now.

Believe it or not, if you operated from these two propositions, then you would be operating very much like a successful business.

This book shows how individuals, couples, and families can learn how to more effectively manage their lives and finances by adopting the following practices of the best-run businesses:

- Successful businesses identify and concentrate on what is essential to the enterprise and they spend a great deal of time focusing on the question "What businesses are we really in?"

- Wouldn't we be better off if we had a dependable way to sort out what is central and what is peripheral to our own lives?
- Businesses know that their survival depends on carefully and systematically listening to what their customers and suppliers are saying and then responding effectively.
  - Wouldn't we be better off if we took seriously the concerns and interests of those closest to us?
- The best companies are not afraid to invest aggressively in their plans to build a future, nor are they reluctant to cut their losses when products or programs are not panning out.
  - Doesn't it make sense for us to be more open-hearted about what has the potential to make us happy and more hard-headed about what is not working in our lives?
- Good businesses make sure that their resource commitments will achieve their essential business goals. They do not "save money for rainy days" or retirement; rather, they invest in activities that help them prosper now.
  - Shouldn't we, too, try to match our assets and income to our important goals and plans rather than put money away for some vague future that may never come?

We call this businesslike approach to identifying and pursuing our dreams the Life Business Program.

The Origins of the Life Business Program: John's Story

The Life Business story began 30 years ago with my career as an organization development consultant to a number of large, global corporations including Royal Dutch Shell, ICI (Imperial Chemical Industries), Procter and Gamble, and British Petroleum.

About that time the shift away from production-focused organizations toward customer orientation had begun in earnest. Experience and research was showing that employees who felt supported in taking initiatives responded more appropriately to customers' changing needs. Leading companies were beginning to see the value of helping employees become more empowered and proactive about both business and their own careers.

Like bees to honey, consultants swarmed into boardrooms promoting their favorite employee development strategies. Clients quickly became weary of the newspeak associated with these ideas. My colleagues and I responded by developing an approach based on the language, tools, and thinking of business itself.

Ultimately a 5-day workshop took shape in which the individual applied to his or her own life techniques originally developed for corporate strategic planning and organizational improvement. We encouraged employees to think of themselves as enterprises in their own right, and we helped them identify and plan for the achievement of their most important personal goals. In this way these approaches became deeply embedded in the individual's way of thinking. As we had hoped, our corporate clients found that employees coming out of our workshops responded more effectively to changes in both business and personal situations.

From 1978 to 1988 we undertook Life Business work in several large corporations in the Netherlands and England. We implemented the first ever shop floor career development intervention in the highly unionized United Kingdom manufacturing sector. In another initiative our consulting company had more than 50 of our employees working with Margaret Thatcher's government to help displaced coal miners and steel and chemical workers choose alternative employment opportunities and train for them. During this period more than 3000 people participated in the Life Business Program in the Netherlands, England, France, Belgium, and Germany.

When I moved to the United States in 1981 for family reasons, my professional life continued to be in Europe. My wife and three children lived full time in North Carolina. I bridged these two existences by flying to Europe once a month for 5 to 8 days. Just as things seemed to be going completely our way, things, in fact, came completely apart.

A Time of Loss and Crisis

My wife's chronic illness became acute and rapidly evolved. She died in January of 1989. I was left with a foot each of two continents and needing to make a decision. Because my children were anchored in their schools, I chose to sell my business interests and become a full-time father in the United States.

Having spent nearly all of my work life in Europe, I had very few professional contacts in the United States. At this point my life had literally split at all its critical seams: family, career, and culture. After 3 or 4 months I was beginning to get used to my new routine of not rushing for airplanes, not putting on suits, not going to meetings, and not billing large consulting fees. Then it dawned on me that while my income had nearly ceased to exist, our family's expenses were continuing at a similar or even higher rate.

When I ran our family's financial projections, it became clear that at the present rate of spending, bankruptcy loomed ahead of us, probably sometime during 1998. I knew that if I could reach age $59\frac{1}{2}$, we could probably make it because my retirement accounts would provide new cash flow. But that would not happen until 5 years beyond my predicted bankruptcy date!

The financial planning consultants I talked with were of little help. They were ready to recommend mutual funds and college and retirement savings strategies, but none of them was very interested in helping me think through our precise situation and the daunting perspective of financial collapse. Finally, I realized that no conceivable return on our investments would "float our boat" given our current and projected lifestyle. Like many shortsighted companies facing similar situations, my immediate response was to clamp down on spending everywhere.

In 2 years, we cut costs by 25 percent. My 19- and 16-year-old sons and my 15–year-old daughter were each told how much financial support they could expect from me. Everything else they wanted they had to earn. We scrutinized expenses, compared prices, clipped coupons, and cut corners, and we did right our financial boat. We also discovered it was possible to cut costs down so far that life was not much fun! Our boat was afloat, but did anyone still want to be in it?

A Transforming Idea

I began to realize that I had taken, what in enlightened business terms would have been viewed as, a wrong-headed approach. Our across-the-board cost cutting had gotten in the way of building a positive future. It was out of this cauldron of personal experience that the financial planning component of the Life Business Program was born. We took a new look. Adding businesslike financial management to the same concepts that I had taught my European corporate clients for years, we began to dream like a business.

Prior to my wife's death and while I was still earning a large income, our family had always invested our money in individual and family enrichment experiences like Outward Bound, summer and winter skiing, European travel. Now, after the first shock of adjusting to our new situation, we began to distinguish between what was really important to us and what was not. For the first time we made strategic choices linking our lives and our spending.

Operating under our new dream-driven approach, we got rid of our cable TV contract when it was not basketball season, but we funded other ventures like my oldest son Ben's Chinese language studies and my daughter Vanina's membership in a task force that encouraged low-impact camping in the Russian arctic circle. Ben's hopes of being a competitive skier were underwritten, but he competed in a duct-taped suit rather than in the expensive Lycra worn by his teammates.

Not all our choices were traditional ones, but they worked for us. After his mother died, our second son Josh chose not to go away to prep school as his brother and sister had done, but he decided instead to get a 10-year-old German luxury car which he intensely desired. His commitment was to keep it in the best possible condition with his own funds. For Josh this was a transitional object of major proportions. He now credits that purchase with helping him get through high school. At the end of high school Josh also chose not to go on to college as almost all his friends were doing. Instead he headed to the Caribbean and the challenge of becoming immediately and completely self-supporting.

We freed up funds for some of these ventures by continuing to shop from grocery lists and taking advantage of store specials. Each of us became an expert in getting the best buys in separate realms: groceries, clothes, telephone plans, gasoline, car insurance, etc. In this way, we beat down the costs of everyday necessities and moved any "found money" into life investments that built our future.

The Life Business approach of focusing investment on important dreams and driving down costs in other areas turned out to be the right way to go for our family. Josh, after a successful minicareer of selling jewelry in the islands and much of the southern United States, graduated summa cum laude from North Carolina State University with a degree in history and serious skills in multimedia and the computer sciences. Vanina is an interiors architect in a small architectural firm in Oregon, and Ben and his wife Ginny are living in an exclusive section of Hong Kong where he is a Mandarin-speaking executive in an international real estate firm catering to overseas investors in China.

I'll be the first to tell you that the concepts and tools introduced in this book won't resolve all the challenges of fathering a motherless family. I do believe, however, that these ideas and methods have helped me keep my sanity and enable my children to develop despite the life shattering loss they have had to endure.

Long before my kids got to where they are today, I met and fell in love with Susie and her three children Chris, Megan, and Sarah. Once again Life Business concepts proved their unique value. Susie and I used Life Business as a tool to clarify the important goals for each of our families and the financial requirements of meeting those goals. This work helped us focus directly on who would be responsible for the various aspects of the merged families' expenses. Today, Susie and I continue to maintain separate financial identities while we pursue the achievement of an exciting and challenging collection of shared dreams.

Furthermore, we are pursuing our dreams without the huge financial anxiety I had experienced earlier. When the NASDAQ lost 60+ percent of its value recently and the DJIA (Dow Jones Industrial Average) dropped by over 20 percent, my concerns weren't about the certain loss of money but whether any of our essential dreams had been jeopardized. When I figured out that we could, by stepping outside the box of traditional personal financial planning wisdom, still achieve our most important short-, medium- and long-term goals, I was able to relax. Bottom line, with a businesslike approach to life and financial planning, it is realizing one's dreams, not growing one's money, that is most important. An implicit strategy of "wealth creation" has given way to a conscious commitment to "cash flow management."

In 1991 I met David, my coauthor. David quickly saw the value of the Life Business Program and incorporated its concepts into his consulting practice and into his own life. (David is a well-respected management consultant who helps nonprofit organizations and small businesses address people and strategy problems. David also lives down the street with his wife and 17-year-old daughter.) In the last 10 years David and I have been providing Life Business workshops and counseling to individuals and groups from many different backgrounds: corporate, professional, government, nonprofit, the arts, and education.

What began in Europe as an approach to changing corporate cultures has now evolved into an innovative, systematic, and structured approach to individual life and financial planning. Having lived the benefits of the Life Business Program for nearly a decade, David and I believe it can be of considerable help to individuals, couples and families, organizations, communities, and society at large. We have written this book because we believe Life Business has a big contribution to make to how we think about, plan, and live our lives.

Introduction: The Life Business Program

Your life, the business metaphor, and this book

You can't step into the same river twice, come to think of it, you can't even step into the same river once...

—*Sherman Kingsbury, Arthur D. Little, 1965*

Suddenly you have a choice to make:

- Your company has merged, and you can work in the new headquarters in a city 500 miles away for a higher salary or figure out what else to do to make ends meet.
    - How do you decide what's best for you and your loved ones?
- You have just turned 30 and though you worked for 16 hours a day for 3 years, the IPO netted you more money than you ever thought you would see.
    - Is it time to take a breather and see what else is out there ?
- You've got this great opportunity at work, and you want to do a really good job.
    - How do you put in the necessary time and energy and still have enough left over for yourself and your family?
- Your kids have graduated from college, and you no longer have the same reasons for working so hard.
    - If you didn't continue to work so hard, what would you do instead?
- You woke up this morning and said: "I am going to do something different with my life."
    - What do you do today?

At times like these—and they seem to occur with growing frequency nowadays—"business as usual" just doesn't cut it. You must make a decision. Not choosing is itself a choice. This could be your defining moment: the time to figure out what a successful life means for you. If you really knew where you wanted to end up in 10 years and what was really important to you, you would be in a lot better position to chart your course in any of the situations above.

Life and Financial Planning: The American Experience

What is a successful life? Some say it's living the American dream. If so, what is this dream? Is it 4th of July picnics, 40 acres and a mule, a sense of ecological balance, a golf membership and a full set of Callaway clubs, spiritual peace, an SUV, healthy children, reading the great books, sitting on your front porch as the world passes by, self-acceptance, world travel, living without financial stress? Or is it something else?

As far as dreams go, the only common thread among us may be the idea of having a dream, no matter what it is, and endeavoring to achieve it. Turning dreams into reality effectively and efficiently is surely one of our most significant human challenges.

Ironically, another aspect of the "American experience" works against the achievement of our dreams. We can think of these as the "ought to's" of responsible money management drummed into us as a culture, parent to child, over two centuries of our national experience. These ideas were wired into our common psyche during very hard times. Our ancestors had to tame a frontier, fight wars, live through depressions, and survive wild swings of economic boom and bust. These cultural mandates were designed to provide them and their families with the maximum chance of physical and economic survival. They include:

- It's our patriotic duty to save.
- Gratification today should be delayed for rewards tomorrow.
- You can't be too rich or too thin.
- Whoever dies with the most toys wins.
- Budgets are for curbing your excesses.

Even though the basis for these beliefs may have vanished with the frontier, we still find them embedded in the cookie-cutter type of advice that much of the financial planning industry regularly dispenses. This advice can be characterized as a list of "people shoulds." People should:

- Own their own homes.

- pay off their mortgages as soon as possible.
- stay out of debt—debt is bad.
- save as much as they can—saving is good.
- have retirement income equal to at least 65 percent of their previous employment income.
- invest in equities a percentage of their financial assets equal to 100 minus their age.
- create wealth in order to fund various purposes after they are gone.

These cultural mandates operate mostly at the preconscious level and are defensive in nature. They are dedicated to keeping you from ending up in the poor house or on the bread line, or dependent on your children or society in your old age, or, more recently, they serve as a talisman against the confusions of the age we live in.

These "shoulds" are not geared to helping you live the life you dream about, that life in which you focus on those activities and relationships—that truly represent your uniqueness and your individual gifts, that bring you the satisfactions that are most important to you, that are consistent with your most deeply held values. When faced with life choices such as the ones outlined above, being held hostage to outmoded values and financial concepts can result in a limiting choice rather than an empowering one.

What Successful Businesses Do

Successful businesses:

- start with a systematic process of defining visions, strategies, goals and projects and then work to achieve them; they do not start from a plan to avoid bankruptcy and work backwards.
- emphasize investing, not saving; they invest short, medium, and long term to build the business; they do not put away funds for retirement.
- budget to enable, not limit, their plans.
- commit resources in support of business priorities. While they maintain adequate reserves, successful businesses do not hoard resources against a rainy day.
- assess risk in terms of the probability of achievement, not in terms of stock market volatility.
- manage both the asset and liability sides of their ledgers to achieve chosen goals; they do not liquidate assets when borrowing would improve their bottom line.

- develop powerful analytic, conceptual, and reporting tools to make sure all of these things happen, rather than relying on standard formulas.

This book will enable you to harness the power of business concepts and tools to make positive choices in your life and to finance that life with approaches that are tailored to your needs.

Thinking like a business can lead to a number of financial strategies that you are not likely to hear about from your broker. That's because successful businesses concentrate on liquidity rather than volatility and cash flow rather than "wealth creation." With a similar perspective we are going to challenge you to consider the merits of:

- borrowing even when you may have as much or more than the amount you want to raise already in the bank;
- taking out the biggest mortgage possible and planning never to pay it all off;
- investing in yourself and your family now rather than putting your money aside for retirement;
- seeking, rather than trying to limit, stock market volatility;
- executing your own estate plans now and experiencing the rewards of facilitating others' dreams while you're still alive.

While some of these nontraditional approaches may not fit your situation, others may actually produce the key that unlocks your ability to finance your dreams. The point is that unless you think like a business, you close yourself off from options that may contain the answer to your financial challenges.

Our Goals and Our Methods

It has become commonplace to argue that the cold, hard world of business should put on a more human face. This book stands that conventional wisdom on its head by arguing that we can all be more fully human and much more effective if we pay attention to what successful businesses really do and apply those lessons to our own lives.

Some claim that businesses are narrowly driven, impersonal, and incessantly calculating—the last qualities a moral person might want to have in his or her life. Truth is, much like individuals, some businesses behave immorally, and many do not. As this book makes clear, there is nothing about the techniques and tools businesses use that requires, or even, invites immorality. In fact, quite the opposite is the case. Business techniques and tools can enable us to focus simultaneously on imagination and analysis, feelings and action, hopes and achievements, the short term and the long term, ourselves and others, our desires and our obligations. In other words, business thinking can help us fashion a more holistic life.

The goals of the Life Business approach are, first, to help you establish a more satisfying life and, second, to help you free yourself of financial anxiety. We've chosen a set of businesslike methods for accomplishing our agenda because that's how successful businesses accomplish these same goals. Besides making it possible for you to focus on what's really important to you, these tools and methods offer the additional benefits of being comprehensive, systematic, and repeatable.

It's as Simple as ABC

The Life Business Program is based on the annual business planning cycle (ABC) shown below, which successful businesses all over the world use to guide their long-term planning and development.

The ABC includes four business renewal processes: the Annual Report, the Marketing Report, the Strategic Plan, and the Business Plan. Applied together, these four tools will translate dreams into reality for your Life Enterprise the same way that they do for successful businesses.

The Annual Report tells you where your Enterprise has been in the previous year and how it has performed. The Market Report gives you a snapshot of how your Enterprise is viewed by key stakeholders (e.g., customers, suppliers, etc.) and what present and future stakeholders expect from you. The Strategic Plan evolves a long-term vision for your Enterprise, provides a sense of direction and priorities, and defines the broad-gauged approach you should take in developing your core Life Businesses. Finally, the Business Plan specifies the commitments of resources (energy, time, and money) that will be required to realize your Business development strategies over the short, medium, and long terms. We teach the ABC's of Life Business through a 13 Step method presented with case studies in the next 13 chapters of this book.

The 13 Steps of the Life Business Program

Annual Report

Step 1. Review and reveal your immediate past. Analyze your activities, events, reactions, and expenditures for the past 12 months to identify where your energy and your money are going and where they are coming from.

Step 2. Identify and focus your core Life Businesses. Cluster activities, events, and expenditures into categories that reflect your major commitments. Give these clusters names that capture the specific meaning they hold for you. These clusters are the foundations of your current Life Businesses.

Step 3. Assess your Life Enterprise. Calculate "a return on investment" in terms of life satisfaction for each Life Business and evaluate the overall effectiveness of your current Life Enterprise, paying attention to issues such as high- and low-performing Businesses and overall sustainability.

Market Report

Step 4. Listen to the market. Identify the major suppliers, customers, and other stakeholders for each of your Life Businesses. Assess the messages being sent to you. Assess the trends and events that may be affecting these "markets" in the future.

Step 5. Envision a positive future. Project your Life Enterprise 10 years into the future. Identify changes in your current Life Businesses (e.g., new ventures that emerge, old businesses that disappear or decline in prominence).

Strategic Plan

Step 6. Strategize for success. Plot your Life Businesses on a chart showing their current and future overall value to the Life Enterprise. Based on this analysis, develop a strategy (e.g., leave, maintain, build, create) for each of your current and "new venture" Life Businesses.

Step 7. Set heartfelt goals and identify life-changing projects. Identify promising action projects to carry out chosen strategies for each Life Business (projects involve discussing, feeling, imagining, thinking, investigating, and implementing).

Step 8. Finalize projects and clarify commitments. Create plans and timelines. Make commitments in energy, time, and money for each project.

Business Plan

Step 9. Think like a business. Learn what successful businesses can teach us about the real meaning of concepts like net worth, risk, volatility, budgeting, saving, investing, and cash flow.

Step 10. Budget to enable your dreams. Develop a budget for the short term that enables your projects and reflects your strategies for each of your Life Businesses.

Step 11. Project your future in dollars and sense. Link your budget to projected future revenues and existing assets. Rework both sides of the equation until a viable plan is achieved and is reflected in a modified budget.

Step 12. Manage the way forward. Reorganize your energy, time, and money to make your dreams and projects happen!

Step 13. Pursue a cash-flow agenda in a wealth-creation world. Know what you need to do yourself and when, and for what, you need others' assistance.

Getting the Most Out of the Life Business Program

Last year we were at a birthday party for a good friend, and one of the guests came up to us and said, "I want you to know that the workshop you did with my husband 7 years ago has continued to be tremendously meaningful for him and for us as well. He's still involved with the Program, and it has helped him in many ways."

Life Business is like that. It is not a one-time shot or one-time high. It is a continuous development process. Once you get involved in the Program, its influence grows in your life and changes you in subtle and positive ways. Here are some helpful hints, gleaned from the experiences of past participants, that can help you on your way:

1. Make a commitment. To win the race, you first have to enter. Make a contract with yourself that you will work the Program all the way through.
2. Do it on your own time. We actually encourage you to put our book down if you feel like it. It's really okay if it takes you a while to finish this work. Quality time, not speed, is more likely to get you where you want to go.

3. **Start at your beginning.** Most people start the Life Business Program at Step 1, and we recommend that you do so. Some people, however, make progress quicker when they "follow the money" and start with their "numbers" (Steps 10–13). Once they have made sense of their financial situation, they are then able to ask themselves what their budget says about the nature of their essential Life Businesses; i.e, what is really important to them?

4. **Different strokes for different folks.** The Life Business Program includes topics and activities that fit numbers-oriented people and activities that are for feeling- and relationship-oriented people. As a result, you'll find some of these chapters easier to read than others. Some exercises will seem relevant; others may not give you the return you would like. That's okay.

5. **Stretch yourself.** The paragraph above notwithstanding, you can gain a major benefit and grow as a person by working hard on those aspects of the Program that do not come naturally to you.

6. **Expect resistance.** Business does not always go smoothly. Your life is not always easy, and neither is reflecting on it. Expect that at times you will uncover painful, but ultimately liberating, truths about how you live your life and spend your time. Life Business is about long-term focus and increased life satisfaction, not instant relief.

7. **Overcome your fear of freedom.** Life Business offers you an opportunity to be free of your finances. Yet it is a paradox that many people seem to prefer to dream about a better life and complain about why they can't achieve it. In Life Business we not only dream, but we live our dreams. This implies change. Change is always stressful. Business, after all, is risky, but it is also rewarding.

8. **Practice makes perfect.** Most businesses update their plans annually. Once you have done your first Life Business Plan, you have a framework for thinking about your life that can serve you from then on. Whenever you return to your Plan, you will gain a deeper understanding of the processes and become a more experienced and competent CEO of your own life. But don't worry if you don't return to your Plan. Your Plan will return to you!

9. **Get by with a little help from your friends.** While Life Business is an individual process, it helps to do the Program with other people who can react to your plan as it is evolving. You'll find it helpful to share some of your thoughts and feelings as they come up. You'll also find it helpful sometimes not to share. Your call. Pick people with whom you feel you could be comfortable sharing and whose reactions to your thoughts, feelings, plans, and dreams you'd be interested in having.

10. The metaphor is always with you. Once you have completed the Life Business Program, you will have learned how to apply business planning techniques to your own life. You will have internalized a metaphor that is always available to you when you are facing a key choice or challenge. To make it work for you, just ask yourself, "If a successful business were dealing with a question of this type, how would the CEO handle it?" The advice you get from this type of questioning may be some of the best you have ever gotten, and it may get you out of a rut you have been in with that problem or dilemma. As you work through Steps 1–13, you'll see that we have capitalized key business terms (e.g., Businesses, Personal Net Worth, Saving, Investing, Risk, Budget, and so forth) when these words are being used to help you think through the implications of planning your life in a businesslike way.

Ready, Set, Go

For over 20 years, thousands of participants in Life Business workshops on two continents have benefited from learning how to take a strategic and businesslike approach to the challenge of living. Turn now to Step 1 and begin managing your life like a business.

PART ONE

Annual Report

The past is always part of the present and, left unchallenged, will be a predictor of the future.

Companies take a comprehensive look at the recent past by means of a 12-month Annual Report. This report states the mission of the company, identifies its major lines of business and their costs and revenues, reviews management actions, and evaluates how well the businesses have been performing in terms of profitability, return on investment, innovation, and market share.

Similarly, in Steps 1, 2, and 3 we address the following questions:

- How do you commit your time and money currently?
- How well do these commitments reflect your major interests and your major priorities?
- How satisfied are you right now with the way things are going?

The Process of Review

Assembling, and reflecting on, the information that tells you about your life as it really is

Just the facts, ma'am . . . .

Sgt. Joe Friday, Dragnet, *1950s TV Show*

LIFE BUSINESS TENET

By reflecting on your past year's activities and financial expenditures, you can discover important realities that will give you a new understanding of what you have been doing and what you care about.

The Review Experience: Generating Questions and Awareness

When Jack counted all the pills he was taking on a daily basis, he got more of a sense about how health concerns had become a significant part of what he did and thought about every day.

When Harry did his 12-month Historical Budget for the first time, he was shocked to learn the cost of his life, health, and disability insurance. He began to wonder—do I need all that security? Or would that money be better spent somewhere else?

When Richard reviewed last year's major events, he became aware of the fact that the time he spent in his bible study class was one of his most positive activities. Did this mean that religion and spirituality were becoming more important to him now?

Mary noticed that one of the most time-consuming events of the last year was the effort of deciding whether to take a promotion in another city. Taking the promotion would mean moving her sons out of the school where they had been very happy. She eventually turned the promotion down. Upon review, she began to think about whether she was at a turning point in how she valued her family life relative to getting ahead in the company.

When Bill analyzed his year's activities, he became aware of how one project at work had preoccupied him for months, drained his energy, and distracted him from his family. Now on the other side of this experience, it was as if he had awakened from a bad dream. He wondered how he had let himself get dragged into that mess.

Judy noted how much more time she had spent with her husband last year than the year before. She began to feel more optimistic about where their relationship was going.

Since Helen is very much into the arts, she keeps copies of the playbills and notices from art events she has attended. When she looked at the notices from all the art events that her daughter Rebecca had participated in, she became more aware of how the family's life was both enriched and, in some ways, held prisoner by her daughter's commitments.

The concept of Review is as venerable and important in business (e.g., annual review, performance review, and salary review) as it is in life (e.g., the "unexamined life is not worth living"). The reason that Reviews of the past are so important is that they present an opportunity to examine, and become more familiar with, relevant facts. The Review process also provides the data for evaluating last year's performance.

Review and Evaluation—not visioning, not strategizing, not goal setting—are the foundation stones of the management process. This may seem surprising, but while all of these other actions are also important, they are dependent for their success on understanding the facts of your situation. It is in the Review and Evaluation process that you confront reality and learn the truth about what it is that you do and value in this world.

The purpose of the Review in Life Business is to provoke that confrontation with reality, learn from it, and go forward. This is a version of the Peter Principle—not the modern one that says we will each rise to our level of incompetence, but the earlier, New Testament principle—which holds that unless we build on a firm foundation, our house will not endure.

When we review our lives, like our businesses, we will find things that delight us, events that inspire us, and memories we will cherish. We are also likely to find some things that are disturbing to us, that do not fit with our understanding of how things ought to be. While it is unpleasant to confront failures, shortcomings, and dissatisfactions, ultimately these facts are friendly as well. They will motivate us to search for ways to change for the better. An important psychotherapeutic principle is "All change rests on the complete, if provisional, acceptance of the status quo."[1]

How Businesses Conduct Annual Reviews

Effective corporate business planning is fact-based and multifaceted. It uses financial data, customer data, product data, and data from suppliers in conducting its review. Today's corporations understand themselves by defining profit and cost centers within the enterprise. They do this by clustering activities that are related to financial flows. The corporate annual report shows the "sources and applications" of income and the net change in the company's assets over the year.

Corporate reviews also look at reports of customer satisfaction and dissatisfaction. They consider changes in the customer geographic and demographic base and changes in market share.

Annual reports look at key events: whether or not a product won awards or recognition from experts and consumer groups, or whether there was a damaging product recall required which generated a huge amount of publicity. Annual reports also address one-time charges in accounting for major capital investments, mergers, and downsizings as well as losses due to strikes and natural catastrophes.

Corporate annual reports have become increasingly reader-friendly. In most companies a lot of effort and skill are now being dedicated to producing attractive and informative reports. Today annual reports serve both as communication and advertisement.

Doing the Review

Get the Facts

Our current Life Enterprise has its roots in the past. In the Life Business Annual Report, the past we are most concerned about is the last 12 months. This is not an ironclad time frame, but the past year is usually a good indicator of our major commitments. If the past year has been an exception in some way, it is good to acknowledge that and understand it as a detour, or a new beginning.

In the Life Business Annual Report, you look at the same kinds of things that corporations do, but at an individual level. You look at both your "activities" and "finances." A complete Review requires knowing where your time and money went and came from. From your time commitments you understand your current priorities, and from your financial cash flows you can reflect on the degree of fit between your economic behavior and the rest of your life.

Create a Process of Recollection

Use a variety of sources. Like a successful business, Life Business participants use a variety of sources for the facts that comprise their Review. The most common sources of information about past realities are calendars for the past year and financial records (check stubs, credit card records, etc.). Other common sources of data are diaries and journals.

Reflect on the past year. For those who don't keep diaries or journals a process of reflection may prove very useful. Going over the past year's calendar will bring significant events and emotions to mind. These can be written down as part of the process. Similarly, going over financial records can help you recall what has been important over the past year. For example, looking at a credit card record of plane tickets and rental cars can evoke your memories of an eventful vacation with your family.

Reconstruct the past with others. Once you have gone through the process of personal recollection, you can gather more data by sharing your memories with those who participated in these events with you. For example, if you feel a beach trip with your family was a particularly meaningful event and you have written down your memories of what made it meaningful to you (the moonlit walks, the scrabble game with the kids, etc.), you can take time to review those recollections with your spouse and children and enrich your memory with theirs.

Use a structure to record your information. It's useful to keep in mind the IRS "Record Keeping Guidelines." For each entry try to record who, what, where, when, and why. Your Review should list the activities and finances of your life over the past year, as follows:

- Recurring activities and roughly the amount of time you spent on each activity (e.g., eating, sleeping, exercise, vacations, work, time with family members, friends, hobbies, and pastimes).
- One-time events and activities and roughly the amount of time you spent on each, including significant projects or occasions (e.g., hiking trip with friends, daughter's wedding, building the cabin, etc.).
- Significant external events or periods that gave or took energy (e.g., finishing the big assignment at work, the hiking trip with friends); note the thoughts and feelings associated with those periods.
- Strong internal events or periods that gave or took energy (e.g., worry about daughter's performance in school, stewing over the conflict with your boss, writing in your diary, daily prayer); note the thoughts and feelings associated with each of these events.
- Your relationships: people with whom you spent more or less time than the year before, new acquaintances.

- Your money: where it came from and where it went.
- Your financial and material assets: record any changes from the previous year.

Meet Life Business Program Participants Brad, Betty, and Harry

Brad, Betty and Harry are three typical Life Business Program participants. Below are some snapshots of their Life Enterprises as they began the Life Business Program. These snapshots provide useful background for understanding their 12-month Reviews in Step 1.

Brad, 46, had a horrendous year. His brother died suddenly, and, in the midst of helping his sister-in-law and her family deal with the aftermath of the death, he had to go into the hospital himself for an angioplasty. His wife changed jobs, and, although she likes her new position, it has still been an important adjustment. Brad's younger son is not doing well in preschool. His teacher has concerns about his behavior. At work Brad continues to experience the same chronic stress he felt prior to his operation. As the head of an important department of city government Brad feels constant pressure from the manager and city council to deliver major projects on time and under budget. Also there is a host of sometimes recalcitrant city workers, neighborhood leaders, developers, etc. who have to cooperate—at least minimally—for this to happen. Brad is very well read and quite literary; he has dreams of writing and of owning his own business. Despite being a two-income family, Brad is on a tight budget. He hopes that next year will be better, but right now he is not sure how to make that happen.

By all accounts Betty, 51, is a person of extraordinary energy and drive. Her two bright and talented children are off at college, one about to graduate. She has had some success in wooing her physician husband from his love affair with medicine and 14-hour workdays for the occasional weekend hiking or biking trip to the mountains. She works as a counselor for a nonprofit drug rehabilitation agency and is known for her success in dealing with the most difficult cases. She has also become a trainer of some renown. She has a huge garden she looks after, a Great Dane, and an ailing mother in a nearby city whom she tends to regularly. Still she feels there is something missing in her life. In the last few years Betty and her husband have had a comfortable income, but since her husband started his medical career relatively late in life, they have no real savings. How does Betty figure out how to deal with her "empty nest" feelings and construct a life for herself that is more satisfying?

Harry is a management consultant who works a lot with nonprofit organizations. He has a 15-year-old daughter and a wife who is an aspiring novelist. Harry and his wife are now in their midfifties. Harry has always been somewhat obsessed with work, but he is trying hard to achieve more balance in his life. Harry has a cholesterol problem, so he watches his diet and gets plenty of exercise. Harry makes a good living, but still his family lives somewhat beyond his income. This was not a problem as long as the market kept rising. Now, with a prolonged downturn, the family's lifestyle will have to change. Harry has been working with the Life Business Program for several years and feels he is moving ever closer to the life he wants to lead, but he still needs to make some major decisions if he is going to break through to a new level of personal satisfaction.

Assessing Key Events, Time, and Money Allocation

Brad, Betty, and Harry were each given the following prompt: "Step 1. Review and reveal your immediate past. Analyze your activities and expenses over the past 12 months to identify where your energy, time, and money are going and where they are coming from."

Below we show a partial list of Brad and Betty's key events for the last year and Harry's time and money numbers. In the Life Business Program all three participants would report on both their activities and their numbers.

Selected Key Events for Two Life Business Program Participants

Selected Key Events for Brad	*Selected Key Events for Betty*
Dealing with death of my brother	Took mountain bike trip with husband
Got counselor for older son	Frequent diary entries about the fact that son does not write more about what is going on with him at college
Process of recovery from my heart operation	Several counseling patients died of AIDS this year
Wife got new job	Got good feedback on training program I designed
Completed the Amity Square Project for the city	Daughter decides to go to the school of social work

(continues)

8

Selected Key Events for Two Life Business Program Participants (*continued*)

Selected Key Events for Brad	Selected Key Events for Betty
Read several novels	Squirrels got in the garden again and destroyed plants I had just put in
Had a good family vacation	Mom had a ministroke
Spent time sending thank-you cards and speaking with people, thanking them for the support I got during my illnesses	Buyout of husband's practice caused him to be preoccupied with the financial arrangements because he served on the executive committee
Doctor's insistence that I lose weight and get more exercise	Trip to NY with girlfriend
	Watched TV a lot in the evenings when husband is not home

Time and Money Review of Life Business Program Participant Harry

Time

Exercise/jogging, walking:	3–5 hours per week
Work:	45–60 hours per week (out-of-town trips: 4)
"Vegging" in front of the TV:	3–5 hours per week
Time with spouse (walks, dinners, etc.):	3–5 hours per week
Driving with teenage daughter:	2 hours per week
Vacation:	15 days (5 days with wife's family, 5 days with my sister, 5 days hiking)
Training group:	10 days, 1 day per month
Continuing education:	5 days
Community service:	5 days
Lunches etc. with friends:	2 hours per week

(*continues*)

Time and Money Review of Life Business Program Participant Harry   (*continued*)

Expenditures in Dollars

- Total taxes 31,000
- Mortgage 17,000
- Savings (IRA) 15,000
- Medical 9,500
- Vacations 8,500
- Food 8,000
- Insurance 7,000
- Autos 6,500
- Domestic help 5,000
- House repair (heater) 3,500
- Utilities 3,000
- Clothes 2,500
- Restaurants, entertainment 1,000
- Miscellaneous child expenses 1,000
- Other 2,500

Total expenditures $121,000

Income in Dollars

- From consulting 94,000
- From stock sales 27,000

Total income $121,000

Changes in Liquid Financial Assets in Dollars

- Appreciation of portfolio 14,000
- Savings 15,000
- Liquidation of stock .... (27,000)

Net change in financial assets ... +$2,000

When you look over these key events from Brad and Betty, you begin to get a sense of what was important to them in the past year, what sustained them, and what took energy from them. These insights will be very important in defining and assessing their Life Businesses later.

When we look at where Harry's time and money went last year, we begin to understand his situation more completely. We see that Harry has been living

10

beyond his current income, but his financial assets were, until recently, buoyed by rising stock values. The amount of time he spends on work compared to the amount of time he spends with his family might be a cause for concern. These are just some of the patterns that begin to emerge when we do this kind of analysis.

These examples show that what we get from a Review is a heightened awareness about the state of our lives. We encounter the facts and gain a better idea of where our pains and joys come from. Most importantly, like Jack, Harry, Richard, Mary, Bill, Judy, and Helen at the beginning of this chapter, we begin to form questions that can lead us ultimately to significant improvements in how we feel about our lives. It all begins with gathering and reflecting on the facts.

Henry David Thoreau: A Pioneer of Life Review

The great American essayist and thinker, Henry David Thoreau, is the "patron saint" of Step 1, the process of life Review. According to the jacket of his famous *Walden* in the New American Library edition, "Henry David Thoreau . . . was . . . an epitome of the Yankee spirit. In March 1845, he set out to live in a new way . . . and retired to Walden Pond where he lived in a hut of his own construction. There he read, wrote, and made friends of beasts, birds, and fish, recording his fascinating woodland life in his book *Walden* in 1854."[2]

While his conclusions about what makes life worth living might not be agreed upon by all, he did demonstrate the value of paying attention to your life. Specifically, his writings show the meaning that can be derived from reflecting on how one invests one's time and money. Not only did Thoreau keep detailed records of how he spent his time but also of the money he earned and spent. The first chapter of *Walden* is dedicated to "Economy." His expenditures for 1845 were:

House	$28.13
Farm	14.73
Food	8.74
Clothing	8.41
Oil	2.00
Total	$62.01

Thoreau immediately grasped an essential Life Business principle that your life experience is very much bound up with how you spend your time and money, how you spend your time to earn your money, and how your beliefs about time and money affect the quality of your life. In his perhaps overly meticulous record keeping and exquisite reflection, Thoreau set the standard for an examined life and the process of Review.

Tips on How to Do the Review

You do not have to go into the woods as Thoreau did, but you should set aside whatever time it takes for your Review. Like all parts of the Life Business process, the benefit you gain from it will be proportional to the quality of effort you put in. Don't try to do your Review in one afternoon. Set aside several periods of time over a week or two so you have time to recollect, reflect, and reconsider.

Gather the data systematically. We find that tax time is a good time to go the extra mile and reconstruct an account of expenses for the past year. Do this as a matter of course, and the data will be there when you need them. Of course, if you use a computer to write your checks and deposits, you have those expenditures and income figures at the press of a button. Many people find keeping a journal or diary a good way to track their experience over time. Others like to keep an ongoing scrapbook that will remind them of significant events. Either way they have a ready source of data to spur their reflections. Dreams, poetry, and letters can be a source of information for your Life Business Review if you make the effort to collect them as you go. Some people use a sampling approach to keep track of their time. This might include keeping detailed notes on what you did for a typical week, such as writing down your activities for each half hour.

Be prepared for the emotional impact of the review. Ups and downs are normal. Of course businesses have their ups and downs, too. Some downs are attributable to the business cycle, some to competition, some to unique external events, some to declines in performance. But businesses that do not keep good track of their ups and downs are clueless about how to improve their performance. Those businesses that fail to gather data about how they have performed in the past are much more likely to be among the thousands of businesses that fail on an annual basis. Personal failures are likely to persist as well if we don't do the hard, but ultimately rewarding, work of the Review.

Face up to and then try to understand your shortcomings, but do so with a sense of humor. Nobody's perfect. When you find out from your Review that you spent $12,346 more than you took in last year or you spent less than 15 minutes a day talking with your spouse or, despite your best efforts, you gained 10 pounds instead of losing the 10 you promised yourself you would, you may well feel let down or disappointed in yourself. Feeling that way is okay; it's part of the process.

However, once you have experienced that disappointment, you are in a position to play Life Business detective. You can investigate more dispassionately why you did not achieve the results in your life you had hoped for last year. Or maybe you find out that you hadn't really hoped for any particular results. To help you get through the hard part, you may want to use some humor. For example, you might want to take a David Letterman approach by listing your "top 10 screwups for the year past." Make sure you quickly follow this list with your "top 10 finest moments." Businesses know that they have little chance of achieving what they haven't envisioned.

The best businesses know that realistic goal setting is dependent on a thorough understanding of the conditions that affect their past performance. The result of exploring your annual results will give you a more realistic understanding of the conditions affecting the success of your Life Enterprise, and put you in a better position to set goals and make plans that are more realistic.

Understand your own approach to responding to evaluation—self-evaluation and the evaluation of others. Some people are hypercritical and perfectionist. When they were students and they got a report card that was all A's and one A – they would obsess for days and flagellate themselves over the A – rather than celebrate and appreciate their hard work. Some people are in denial. Upon getting a report card that is all D's they will say: "The teachers had it in for me," or "No problem, I'll do better next term." Be aware of your tendencies to overreact or underreact to the Review. One well-regarded psychotherapist has formulated a multistage process for learning from experience. The first three stages are: awareness, acknowledgement, and acceptance.[3] Through the data-gathering process we can become aware of things we need to take into account about how we are running our Life Enterprise. By a process of reflection we acknowledge certain facts, and through our capacity for self-forgiveness we can accept these truths as a basis for going forward in our lives.

Dealing with the Emotional Impact of the Review

Here are some additional tips for dealing with the emotional impact of the review:

- Have someone to talk to. If you, by nature, tend to blow off bad news, find a friend who will hold your feet to the fire. If you are self-critical to the extreme, pick a friend who will remind you of what you have going for you and can help block your destructive self-criticism.
- Spread the Review out over time so that you can assimilate new learning.
- Do the Review with a friend who is also doing the Review so you can compare notes, celebrate, commiserate, and support the process.
- Better yet, do the Review in conjunction with the Life Business Program so you have the support of the instructor and the Program as well.

Enriching the Review Process
with Additional Questions

The Life Business Program is constantly evolving, and we are constantly looking for new ways to help people do a better job of focusing and balancing their lives. In recent years organizations have turned to at least three new approaches to help them grow and develop more effectively. These approaches are: Appreciative Inquiry,[4] Assets-Based Assessment,[5] and Future Search.[6] Life Business Program participants who want to enrich the Review process may make use of these ideas.

Appreciative Inquiry emphasizes the importance of celebrating the life-giving forces of the enterprise and building on those instead of focusing on the organization's problems. Organizational developers operating out of this model conduct surveys that ask the questions: "When, in the past have you felt most engaged, productive, and vital? What helped you achieve that state?" These questions are a variant of the Review question that Life Business asks, "What activities gave you energy in the past year?" Appreciative Inquiry focuses on the most intense experiences of effective functioning and for this reason might be usefully added to a program of Review.

Assets-Based Assessment emphasizes the resources that exist in communities that can be used for development. Like Appreciative Inquiry, Assets-Based Assessment argues that it is better to work with the positive rather than focus on deficits when developing a community. When assets-based developers go into communities, they do extensive interviews to uncover the talents of people living in neighborhoods along with the organizational and physical assets that exist in a neighborhood. Applied to Life Business, we could add to the Review process questions such as:

- Which of my own skills and abilities did I use that made me as effective as I was this year?
- Who were the individuals that helped me most last year and how did they do that?
- What other factors aided me in the last year to be as effective, energetic, and constructive a person as I have been?

The Future Search model is a highly developed, interactive intervention process used in organizations and communities. Particularly in its initial stage, the Future Search process offers an interesting dimension to the Review process. Participants are asked to list the events in the society, the community, the nation, and the world which have, over the last 10 years, impacted the issue they are working on. You may want to enrich your Life Business Review by noting the local, national, and global events that made an impact on you this year. In this way you can be more aware of the context of your Life Enterprise.

Exercises for the Reader

1. Do your own expense summary for the past year. (See Appendix A for possible expense categories.) Also identify sources of income and changes in assets.
2. Review major events for the past year. Use your calendar to identify the major events of each month.
3. Create a chart of recurring events either by keeping detailed records of your activities for a typical week or by going back over your calendar. List the daily and weekly recurring activities (e.g., exercise, meals, sleep, doctors' appointments, time spent at work). Your chart should show how much time you spent on these activities each week.

For more Review exercises and discussion visit our Web site at the following address: www.lifebusiness.com.

The Benefits of Committing to a Process of Life Review

If you put this book down right now and do not read another word but incorporate Review in your life, you will have immeasurably enriched your life prospects. From now on you will be more in touch with your temporal, emotional, and financial realities. You will have considered the things that give you energy and those things that drain life from you. This awareness cannot help but work on you unconsciously and gradually lead you toward more self-enhancing choices and away from life-denying ones.

However, you'll get a great deal more benefit if you next use the Review process to consciously focus and actively shape your Life Enterprise for the better. "What businesses are you in?" This is a fundamentally important question, but the answer is not entirely obvious for either all readers or all businesses. Getting the answer wrong can have serious soul-denying consequences. Getting the answer right builds a foundation for focusing and balancing your life and finances. The good news is that getting the answer right depends in part on your just completed Review of your recent past experience. Read on!

Notes

1. Paraphrased from a statement at a workshop by Carolyn Lukensmeyer-Hirsch in spring 1979, Wrightsville Beach, NC.

2. Henry David Thoreau. *Walden.* Signet Classics Edition, New American Library, 1960. See the first chapter, on "Economy."

3. Jean McLendon. *"The 7& A's" Congruent Leadership Workshop Notebook.* 2002. Go to www.satir.org for more information.

4. Jane Watkins and Bernard Mohr. *Appreciative Inquiry: Change at the Speed of Imagination.* John Wiley & Sons, 2001.

5. John Kretzmann and John McKnight. *Building Communities from the Inside Out: A Path Toward Finding and Mobilizing a Community's Assets.* ACTA Publications, 1997.

6. Sandra Janoff, Marvin Weisbord. *Future Search,* 2nd ed., Berrett-Koehler, 1996.

Discovering and Naming Your Life Businesses

The fabric of your life is in fact a quilt

Umpire One: I calls 'em like they are!

Umpire Two: I calls 'em like I sees 'em!

Umpire Three: They ain't nothin' till I calls 'em!

LIFE BUSINESS TENET

What your commitments truly are is best shown by your personal calendar and your checkbook register. By analyzing last year's activities and expenditures, you can sort out what your commitments have been and begin to determine whether these are right for you going forward.

Few people today invest in their lives so much as they just spend them. Even if they aren't living lives of quiet desperation, they may come perilously close. Many feel hurried, harassed, swept along by the flow of everyday activities: coping with challenges at work; ferrying, clothing, feeding, counseling the children; taking care of aging parents. Many of us certainly do not feel in a position to control events.

Part of the problem is an inability to understand at any given time what's important in our lives. Is a specific commitment or obligation central to your purpose? Or is it really more of a forgettable "blip" that just ends up costing you your valuable energy, time, or money? When we can make these judgments, our sense of control and well-being is enhanced.

In business, priority setting is evident in the definition of a company's products and services. If an event affects the long-term profitability of a product or service, it is important; if not, it is really not worth an investment of energy, time, or money.

In the Life Business Program, you obtain greater focus by using the information you collected during the Review process to help you define the core commitments that you want to pursue in your life. Ultimately, you will define these core commitments so clearly that you can call them your essential "Life Businesses."

The Importance of Whole-Brained Planning

A basic principle of Step 2 is using all parts of the brain. This process has also been termed "whole-brain thinking."[1] Increasingly, smart businesses are recognizing that they need to be both analytic and creative in defining themselves and in planning.

They use methods that emphasize data, numbers, and analysis to be in touch with the reality of their situation. They also use methods that are more holistic, interpretive, and relational to define, understand, and present themselves in a way that makes continuing sense to themselves and their customers.

These days you will see technical organizations training their bench scientists in creative approaches to problem solving. On the other side of the ledger, you will see freewheeling, nonprofit arts organizations turning to MBA-type analytical techniques to help them gain control of their finances so that creative work can continue.

In the Life Business Program we try to embody this principle of *whole-brained planning*. In order to achieve an effective clustering of activities that leads to a definition of commitments that are both meaningful and verifiable, we use a right-brained collage technique called the *Big Picture* which relies more on an intuitive understanding of our participants' life situations. We then test the product of this work with a more analytic technique called *Got-Gone Analysis,* based on "where got—where gone" (or sources and applications) accounting methodology.

It is important that the results from left and right brain approaches add up to a coherent whole. In the early 1980s an annual report from Chrysler argued that the company was bouncing back from a bad year; however, the cover showed its new model located in the middle of a desert. Despite the beauty of the desert, the visual message sent was that the company continued to be in a particularly harsh business environment. This visual message undercut the upbeat text, charts, and graphs inside the report. Which message were investors to believe?

The value of looking at one's life from both analytic and intuitive approaches is that we get perspectives on the whole that can then be built up into a more comprehensive, accurate, and credible picture. If we don't use both sides of the brain, we can wind up with a muddled self-understanding that does not play well in the marketplace.

Developing the Big Picture

Annual reports in business are visual documents. They have illustrations and photographs in addition to numbers and facts. In a well-designed annual report these features communicate the main message that senior management wants to get across to shareholders. In the Life Business Program we encourage our participants to "get visual."

Once participants have made their lists of the past year's significant activities, we ask them to put these data together for themselves and create their personal "Big Picture." We give them an assortment of popular magazines, a pair of scissors, a pot of glue, and a large sheet of poster paper. We ask them to cut out images and words that are particularly meaningful to them and create a collage that represents the year just gone by.

In these collages, participants make meaning of their past year. In explaining their work to other workshop participants and getting comments, participants find significant connections that they may not have seen initially. They also begin to create pictures of their hopes and dreams.

One participant told us that in her collage she evoked the vision of the home she wanted to create and felt she was missing. She took the poster home and hung it in her office as a reminder. A year later she found that home, bought it, and decorated it almost exactly as she had done in her collage. This is a tangible example of how an exercise in literally "picturing" one's dreams can actually help people shape their future lives.

In Brad's case, his Annual Report was punctuated with images of clocks and time. His own brush with death and dealing with the death of his brother made him acutely aware of the time we all have or don't have.

Betty's Annual Report had white space at the center of her collage—a void that was asking to be filled. Mary's Report showed a skyscraper, which represented her career achievement, but also a small child who she said symbolized her baby steps toward getting interested in finding a new primary relationship. Richard's Annual Report showed a rocket launching, symbolizing the energy that was liberated for new activities after the sale of his family business was finalized.

The collage produces a deeper, more personal understanding of the meaning of life events and challenges for each person. It also helps us get a more substantial grip on the intangible aspects of our lives and so creates a more complete understanding of the current state of our Life Enterprise.

The collage is an intuitive way of clustering and grouping the major activities of the past year. Collages often introduce categories that describe the major activities of one's year, such as "getting adjusted to the new job," "dealing with mother's terminal illness," "helping the eldest choose a college," "staying fit," "quitting smoking," "falling in love," "making a push on the novel," "the ups and downs of the stock market."

The collage is a particularly good visual method of creating meaning from the data of participants' Life Enterprise Review. Other people may benefit from a more tactile or auditory approach. We have had workshops where we have given people art construction materials and asked them to create three-dimensional pieces that describe their lives. Those people who are enthusiastic about music may find it congenial to create a tape that captures the major themes of their life. The essence of this approach is to find a nonverbal, nonlinear method to express your feelings and reflections on your life's data, thereby tapping into the creative side of your brain.

Charting Gots and Gones

We also use the mathematical analytic side of our brains in defining our Life Business. Accountants chart cash flow in and out of the business. In Life Business we translate cash flow into the intuitively meaningful term of *life energy*—that feeling of a sense of motivation, meaning, and power in participants' lives.

When looking over the lists of the past year's significant activities, participants are asked to distinguish between those which gave them energy—"The Gots"—and those which "cost" them energy—"The Gones." In doing this, certain entries naturally cluster together in common themes as in Harry's example below.

Typical Life Business participants may have 5 to 10 meaningful clusters with unifying themes around such topics as child care and rearing, hobbies, travel, spirituality, business ventures, spousal relationships, and the like. Participants sometimes go another step and label their Gots and Gones using accounting terms that make these entries even more meaningful. For example, the label "windfall profit" might be used when there is no "gone" associated with a "got," such as a "free gift" of energy. Another example is when the words "lost" or "stolen" are used, as in "Where did all that time in front of the late night TV go?"

Naming Your Life Businesses

Giving each "unifying theme" a name that is particularly meaningful to you is an important part of the process. Harry realized that a significant portion of his time

Part of Harry's Got–Gone Chart

Energy "Got" Events	Energy "Gone" Events	Unifying Themes
Walking every day and taking hiking trips	Buying, and taking, two cholesterol medicines and many heart-protective vitamins	*All of the activities involved in working to maintain my health and well-being*
Beginning a meditation practice	Dealing with acid stomach	
Getting a good night's sleep	Reading the Harvard Heart Letter	
Feeling successful when I have lost some weight	Doctors' appointments and health insurance filings	
	Getting counseling for high anxiety	
	Watching my weight rise after I have lost some weight through dieting	
	Dieting	
	Worrying about health matters	

(maybe 10 to 12 hours a week) was devoted to worrying about and doing things to prevent the onset of heart disease. (He has very high cholesterol.) His time, energy, and financial expenditures include health insurance, running shoes, doctors' appointments, and a whopping pharmacy bill. This was clearly a major commitment. He called this cluster of activities Harry's Health Maintenance Organization. The name captured the essence of the business for Harry: staying healthy so he could enjoy life. Therefore, it was a very powerful label for, and description of, that Life Business.

In the Bible's book of Genesis we are told that Adam's job was to name the animals. By doing so, he took the first step in assuming dominion and stewardship over life in the Garden of Eden. In the same way discovering and naming your Life Businesses is a first step in rising above the chaos of everyday experience and becoming the CEO of your own life.

The authority for our approach, however, is not biblical. It only goes back to Ted Levit, Harvard Business School professor and a leading business strategist in the 1950s. Levit taught us that organizations will become and remain vital and robust only if they concentrate on identifying and developing their core or key businesses.

What Businesses Are You In?

Earlier in this chapter we talk about how this step will help you gain focus in your life. Here is where we deliver on this promise. There is an important mental shift that takes place as we identify our key Businesses. The noise and confusion of daily life quiets down. Our major commitments move into the foreground. What is less important fades away. On the financial side of things, it becomes possible to differentiate investment in core Businesses from expenses for basic Support, and both of these from expenses that are simply "fudge," that is, those expenses which contribute no enduring value to our Life Enterprise.

By sorting the truly important activities from the merely convenient or habitual, you are beginning to take control of your own life. In the words of two current self-help gurus, Life Business participants are better able to "put first things first"[2] and not "sweat the small stuff."[3] In identifying and naming the activities to which you commit your energy, time, and money and which give energy back to you, you are making significant progress toward answering the fundamental question: What (Life) Businesses are you in?

These Life Businesses may be any pursuit important to you: hobbies, relationships, work or professional activities, spiritual or psychological goals. As we shall see, these Life Businesses may be net energy gains or net energy losses. Not all Life Businesses are positive and forward-looking, nor are they necessarily freely chosen. Some are imposed by circumstances and may be challenging (e.g., looking after a dependent close relative to whom actual caregiving is very difficult).

As a result of this process of creating broad themes and activity clusters, participants come to see themselves as having certain critical or core commitments in their lives. They then come to understand how these commitments intertwine and interact to create their unique Life Enterprises.

Life Businesses We Have Known

The classic definition of the mission statement of a business has three aspects: (1) it identifies the goods or services the business provides; (2) it specifies the customers in some way (e.g., demographically, geographically); and (3) it makes a claim for what is distinctive and attractive about that business in terms of its scope, quality, cost, or some other competitive dimension.

We encourage Life Business participants to capture the essence of their Businesses with meaningful titles and then describe the theme or cluster of activities that fit under that banner line. In the description they create, we challenge them to declare what makes that Business uniquely important or special to them.

The Business lists of Harry, Mary, and Sandy that follow show typical results of this process. While their Businesses tend to focus around social roles of parent, spouse, and friend and the major categories of vocation, spirituality, health, etc., they also have a distinctive quality and are deeply meaningful to the individuals who "own" them.

Harry's Life Businesses in His Own Words

1. Connections Unlimited: The Business of maintaining and developing intimate relations with my wife and 15-year-old daughter, my close relatives, and a wide circle of longtime friends and clients. This includes staying in good communication with my wife so that we don't lose track of each other's concerns, scheduling regular activities with my daughter and keeping abreast of her thoughts and feelings, maintaining regular phone contact with close relatives like my sister, and making periodic contact with that wider circle of old college buddies and other friends who are important to me. This Business includes the social roles of father, husband, friend, brother, and stepson.

2. HHMO (Harry Health Maintenance Organization): The Business of preventing heart disease (I have congenitally high cholesterol) and maintaining good physical health through exercise, preventive medication, good diet, and by trips to dentist, doctor, ophthalmologist, etc.; also includes funding my wife and daughter in their health activities.

3. PP&G (Personal and Professional Growth) (I know the ampersand is in the wrong place, but I like it better between the P and G): The Business of developing myself, and my abilities, through activities such as seeking personal counseling, skills training activities, and taking on projects to keep me on the leading edge of my field.

4. TGAL (Think Globally, Act Locally): I like doing things that make me feel that I am contributing to the solution of problems in my community and in my state. These activities include charitable and political donations, pro bono activities in my professional work, and the development of paying projects that address societal problems or use my consulting skills to help those organizations which do.

5. IGUANA (I guana be me): I have a small, but persistent, Business that concerns doing what I like to do for no other reason than I like to do it—hiking and walking in beautiful places; reading magazines about current events, philosophy, government, and politics; cooking; playing bridge; foreign travel; going out to plays, music, museums; checking out the world of art; following our university's basketball team; watching late night TV; etc. (P.S.: The "iguana" comes from a great image in my "Big Picture" of an iguana sunning himself on a ledge overlooking a beautiful rain forest.)

6. HEWT (Have Ear, Will Travel): This is my consulting Business, which is actually the biggest consumer of my energy and time. I spend my time helping organizations solve problems and seize opportunities by learning to work in more creative and productive ways.

Mary's Life Businesses in Her Own Words

1. SOUL FULL ME: Spiritual transformation, meditation, women's group, attending personal development programs, aroma therapy, massage, a category that never existed before in my life where I take care of myself.

2. THE GUYS: My two sons. It takes time to really listen to what they are saying. I want them to say, "she really hears us, she respects our opinion, she backs off appropriately." I realize this is a critical time for them and for our relationship. I want to do it right.

3. MAKIN' A LIVIN': This is where I figure out what I really want to do versus what I think I have to do to make the money I think I need to have. I need to analyze my personal financial situation, analyze my portfolio, and analyze my savings. It really clicked for me to analyze my personal life as a business because I know how to pay attention to business. I just haven't given myself permission yet to pay the same level of attention to the rest of my life.

4. THEM TOO!: I became custodian of my 90-year-old grandmother, when my mother became too ill to look after her. This is a major energy, time, and money commitment. It is not what I would choose to do but, living where I do, I am "it."

5. CP/PS (Consulting Practice/Place to Stay): The work here is exploring various locations where I want to live and work in the future after I leave the corporation—like the mountains. I hope to go out on my own as a private consultant. I need to explore this possibility as well.

6. MSO (My Significant Other): Having been unmarried for more then a decade with an exclusive focus on my job and my two sons, I think it is time for me to begin thinking about finding someone to share the rest of my life with. I am not excited about dating again, but I do need to think about this.

Sandy's Life Businesses in Her Own Words

1. BEING & BECOMING: The quest to continually identify and exercise the essential me, professionally and personally.
2. CALL ME MOM: Continue in the manner I've begun to be a mother and stepmother to all my children.
3. REALIZING POTENTIAL. More than being a Mom in a day-to-day sense, being there as the children, in turn, seek support on their own journeys.
4. MRS. P., WIFE & PARTNER: To balance on a day-to-day basis my marriage commitments and hopes with the rest of my life.
5. OUR TIME: A special time sometime in the future for Peter and me to live out our shared dreams.

Defining the businesses you are in is not always easy, in business or in Life Business. Take, for example, the situation of one of our business clients, a rapidly growing start-up that specialized in computerizing the government paperwork that school systems have to fill out for all special education needs. Originally, the client was in the business of selling software to school systems throughout the country. In the process of doing this it realized that with the information it was collecting it could help the school get Medicaid reimbursement for eligible students. Since it could charge the schools a per child fee for handling the reimbursement, it suddenly became more profitable to give the software away in exchange for the contract to help collect the Medicaid reimbursement due the school districts. In one year the client had gone from the software sales business to the services business. Recognizing this was quite a shock and a strategic breakthrough. It realized it could create more value by giving its software away and profiting from reimbursement services. This redefinition made the company much more attractive to investors.

A client in one of our workshops had set himself the goal of starting a new business, but, in looking back over his calendar, he found that he had made little progress in developing his business idea. He was instead spending a lot of time talking with family, making trips, consulting with lawyers, brokers, etc. When he checked his calendar, it became clear that much of his time had been taken up with dealing with the estate of his recently deceased mother. In the past year, he really had been in the business of managing his mother's estate, but he hadn't realized it.

The businesses you are actually in may or may not turn out to be the businesses that you want to be in or need to be in, or what, upon reflection, you would determine to be best for you. Yet they are the businesses you are in, and it is there that you must start.

Life Business participants find that naming their Life Businesses is sometimes a painful process, sometimes a delightful process. However, it should always be a process of self-discovery and self-acceptance, which can create a solid foundation for moving to a position of more empowerment, control, and direction in your life.

Exercises for the Reader

You can get a start on defining your current Life Businesses by doing some of the exercises suggested in this chapter.

1. After doing the Review introduced in Step 1, construct a multimedia Big Picture describing last year.
2. Discuss it with close friends or advisers.
3. Identify the main themes.
4. Do your own Got–Gone chart.
5. Make a start at naming your Life Businesses.

For detailed instructions and more tips on discovering and naming your Life Businesses, see our Web site at www.lifebusiness.com.

Now You're in Business

If you have completed the foregoing exercises and identified your current Businesses, you have taken a big step toward understanding what you are doing with your life. You are on your way to becoming the CEO, rather than an observer, of your life! You can answer the critical question "What (Life) Businesses are you in?" This puts you way ahead in the game, but not nearly at the finish line.

You now know how you spent your time over the past year, the major events and recurring activities, your feelings about what happened, where your money went and where it came from. You know what energized you and what depleted you.

When you get to this point, stop a moment and pause to appreciate yourself. You have done what few other people have done. You have actually looked at what you are doing with your life and can say with some confidence what that is. Even if what you have found is not entirely pleasing, you have taken the courageous step to look the reality of your situation in the face.

You have done for your life what a responsible CEO of any corporation must do for his or her business. You have gathered the facts and created an intelligible narrative about the nature of your Life Enterprise. This is a critical part of your Annual Report and a big step toward greater accountability to your stakeholders which include you, your significant others, and the many more who depend on you in certain ways.

The results of Step 2 may be surprising. You may find that some of the Businesses you are in are unexpected. You may have not been really aware of where your time and energy were going. You may find the result either delightful or appalling (I still cannot get over how little time I actually spent with my family!). Your gut feeling might be that "I have got to get out of this or that Business and into something more rewarding." Or "Wow, now that I understand better what I have been doing, I have to find a way to make this or that happen more often."

We are ready for the final step in the Annual Report. Now that you have identified your Life Businesses, you need to do a businesslike job of evaluating them. Evaluating your current Life Businesses is a necessary prelude to improving the value of your total Life Enterprise. In Step 3 you will find out how to apply business concepts to the task of assessing the performance of each of your Life Businesses and ultimately the value or values of your life as you are now living it.

Notes

1. Ned Hermann is the psychologist who has done the most to introduce "whole-brained thinking" to industry. He is the author of the Hermann Brain Dominance Instrument, which measures individuals' cognitive styles. He spent most of his career with GE and then established his own firm to promote the use of these concepts in organizational thinking and planning.

2. Stephen Covey, Roger Merrill, Rebecca Merrill. *First Things First: To Live, to Love, to Learn, to Leave a Legacy.* Simon and Schuster, 1996.

3. Richard Carlson. *Don't Sweat the Small Stuff . . . and It's All Small Stuff: Simple Ways to Keep the Little Things from Taking over Your Life.* Hyperion, 1997.

Assessing Your Businesses

Giving and getting don't always match up

The cost of a thing is the amount of what I will call "life" which is required to be exchanged for it, immediately or in the long run.

Henry David Thoreau

LIFE BUSINESS TENET

You are the best judge of whether your Life Businesses are performing as you would like . . . but you gotta think about it! Using both imaginative and analytic processes, you can come to a sound judgment as to which of your major investments in energy, time, and money are truly returning positive meaning and vitality to your life.

Step 3 empowers you to take a quantum leap in businesslike thinking. You face the facts of your Life Businesses, assess your situation, and gain insight into how to evolve a more rewarding Life Enterprise. You can make the most of Step 3 if you apply several important businesslike principles: (1) separate fact finding from analysis; (2) look for opportunities for improvement; (3) suspend blame, take responsibility, and shun the "quick fix"; and (4) catch yourself doing something good.

Separate Fact Finding from Analysis

We can learn from unsuccessful businesses as well as successful ones. The precipitous fall of accounting giant Arthur Andersen was in large part due to a failure to create adequate separation between its evaluative accounting arm and its fee-based consulting business. When it comes to assessing our Life Businesses, we need to differentiate the fact finding (Step 1) and business definition (Step 2) phases from analysis (Step 3).

Successful businesses employ professionals who prepare a profile of hard facts about the enterprise's past-year performance. A synthesis of this information appears in the enterprise's annual report. Management must weigh these facts, decide what they mean, and determine the most appropriate organizational response. Finally it is the industry analysts and shareholders who read the annual report and bid the company's stock up or down. This division of labor and accountability help ensure that reality rules and good business decisions are made. When the facts are distorted or hidden as in the Enron debacle, a business, even if once hugely successful, can end up in receivership.

Look for Opportunities for Improvement

Many of us are in constant inner struggle about those things in our lives that are real or potential problems for us (e.g., the few pounds we put on each year, the failure to save quite enough for the college fund, the drifting apart of close relationships). Often we don't tackle those problems because we lack the self-confidence and the optimism to believe that our lives could really be better. We let things build, erect a wall of denial, and then drape that wall with complacency. When reality finally breaks through, we may have a big problem on our hands: the heart attack, the divorce, the troubled child, the financial crisis.

The best leaders are able to sustain a creative tension in their organizations. These leaders are able to acknowledge that there is a problem in the present, but also to envision a more positive future and direction. This attitude allows them to build on shortcomings, disappointments, and failures. It is this attitude that has allowed major businesses like IBM, Xerox, and Ford to face up to, confront, and overcome major problems that have been allowed to build up over years. An attitude of continuous improvement helps us spot problems early, before they become too large.

Seeking Improvement in Business

The following excerpts are from a study of businesses that won the North Carolina governor's award for environmental quality improvements.[1]

> At the Crown Cork & Seal plant, they identify all the waste streams for the corporate organization.
>
> Hornwood textiles established a cross-departmental team to survey waste composition to identify where it was generated in the manufacturing process.

They involved customers and suppliers to help the team. The team then determined which strategies of elimination, recycling, and reuse would be feasible.

At Kemet Electronics, they are continually tracking all waste by area within the plant. Tailored spreadsheets are used for each process, calculating waste reductions, cost savings, and return on investments. Costs for labor, disposal, materials, and implementation are all factored into these calculations.

At the Cherry Point Naval Aircraft Station, the pollution prevention team has categorized 97 active waste streams and has analyzed each stream in terms of quantity of waste, hazardous waste production, and potential cost avoidance.

Maola Milk Company's suggestion program is highly structured and is personally led by the Company Vice President. This system has resulted in hundreds of thousands of dollars in annual savings and major waste reductions.

At the Bowman Gray Medical Center, which employs over 3000 people, they launched Project Waste Watch. The hospital asked employees to submit ideas for environmental protection. If their idea was selected, they were publicly presented a certificate of commendation.

The best businesses know that there are always opportunities for improvement: in cost, in service, and in product quality. With this attitude, the facts are always friendly. However, it takes an analytic effort to understand where to seek improvement.

Suspend Blame and Take Responsibility

The executive at General Motors who, with the authority of GM's top management behind her, brought Cadillac back to top-ranked quality ratings for luxury cars after they had dropped to 14th worldwide taught two principles to senior management and employees alike: (1) suspend blame and (2) take responsibility. For example, the engineers who were working to improve Cadillac's trunk space came to management and said: "We designed this wrong five years ago and it's costing the company $2 million a year and we want $1 million to fix it." To counteract the executives' natural instinct to leap over the desk and rip out the throat of the offending engineer, she taught management to respond: "We appreciate your honesty and analysis, and management will assess this opportunity for improvement very seriously."[2]

One of the reasons we all hate to assess ourselves is because we know we are in for a big dose of guilt for our failures and shortcomings. If we can work on suspending blame, and take responsibility instead, we can start the process of righting the ship. If we can't, we are likely to continue to sail around in circles.

Don't Leap into Corrective Action

Problem solving is an expensive business. It takes energy, time, and often money to correct a pattern that has gone wrong. When there are several problems to be corrected, it is an important act of judgment to decide which one to tackle, rather than go after the first problem found. Management consultants often encounter the "ready-fire-aim syndrome" in business. The solutions that are created in this way can cause more difficulties than the original problems. In Step 3 of the Life Business Program we encourage participants not to seize on a "quick fix" for the problems and shortcomings they uncover in assessing their Life Businesses. Hang in there and let the "creative tension" work for you until the time is right to act!

Catch Yourself Doing Something Good

The best-organized companies have systematic programs of recognition and encouragement. High-performing individuals and teams are recognized with rewards and bonuses. Company communications feature the employee of the month and so on. This is all part of creating a culture of continuous improvement and corporate pride. When you assess your Life Businesses, you have the opportunity to identify not only problems to be fixed but also areas where you are doing really well, accomplishing a lot, and taking good care of yourself. The assessment phase of the Life Business Program is the first of many opportunities in the Life Business Program to recognize and appreciate yourself for the good work that you do and the progress you have made in getting your life to move in a positive direction. As you work with the Life Business Program, this capacity for self-appreciation will become an even more important force for propelling you toward your life goals.

How Is Your Life Enterprise Performing?

The performance of your Life Enterprise is determined by the performance of the Life Businesses that make it up. So, having identified your current Life Businesses, you need to assess their performance. Companies have a simple way of doing this. They calculate the return on investment (ROI) of the separate businesses in their corporation.

Return on Investment (ROI) as a Business Evaluation Tool

If you buy a share of stock for $10.00 and after one year the value of the stock has risen to $10.75 a share and you also received a $.25 dividend on each share, your ROI totaled $1.00 on a $10.00 purchase or 10 percent. Businesses calculate expected ROIs before they invest in new plants and equipment or increase staff.

ROI helps companies choose among a variety of options: Should we increase staff in the sales department to accommodate new demand? Or should we buy equipment in order to increase efficiency? Or should we invest in closing down this product which is no longer popular and sell or redirect the assets associated with its production? Which set of choices provides the greatest long and short-term benefit? ROI, calculated over a number of years, helps businesses decide which choices to make.

In the Life Business Program we calculate a type of ROI that has to do with the amount of energy a Business returns to you compared to the amount of energy you invest in it. We call this the *Got–Gone ratio.* In life all we really have to invest is our human energy, our vitality. Once this energy is gone, we are gone. So we use the concept of energy flow as a way of talking about whether specific life activities are relatively good or poor (life) investments.

For example, within his HHMO Life Business, Harry has made the following assessment: Taking vitamins is a small nuisance but they are low cost and have a potentially big payoff given his cholesterol problems, so the ROI is relatively high—perhaps two to one (2:1). Exercising takes time and energy, but Harry has always enjoyed jogging and hiking. It gets him outside, in the air, moving along. It has a big payoff for his mental health, his feeling tone (he loves those endorphins!), and positive spin-offs for his other Life Businesses, as when Harry generates new business ideas or solves clients' problems while tooling along at 4 mph. So overall, Harry estimates that his HHMO Business has a relatively high ROI, perhaps as much as four to one (4:1).

On the other hand, Harry took on the project of bringing in a new partner who he thought would complement his practice. It turned out that after about 2 years of working together, all Harry was getting was aggravation. Harry and his new partner tended to irritate each other when they worked together. The new partner did not bring in any new business for Harry, while Harry provided new business for him. Harry began to see the partner as less creative and effective than he had thought when he first recruited him. In short, the energy return in this relationship was negative. He calculated it at a 1 to 5 ratio (1:5)! As a result of this review, the two parted company, painfully, but successfully.

Calculate the ROIs for Your Life Businesses

In the Life Business Program, we calculate ROIs by using the following method: Draw two pie charts. One pie chart represents the total energy you "get" (Got Chart) from all of your life's activities. The second pie chart represents the total amount of energy you "give" (Gone Chart) to your life activities. Carve up your Got pie by

Energy Got–Gone Calculations for Harry

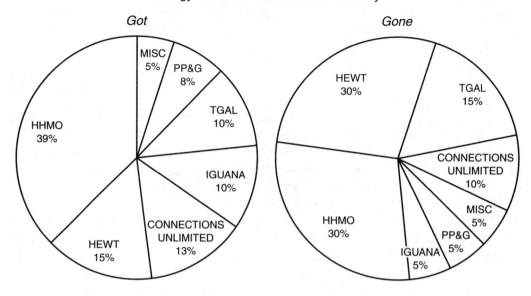

assigning a percentage equal to the amount of energy you get from each of your Life Businesses. The percentages of all your Life Businesses must add up to 100 percent, because, by definition, it is from your Life Businesses that you get all your energy. Do the same with the Gone pie. The accompanying illustration shows Harry's "pies."

    With the data from his pie charts in hand Harry is now in a position to pull all of his information together in one place: the Life Business Assessment Chart. To do this he lists his Life Businesses down the left side in column 1. In columns 2 and 3 he enters his "Got" and "Gone" percentages. In columns 4 and 5 he puts in his "Got:Gone" ratios and the fractions those ratios represent. Finally he records the information that he collected in Step 1: time spent, money costs, and revenues, allocating appropriate amounts to each of his Life Businesses. Now Harry has all his information together and is ready to put on his business analyst hat.

Harry's Life Business Assessment Chart

Business	Got	Gone	Got:Gone	Got/Gone	Time	Cost	Revenue
HEWT Have Ear Will Travel (consulting business)	15%	30%	1:2	0.50	35%	$11,500	$105,500

(continues)

Harry's Life Business Assessment Chart (Continued)

Business	Got	Gone	Got:Gone	Got/Gone	Time	Cost	Revenue
HHMO Harry Health Maintenance Organization	40%	30%	4:3	1.33	35%	$9,500	0
TGAL (1)* Think Globally, Act Locally	10%	15%	2:3	0.67	10%	$3,500	0
Connections Unlimited (2)	12.5%	10%	9:8	1.125	5%	$100,500	0
PP&G Personal & Professional Development	7.5%	5%	3:2	1.5	5%	$3,500	0
IGUANA I gonna be me (personal time)	10%	5%	2:1	2.0	5%	$500	0
Misc. (3)	5%	5%	1:1	1.0	5%	$3,500	$27,500
Totals (4)	**100%**	**100%**			**100%**	**$132,500**	**$132,500**

*See text for notes.

Notes for Harry's Life Business Assessment Chart

1. That proportion of Harry's consulting business and other activities which have a *pro bono publico* aspect.
2. Includes the main expenses that go to support those he is most connected to: mortgage, food, insurance, child care, summer camp; medical expenses for loved ones, annual trip to beach with sister's family, family vacations, etc.
3. Time and money cost categories include lunches, breakfasts, personal hygiene, errands, late night TV, daily papers, etc. Revenue figures represent proceeds from the sale of stock that Harry needed that year to cover his expenses. (Had Harry borrowed the money instead, it would have shown up here as well.)

4. Total cost figures include $121,000 for Harry's household and personal expenses plus $11,500 for Harry's business costs. These were not shown in Harry's "numbers" in Step 1. Total revenue figures include the gross revenues from Harry's consulting business, not the net as shown in Harry's numbers in Step 1.

Answer the Critical Questions About Your Life Businesses

Harry is now in a position to complete the assessment of his Businesses. Using the data from his Life Business Assessment Chart, Harry can answer the following seven critical assessment questions:

1. What are the surprises for you when you look at your Life Business Chart? What is important about these surprises?
2. Which of your Life Businesses are currently returning good value for your investments of energy, time, and money? Which are returning relatively low value?
3. Is the overall Enterprise currently profitable (i.e., more energy coming in than out, or vice versa)?
4. What is the volume of each Business in terms of energy, time, and money? Is overall volume growing or slowing?
5. For each Business: Is the current Business sustainable? For how long at its current ROI?
6. If you were an outside investor, what questions would you want answered before you decided to invest in one or more of these Businesses?
7. If you were an outside investor, would you invest in an Enterprise with these Life Businesses? Why or why not?

Harry answered these questions as follows.

Question 1: Surprises. One interesting feature is that most of Harry's expenditures are allocated to his Connections Unlimited Business in which he has lumped the important social roles of husband, father, brother, and friend. Perhaps he needs to "unpack" this Business a bit to better understand his Life Enterprise.

Question 2: Return on Investment. Harry's ROI analysis reveals that his most "profitable" Business is IGUANA (the time he spends on things that are fun and interesting for their own sake), but he only spends about 5 percent of his time there. Learning new skills as a consultant (PP&G), going to workshops, etc. are also relatively rewarding.

Harry's Connections Unlimited Business has a net positive return, despite the fact that his daughter is 15 and is an intense teenager. The biggest plus has been the time he has spent walking and talking with his wife on a weekly basis, which results in the coordinated child-rearing strategies required especially in dealing with a teenager. HHMO is net positive mostly because of the value of exercise and getting enough sleep. These positive results more than outweigh the negative psychic effect of taking a lot of pills to reduce cholesterol. Harry's Miscellaneous Business includes mundane things like going to the cleaners, eating lunch at work and reading the newspaper, and watching late night television. It is a breakeven Business.

Harry's smaller energy drain is in his social activism Business TGAL (Think Globally, Act Locally). That's not surprising, because Harry's way of giving, mostly, is to donate or provide his services as a consultant to worthwhile organizations. Therefore, TGAL is a lot like work. While Harry gets a sense of satisfaction from feeling that he is really helping people who need his help, he is using the parts of his brain that are perhaps already overused on many other projects.

HEWT is the big energy drain—only a 50 percent return on every unit of energy put in. The good news is that Harry gets money to compensate him for this activity. Actually Harry likes his work—a lot. It's the volume of it and the pressure that comes with it that makes it a drain.

Question 3: Overall Enterprise Profitability. Things are going well for Harry at the moment according to this analysis. He works a lot, but apparently not to the detriment of his personal relationships and personal health. Harry has paid a lot of attention to himself over the years—much of this via the Life Business Program—and has made some positive adjustments in his workaholic tendencies, notably, spending more time with his wife and daughter. He has also systematically cut down on the most draining parts of his practice (e.g., putting in long-shot, high-effort bids for consulting work). As a result, his total enterprise is more profitable and less draining than it has been in previous years and overall is in fairly close balance.

Question 4: Life Business Volume. This is still a very high-energy Enterprise overall. Almost all of Harry's time is scheduled. He puts in 50–60 hours a week on his job, sometimes more. He is tired at night. There is not a lot left over for spontaneous activities, creative arts, nights out with the guys, etc. The big volume Businesses in terms of time are still work (HEWT) and staying healthy (HHMO), getting enough exercise, sleep, etc. Harry still works a lot, but less so than in past years. The volume of the nonwork Businesses, in terms of time, is increasing a bit. That is good in terms of life satisfaction.

The Enterprise as a whole is definitely on the plus side. This is better than a few years ago when Harry was tired and pressured and anxious most of the time, due to overwork and stressed relationships on the home front. The Enterprise was definitely in a deficit then. This year the family has dealt fairly well with the need to provide a costly medical treatment for his daughter requiring daily attention, managed a vacation that was very positive, and all members seem to be achieving well in their chosen fields. Things could be a lot worse.

Question 5: Sustainability. The overall Enterprise is profitable now in terms of life satisfaction. Underlying conditions are quite favorable—no major illnesses, no relatives in distress, the consulting business is good, etc. Harry and his wife still spend more than they are earning on a yearly basis, however. In the past this shortfall was covered by increasing stock values, and net financial assets are still sufficient to provide a basis for eventual retirement. But the recent economic downturn may well force a reevaluation of life style and spending habits, since net financial assets will actually decline at this rate of spending if there is no run-up in the market. Sustainability is also a factor in Harry's HHMO Business. Not unlike most 50-year-olds he continues to put on a pound or two each year. This is not a sustainable trend.

Question 6: Investor Questions. An outside investor would probably want a greater breakdown of expenditures in the Connections Unlimited Area. This is actually available in Harry's current financial data. The investor would be interested in seeing if there are really several different Businesses that might usefully be broken out as independent profit centers. "Following the money" might lead to clearer distinctions among possible Businesses.

Question 7: Good Investment? An outside investor might say the Enterprise is profitable, but hardly efficient. The investor would want to see higher ROI in the HEWT areas. He might say that Harry should work less and invest more of his time in other areas of his life that give a higher ROI. Harry should find a way to do that without negatively impacting the overall financial health of the family. He needs to think about increasing income or reducing expenditures, or coming to understand his financial situation in a new way by having a more accurate projection of his long-term needs. These considerations, as we shall see in later Steps, are critical dimensions of the Life Business Program.

Other Participants' ROI Analyses of Their Life Businesses

Brad, having just come through a life-threatening illness and the death of several relatives in one year, assessed himself as deeply in the red for the year. He needed a turnaround plan to protect his health, to secure his marriage, and to help his children with the trauma of the previous year.

Mary analyzed her Life Enterprise and saw that she had been on a downhill trend in her job satisfaction for some time. She had a high position in a Fortune 100 company, and was well taken care of financially, but now she saw that there were other areas of life that were crying for attention.

Jena realized that all of her activities had a positive ROI except work, but that is where she spent most of her time and earned almost all of her money. This emerged as an area in her life she needed to do something more about if it was not going to drag down the rest of her Life Enterprise.

Peter depends heavily on his retirement funds to finance his Life Enterprise. The fall of 2000 and the spring of 2001 saw Peter's accounts lose more than $300,000. Peter's assessment was that while it was no fun watching his finances crash and burn, it was great to realize that he still had the necessary resources to develop his Life Businesses and pursue his dreams. In other words, the real "net worth" of his Life Enterprise hadn't suffered at all.

Additional Methods of Assessing Your Life Businesses

Value Analysis

It is entirely possible to have high ROI Life Businesses and still be in the wrong Businesses. In Life Business work, in order to get a sense of whether one's overall Life Enterprise is meaningfully anchored, we suggest Value Analysis. In Life Business we ask, What are the critical values that determine for you whether your life is in balance?

Value Analysis is another way of summing up what your commitments to various activities over the past year "bought" you in terms of what you really care about. Businesses are always talking about "value added" as a way of assessing the utility of certain activities or even of justifying their prices. Value Analysis gives you a way to look at what was present or lacking in the return you achieved in the past year.

In Value Analysis we present participants with a list of values such as creativity, security, integrity, friendship, family, recognition, and so on. We ask them to rate on a five-point scale the degrees to which those values were present in their lives in the last year versus the degree to which those values were important to them. The resulting agreement or discrepancy between the two ratings yields important insights about whether you are in the right businesses, no matter how profitable they are.

For many people who have gone through the 13 Steps, the Value Analysis turns up big deficits and becomes a key factor as they guide their Life Enterprise.

They may find themselves lacking in intimacy, health, or financial security. When big gaps appear in the Value Analysis, they are almost always reflected in low Life Enterprise ROIs or missing Life Businesses and are powerful indicators that change is needed.

Internal Management Team

Another Evaluation activity we use in Step 3 is the Internal Management Team.[2] This activity is based on the common idea that we all have different aspects of ourselves that we bring out on various occasions. You may at the same time have a "soft" side, a "hard edge," an "artistic" side, a "big kid inside," and so on. You can make use of this everyday insight to see how you are running your various Life Businesses and how to improve the management of your Life Enterprise. In this activity, you give each of these traits a name and a personality and analyze how they interact with one another to produce Life Business results. Below we can see how Harry described his Internal Management Team.

Harry's Internal Management Team

- Isadore the Intellectual: The part of Harry that gets carried away by ideas and likes to make connections between ideas. Sometimes Isadore can write interesting essays that clarify connections between different aspects of a given problem. He is good at writing reports for clients. Isadore can be very absentminded and abstracted and is considered dangerous behind the wheel by his friends.
- Friendly Frank: The part of Harry that likes to get along with people, is a good listener, and genuinely wants to help others. He is good at cocktail parties, general marketing, and talking with clients. Unfortunately, Friendly Frank will often say yes to things that Harry really does not have time to do. Friendly Frank is in charge of Connections Unlimited.
- Explosive Eddie: When Friendly Frank gets worn down, Explosive Eddie can sometimes appear, particularly at home. Explosive Eddie will snap and fume and on occasion rage when he feels he is being pushed beyond his limits. The good thing about Explosive Eddie is that he knows what Harry needs at that moment. The bad thing about Explosive Eddie is that he is likely to put a dent in whatever relationships happen to be around at the moment. Explosive Eddie, when contained, has energy for the long-term struggle in a conflict. Explosive Eddie was most in action when Harry was on the high school wrestling team. Now mostly he is in the closet or trotted out to handle really extreme situations. Sometimes he does well in those situations. Sometimes he blows it entirely.

- Anxious Al: Al is worried about the future. He considers the possibilities and the downside risks of situations. Al is good at understanding the dynamics of a situation, but he is bad at action. He can get into analysis paralysis, even obsessive ruminations, and slightly paranoid fantasies. These fantasies sometimes get Explosive Eddie engaged, Anxious Al is Chief Financial Officer of Harry's Life Enterprise.
- Honest Abe: Honest Abe is up-front about his feelings and perceptions, both positive and negative, and is good when problems need to be solved and trust needs to be built.
- Disciplined Dave: Disciplined Dave is very hard working, ambitious, and achievement-oriented; he always needs to be doing something that advances the ball down the field. Dave wants to look good, be respected, and get a lot of recognition. Dave is not very good at relaxing. When he reaches the exhaustion point, Explosive Ed is sometimes evoked. Disciplined Dave runs HEWT, HHMO, and TGAL.
- Playful Paul: He has a good sense of humor and likes word jokes and composing doggerel. He loves being outdoors, sightseeing, reading for fun, enjoying life, etc. Paul leads Harry's IGUANA Business.

Disciplined Dave (CEO) and Friendly Frank (Marketing and Sales) run most of Harry's Life Businesses most of the time. Anxious Al operates as CFO. With Friendly Frank loath to say no and Disciplined Dave eager to respond to any demand, you get the picture: overwork. Anxious Al is evoked to worry about how he will get it all done and to pay for what needs to be paid for. Isadore comes up with the ideas for clients, family, and friends. Explosive Ed sometimes gets aroused, and Honest Abe has to clean up the mess he creates. Playful Paul does not get the outdoor time he might like—not enough company outings!

It is interesting to speculate what might happen if Harry's management team made better use of its strengths. For example if Disciplined Dave helped Anxious Al with the finances, he might find that by managing the money better he would not have to work so hard. This might allow Playful Paul to develop his business to a greater degree. Once that happened, Explosive Ed might be less needed in his gorilla-in-the-closet role and could take up more productive pursuits. These are some of the lines of analysis we will pursue as the Life Business Program advances.

Exercises for the Reader

To develop your own draft Annual Report as you read, or just to "get the hang" of the Program, do the following activities.

1. Do Got–Gone pie charts for the Life Businesses you identified in Step 2.
2. Use the Got–Gone pie charts to calculate an ROI for your various Life Businesses.
3. Create your own Life Business Assessment Chart.
4. Answer as many of the Life Business Evaluation questions as you have data to answer at this time.

More information and discussion about Values Analysis, the Internal Management Team, and other assessment exercises can be found on our Web site at www.lifebusiness.com.

The Value of Step 3

At the outset of this chapter we said that Step 3 was empowering and represented a giant leap in applying business thinking in your life. In Step 1, you built awareness on a firm foundation of facts. In Step 2, you created focus by organizing those facts into a number of meaningful themes we call "Life Businesses." In Step 3, you begin to define key concerns using a variety of analytic tools. Put it all together and you have last year's Annual Report, the story of your Life Business in the recent past.

This is the empowering element. It has been said that "those who ignore the past are condemned to repeat it." You have lessened the chances that you will continue with the "same old, same old" situations because you have been willing to look at things as they are and identify those things that are not working well in your life. At the same time you have given due recognition to the sources of your positive energy.

You are now ready to move on to the next phase of your Annual Business Planning Cycle: The Market Report. You are like a business that has begun to better understand which products and services are profitable and which are not so profitable. Your Life Enterprise is now in a good position to improve its balance sheet, but only if your Internal Management Team is willing to restrain its impulses to execute quick fixes. Quick fixes distract attention from the important messages the market is sending and from those trends and events that may have an impact on future success. Understanding these important strategic factors is the primary focus of Step 4.

Notes

1. The "Internal Management Team" exercise was created for the Life Business Program by Dennis Bumstead, Ph.D., a certified Life Business trainer in Europe.

2. This anecdote is from a presentation at the Research Triangle Chapter of the American Society of Training and Development, which David Kiel attended in the early 1980s.

PART TWO

Market Report

We live our lives in relationship with others in the past, today, and in the future.

Companies look at their relationships with competitors, partners, suppliers, and customers both now and in the future by means of a Market Report. They assess significant trends and events impacting their business and create a vision of what their business can be in the future.

Similarly, in Steps 4 and 5 you address the following questions relative to your Life Businesses:

- Who are the individuals and groups most closely associated with your Life Businesses?

- What do they want and need from you now and in the future?
- What are the predictable trends and events in your life that will have significance for your Life Enterprise in the future?
- How do you want your life to be 10 years from now? Are you in the right Businesses now to get you there?

Listen to the Market

How to truly hear customers' thoughts, feelings, and needs

I get by with a little help from my friends.

Paul McCartney and John Lennon

LIFE BUSINESS TENET

You have significant others! You can determine who is most important in your life and what you need to do to build positive relationships with these individuals and groups. You can also learn to appreciate yourself as a significant "customer" of your own Life Enterprise!

As the past is prologue to the present, the Annual Report is the backdrop for the Market Report, the second stage of the Annual Business Planning Cycle. In preparing the Market Report, companies take into account both what key stakeholders (customers, shareholders, employees, suppliers, regulators, etc.) are thinking and planning and major trends and events that will likely affect their businesses.

Appreciate the Importance of Your Stakeholder Network to Your Life Enterprise

Corporations understand their history, but they also pay attention to the messages they are getting from the markets right now and the trends and events that may affect their future prospects when planning. You should do the same in thinking about your life.

At least since the rise of the Total Quality Management movement of the 1980s, talking with, and listening to, customers has been a driving force for much business planning. The watchword in quality is understanding and then meeting or exceeding customer requirements. Tom Peters, the ubiquitous business guru, has argued that in assessing the health of a business, customer satisfaction is often a better predictor than looking at the company's current balance sheet.

In addition to customers, there are other key stakeholders who affect the "Gots" and "Gones" of any business. Taking their perspectives into account when planning is also critical to success. Research shows the importance of a fully functioning network of advisers, investors, and suppliers to the success of new business ventures. As a consequence, one of the main strategies for strengthening new businesses is helping them gain access to the sources of expertise, capital, and information they need to be successful.

In your own life, too, the success of your Life Businesses depends on the continued support from your key stakeholders. For example, it has been found that for men recovering from a heart attack, the quality of their relationship with their spouses is a key predictor of the success of the recovery. In how many more mundane ways do you "get by with a little help from your friends"?

Define Your Network of Stakeholders

The best-run companies make every effort to understand who their customers are: their ages and genders, their buying power, their cultures, their outlooks, their needs, their interests. The companies conduct surveys, focus groups, and interviews to determine present and emerging customer needs and to gauge customer satisfaction with their products and services. They monitor chat rooms on the Internet where customers talk about their experience with their products and comparable services. They know that if they begin to lose the loyalty and interest of the customer, their business is heading for trouble and the sooner they do something about it, the better off they will be.

The managers of well-run businesses pay exquisite attention to other elements of their stakeholder network as well. For example, they work with suppliers to ensure that the parts or ingredients provided meet high quality standards. They have lobbyists in Washington and in state governments to monitor and influence governmental policies that might affect their businesses. They have corporate foundations and public relations departments to influence the opinion of stakeholders, the general public, and the local community about their business.

You are the CEO of your own Life Enterprise. You also have customers, suppliers, regulators, and a general public for each of your Life Businesses. You need to understand who they are and appreciate the importance of your relationships with these Stakeholders. In your Life Business these Stakeholders may have titles like spouse, brother, sister, child, parent, physician, broker, business partner, best friend, and colleague.

Defining Stakeholder Relationships in Organizations

In our consulting practice we recently went through an exercise where we helped a large, urban, nonprofit, housing agency set priorities within its newly developed strategic plan. It listed its key stakeholders which included partner banks, the city administration, its own staff, the neighborhoods it served, community organizations it worked most closely with, and foundations and other funding groups. We went further and asked people at the agency to identify an individual who represented each of those stakeholder groups. Then we listed the key results we thought those stakeholders wanted from the implementation of the strategic plan in the first year. This list was then used to set internal priorities, which were then validated with the board of directors on which many of these stakeholders were represented.

Leaders of organizations use this concept as well to define their role and prioritize their time. We helped the dean of a new and innovative school of public health use stakeholder analysis as a means of ensuring that his leadership was touching the right bases to garner the support he needed in the fledgling school's first year. He created a grid of the key stakeholders he wanted to be in contact with and then, using his calendar, established the desired pattern and frequency of contacts. He reviewed this communications plan with his advisers on a regular basis.

Stakeholder analysis is important in communities as well. In conducting a study of economic development potential for minority communities in a southern state, one of the first steps we recommended was to analyze the network of existing business and agency relationships in those communities. We could then see how they needed to be strengthened, leveraged, or modified to help those communities do a better job of providing employment and building assets.

Take time to listen and understand the messages your network of Stakeholders is sending to you.

It's one thing to understand who your significant others are, even to be in contact with them; it is another to really listen and respond to what they are saying. There's nothing so annoying as to hear the message on an answering machine, "Your call is really important to us" and then not get a call back. We all get those evaluation forms from hotels about their service, and we wonder whether anyone ever reads them. However, when you have given people feedback and they respond to your needs in a timely manner, you are reassured there is someone, a real person with whom you are in relationship. And this is the important point: You have found someone who cares enough to act on your behalf.

It is a challenging step to commit to be open to what your significant others are saying to you and to respond to them in a way that meets both your needs and their desires. However, without making this commitment, it is doubtful whether your Life Businesses can progress beyond a certain point. One of Steven Covey's Seven Habits of Highly Effective People is to, "Seek to understand and then be understood." This prescription for effective communication is made even more powerful when you are in dialogue with "a significant other" for one of your important Life Businesses.

Take Time to Understand the Trends and Events That Could Affect Your Important Life Businesses

The most effective businesses appreciate that the markets they operate in are dynamic and changing, not static. Management teams need to anticipate trends and events that will affect the market performance of their business. They map the environment and scan that environment regularly for potential threats and opportunities. They look at all kinds of trends—demographic, technological, political, natural resource, economic, and social—as they relate to their industry, customer base, and competition.

On the basis of the results of their trend analysis, they make plans that affect their choice of suppliers, their prices and promotions to customers, the recruitment of staff, the securing of financing, and the adoption of technical innovation. Successful businesses know that the effective anticipation of the short- and longer-term future in all these areas is crucial for their success.

In the Life Business Program we ask participants to scan the environment of their Life Businesses and identify trends of importance. These trends may include economic prospects, health prospects, social relations, the predictable developmental phases of children, parents, and families as a whole.

The Voice of the Customer: Understanding the Markets for Your Life Businesses

In Step 4 the first activity is identifying the key Stakeholders in each of your Life Businesses. Harry, whose Life Enterprise we analyze in detail in Step 3, developed the Stakeholder list shown on the next page.

List of Stakeholders in Harry's Life Businesses

Life Businesses	*Key Stakeholders*
CONNECTIONS UNLIMITED: the business of maintaining and developing intimate relations with my wife and daughter, close relatives, and a wide circle of longtime friends; the upkeep of the physical and emotional home, which is the center that keeps it all together	Shareowners: wife, daughter, sister Customers: cousins, friends Suppliers: child psychologist, tutors, teachers, my daughter's summer camp, people who keep our yard and house presentable
HHMO (Harry Health Maintenance Organization): the business of preventing heart disease and maintaining good physical condition	Shareowner: me, wife, daughter Customers: relatives, friends, and clients Suppliers: internist, cardiologist, counselor, friends who have similar concerns and access to information, friends who are physicians, the Harvard Heart Letter, sports outfitters, the Spa
PP&G (Personal and Professional Growth): the business of developing myself and my abilities	Customers: me and my clients and family Suppliers: my counselor, my friends and colleagues who challenge and support me, my professional association
TGAL (Think Globally, Act Locally): contributing to the solution of community problems	Customer: my conscience Suppliers: the organizations I donate time and money to
IGUANA (I gonna be me): doing what I like to do; having fun; recreation	Customer: me Suppliers: hiking buddies, travel agents, the Spa, the beautiful places, the bright lights of the city
HEWT (Have Ear, Will Travel): Harry's consulting business	Customers: me and my clients Suppliers: accountant, computer consultant, Web provider, subcontractors, business partners, referral sources, etc. Regulators: my wife and daughter (They let me know when I am working too much.)

In Harry's CONNECTIONS UNLIMITED Business he has listed his wife and daughter as shareowners rather than customers. He likes this way of thinking about them because it recognizes their central place in his life. It may be hard to replace your friends, but it's a real pain to have to replace your wife and kid!

Recently, Harry asked his wife what she thought was important for the development of their relationship. She stated what he already knew—that she felt it was important for them to have time together, preferably walking time at least every two weeks. She also said two things Harry didn't know: first, that it would be good to have a set time, say lunch once a week, to go over family business items that accumulated during the week that she needed to talk with him about; second, that what was offensive to her in their relationship was that Harry seemed too busy or distracted to pay attention to her when she had something to tell him at odd times when they were together in the house.

Because his wife is an important stakeholder in an important Business whose performance Harry wants to improve, he agreed to work on his everyday interactions. Harry concluded that he really could break off from what he was doing to give his wife his full attention—who else is more important? This is an example of the kind of useful, if sometimes challenging, information you can get when you consult the important customers of your Life Businesses.

Harry's teenage daughter, a significant Stakeholder in CONNECTIONS UNLIMITED, is saying: "support me but give me space and recognize my growing abilities" and "cut out the yelling." Harry's sister seems to be saying: "stay in touch," based on the fact that if he does not call every few weeks, she will call him and say "What's up?"

In HHMO, there are a lot of players. Harry is the main shareowner, and his wife is a Stakeholder who also holds his daughter's proxy. Harry's consulting customers, his relatives, friends, and clients, are definitely involved. His suppliers are physicians, pharmacists, the publishers of the Harvard Health Letter, and other health professionals that Harry consults. There is also synergy here with his other Businesses because if his wife does not feel that he is taking good care of himself, Harry will hear about it, that is, CONNECTIONS UNLIMITED is affected. Of course, HEWT, Harry's consulting business does not function unless HHMO is up and running. In planning the next steps in this Business, Harry needs to take into account what these Stakeholders are saying to him.

Harry's doctor is telling him that since he is over 50, he should come in more than one time a year to be seen. His wife is telling him that she would like him to consider alternative health approaches for stress management.

Do I Really Have to Listen?

If one of your core Life Businesses has to do with being a parent or spouse, then this part of the Life Business Program would involve taking into account what your spouse or children are telling you about what, if anything, you might do differently to meet their needs and desires.

You retain the right to choose how you respond to this feedback, but if you are going to take your life seriously—as seriously as successful businesspeople take their businesses—you do not ignore this feedback in setting your future plans.

In our workshop we provide an opportunity for people to reflect on what others are telling them. Part of their action plan may be to actually check out their perceptions with those who are significant to the success of a given Business. Sometimes you get information you need to know. Sometimes it just is not the right thing to do to ask for direct feedback because the feedback might be too painful, the relationship may be too fragile, or the individual in question might be incapable of giving you a fully honest answer. In those cases you just have to go on hunches and trial and error, but at least you are paying attention.

Techniques for Getting in Touch with Your Stakeholders

There are a number of techniques for getting in touch with your Stakeholders' messages. They are variations on a theme, but the slight variation might make one or another approach more feasible or provide better information to guide your Life Business work. We have used all the following methods in the Life Business Program itself or as part of the follow-up or homework aspect of the Program:

1. Reflect and observe: What has the person or group actually said to you that you need to take into account? What messages does their behavior send?
2. Put yourself in the others' shoes: Even if Stakeholders have not communicated their desires and concerns directly, can you imagine what those might be by attempting to understand their situation in detail from their point of view.
3. "Rent a significant other": Even if you have a hard time imagining what a stakeholder might be feeling, you can describe the situation and get advice from a friend who might be better able to imagine what is going on with the other person.

4. Obtain group advice and try role playing: Do you have a group to whom you could take the question of what a significant other might be feeling? Perhaps you can watch while others role-play a situation, or role-play the Stakeholder yourself and get some insight.

5. Observe: If you have a hunch of what people are thinking and not saying, you can observe the relationship more carefully to confirm it.

6. Assess the relationship: Ask and/or check out whether the relationship is strong enough and the situation appropriate. Consider whether you are a good enough listener to ask directly what a person thinks and feels about the relationship.

7. Get a coach to find out for you. Right now coaching is big in the business world, along with feedback surveys. Many leaders in major businesses have coaches. In a recent issue of the *New Yorker* magazine,[1] there was an entertaining story about a hugely successful business coach. One of his specialties was "360-degree feedback," in which he would interview the circle of the significant others of his client and bring him back the bad news: From the Boss: Jerk! From the Wife: Jerk! From the Kids: Jerk! From the Colleagues: Jerk! From the Aging Parents: Jerk! Undaunted, he would then work with his client to turn these perceptions around. Hopefully most of us are not candidates for a turnaround intervention in our Life Enterprise, but we probably could all benefit from a little more honest feedback. Sometimes a coach is available to collect that feedback for us.

Other Voices from Life Business Programs

The Voice of the Customer exercise has produced valuable insight for many Life Business participants. Here are examples from recent participants.

- Mary, the successful businesswoman working for one of the larger banks, incorporated the voice of her two sons right into the definition of her Business named "My Two Sons." Mary hears her sons saying to her, "Really take time to hear us, respect our opinions, and back off appropriately." Mary realizes that this is a critical time for her sons and for her relationship with them. She concluded, "I want to do it right."

- Brad, when he thought about how his children were reacting to the very stressful (and nearly fatal) year he had, understood the message from his youngest to be, "I need help."

- Nancy, a human resources consultant by profession, who was very people-oriented and "touchy feely" in her communications recognized that her accountant husband was sometimes uncomfortable about the way she communicated. The message intuited from her husband was, "Speak to me more in the language that I am comfortable with—facts, not just feelings."

- Cora is a successful businesswoman in marketing with a global tech firm. When querying herself as a customer of her Life Business that had to do with her professional self, got the message: "The thrill is gone." Things had changed in her workplace so that she no longer enjoyed working there.

- Henry, whose marriage had gone through a difficult time several years back, realized that the most important thing to his wife was that he "tell the truth" from now on out.

- George, an engineer, who was having a very difficult time with his boss whom he disagreed with on a number of on the job issues, used this exercise to put himself in the role of his supervisor. He heard the message, "Don't buck me." While George did not like what he was hearing, he recognized that he now had the key to getting along with his boss. Since he had only one year until his boss would probably be transferred, he decided to focus his efforts on the other Life Businesses in his portfolio where positive returns were more likely.

The voice of an important customer or supplier may not be determinative of your actions, but you darn sure better take it into account in choosing your future directions in business and in life!

Understanding the Trends and Likely Events in Your Life Businesses

The business world has developed numerous techniques to predict and take into account the various trends and events that might effect future market performance. In the Life Business Program we simply ask individuals to take each of their Businesses and identify the likely events and then project current trends that might impact that Business down the road.

You do not need a crystal ball to predict that your delightful 10-year-old daughter will be a teenager in a few years with a very different view of family vacations! You can predict that unfortunately your aging parents may need to move to an extended care facility within the next 5 years. If you have been keeping good records and know that your business has been growing steadily at 5 percent a year, that has some implications. At some point you will need more space. You can predict that the 15-year-old Volvo you have been driving will give up the ghost some time in the next 5 years, and so on.

Yet, amazingly, some people do not take the time to really think through the consequences of some perfectly predictable events for their Businesses. The Life

Business Program gives people the time and the forum for this kind of businesslike thinking.

Business Techniques for Assessing Future Trends and Events

There are a number of specialized techniques that businesses use for assessing future trends and events. These include Scenario Planning, the Delphi Technique, and Mind Mapping.[2] They can be adapted for use by individuals for this part of the Life Business process.

Scenario Planning, a method of preparing an organization to deal with the future, was pioneered by Royal Dutch Shell. The company's planning department first develops well-researched future scenarios based on assumptions about important aspects of its business (e.g., the price of oil). Usually it develops a best-case, worst-case, and middle-case scenario about what could happen in the future on those dimensions. Company management then develops contingency plans for each scenario and implements those elements of the plans that provide it the greatest flexibility in the face of a highly uncertain future. Individuals can do this as well to address uncertainty about their own personal futures.

The Delphi Technique is a method for getting the best possible information about the future from expert advisers. A panel of advisers is selected and queried about a wide range of relevant predictions about future trends and events. When conflicts in predictions arise, the experts are asked to reconcile or explain the conflicts. In that way the organization gets a consensus view from the experts of what is the most probable future and can also define and prepare the areas of greatest uncertainty. Individuals can manage uncertainty about their futures as well by consulting experts (e.g., physicians, stock brokers, psychologists, etc.) and comparing their answers.

Mind Mapping is a method of using a group of stakeholders from a range of different sectors of the organization's environment to pool its information about important future trends and events. Starting with a series of "trunk" lines on a large sheet of white paper titled "technology, economics, politics," etc., the participants list various specific events and trends that become branches and stems off these trunks. The group then prioritizes the trends as to their importance and develops potential responses. Using this method, the organization becomes aware of all the connections among the various trends and events and how they can affect their business. In Life Business you can use Mind Mapping with a group of advisers, or it can be used solo to make sure you have covered all the bases in your personal analysis of future Trends and Events affecting one of your Life Businesses.

When Harry went through the above exercises, he came up with the Trends and Events listed in the accompanying figure.

List of Trends and Events in Harry's Life Businesses

Life Businesses	Likely Trends and Events
1. CONNECTIONS UNLIMITED: the business of maintaining and developing intimate relations with my wife and daughter, my close relatives, and a wide circle of longtime friends	• Mother–daughter conflicts becoming more frequent and intense. • Daughter will be thinking about college. • Daughter will get her driver's license. • Anxiety about balancing of my daughter's extracurriculars and school work. • Wife will be finishing her novel. • Wife after me to get a new car.
2. HHMO (Harry Health Maintenance Organization): the business of preventing heart disease and maintaining good physical condition	• Gaining weight at rate of 2 lbs. per year. • Cholesterol has been creeping up. • New cholesterol lowering drugs. • Knees do not like jogging much. • Health insurance costs are on the rise. • There is a closing window to get long-term care insurance.
3. PP&G (Personal and Professional Growth): the business of developing myself and my abilities	• Many professional education opportunities will continue to be available.
4. TGAL (Think Globally, Act Locally): contributing to the solution of problems in my community and in my state	• There will be plenty of good causes to work on and contribute to.
5. IGUANA (I gonna be me): doing what I like to do; having fun; recreation	• I may be aging out of some of the more strenuous hiking trips, etc. • I will need to use my frequent flyer miles within 3 years. • My wife will be at a conference in July—a good opportunity for a hiking trip.

(continues)

List of Trends and Events in Harry's Life Businesses (*Continued*)

Life Businesses	Likely Trends and Events
6. HEWT (Have Ear, Will Travel): Harry's consulting business	• Referrals have continued to be remarkably steady. • There is a trend toward longer-term projects and more travel.
Other	• Kitchen in bad need of renovation.

When Harry put these Trends and Events together, he noticed several important clusters that were significant for his future plans. Pressure was building up on the home front with his wife trying to finish her novel and his daughter getting involved in big-time teenage events like learning to drive and thinking about college. At the same time his business was growing, and he was traveling more.

Also there was lots to think about on the health front. The Trends were not good: higher cholesterol, more weight, weaker knees, and bigger insurance payments. On the bright side business continued to look good, but would it draw him away from home at crucial times? Finally, there looked like there were going to be some big financial outlays for college, renovation of the kitchen and other parts of the house, and a new car.

Trends and Events for Other Life Business Participants

This Trend and Event analysis is productive in many ways. Here are insights from some other Life Business participants we have been following:

- Mary realized her 90-year-old grandmother was going to require significant attention now that she had fallen and damaged her hip.
- Peter realized there was a likelihood that he would have periodic trouble with his eyesight due to a detached retina problem that continued to recur.
- Sandy realized that going back to school to get her master's degree in order to become a principal would have a broad impact on some of her other interests and commitments.
- Richard recognized that in 2 years the lump-sum payment he had gotten from the sale of his family business would be spent, so he needed to get his consulting operation up and running by then.

- Betty recognized that real estate values were continuing to rise and that she needed to act sooner rather than later on her long-term goal of buying investment real estate.

This activity helps you avoid "future shock." How often do you take the time to think about the upcoming changes in your life and what impact they will have both individually and, very importantly, cumulatively? Only when you make the time necessary to do this kind of thinking will you be investing your life with the focus and seriousness of managers of well-run businesses.

Exercises for the Reader

1. Create your own chart of key Stakeholders and then list their key messages. Which messages are you most certain about? Which do you really need to check out in some way?
2. List the major Trends and Events that will be affecting your Life Enterprise over the next few years. What is the cumulative impact of these Trends on your time? Your finances? Your key relationships?

For additional exercises related to Step 4 of the Life Business Program, go to www.lifebusiness.com.

Conclusion

You have assessed the "marketplace" messages that your Stakeholder network has for each of your Life Businesses. You have identified the short- and long-term trends that impact on your Life Businesses. As a result of these activities you now understand the overall position of your Life Enterprise in the marketplace. Because of these assessments and those in Step 3, you have successfully avoided the Ready-Fire-Aim problem that afflicts many businesses and individuals. You have a firm base of facts and analysis. You are ready to take on the future. That's Step 5.

Notes

1. Larissa MacFarquhar. "The Better Boss: Whom Do You Call When the Executive Is Unbearable?" *New Yorker*, April 22–29, 2002, pp. 114–136.

2. A good discussion of "Mind Mapping" may be found in Sandra Janoff and Marvin Weisbord, *Future Search*, Berrett-Koehler, 2nd ed., 1996. pp. 79–85; for a discussion of scenario planning, see Charlotte Roberts, et al. in Peter Senge, Art Kleiner (eds.), *The Fifth Discipline Fieldbook: Strategies and Tools for Building*

a Learning Organization, Currency/Doubleday, 1994, pp. 279–285. The Delphi process originated in the RAND corporation in the 1960s and has been widely used in many variations since then to assess future trends. An early article on Delphi is Fusfeld and Foster, "The Delphi Technique: Survey and Comment," *Business Horizons,* June 1971.

Envision a Positive Future

What does the future say about what you need to be doing today?

If you do not think about the future, you cannot have one.

John Galsworthy

LIFE BUSINESS TENET

There is a positive future for you! While considering the trends and events that are likely to affect your Life Businesses, projecting the needs of those who are most important to you, and keeping your core Values in focus, you can paint an imaginative and compelling Vision of the future that you want to live.

The most successful companies spend a lot of time thinking about what the future will be and how they can succeed in it. In fact, the latest strategic planning literature suggests that businesses need to have two organizations going simultaneously, one that implements the current business and one that is busy creating the business of the future! Predicting the future has become a whole industry in itself, and the most successful companies are very much in the business of imagining what new products and services will make them successful players in that future.

Some argue that with rapid change occurring everywhere, long-term thinking no longer makes sense. We beg to disagree. Without Vision you succumb to "drift." With a clear Vision you have a basis that can guide your response to change. While your Vision can certainly change and ought to be revised periodically, having a Vision is fundamental to building a sound Life Enterprise.

The idea of Vision has become a part of the political landscape. "The Vision Thing" was the Achilles heel of the elder George Bush. Now every presidential

61

hopeful has a "A Vision for America." The Vision concept has already gripped popular and business literature. For example, Peter Senge argues that personal Vision is one of the five essential "disciplines" of an effective leader.[1] Visioning is an idea whose time has come! But how do you get a Vision for your own Life Enterprise? In our experience, for a Vision to be effective, it must have at least three characteristics. It must be: (1) positive, (2) grounded, and (3) specific.

Imagine a Positive Future

Hope is the fuel that will propel your Life Enterprise into the future. Vision is the process that injects that fuel into the engine of your Life Enterprise. We live in a time when catastrophic images of the future (e.g., asteroids hitting the earth, volcanoes, tidal waves, epidemics) have great currency in the popular media. We also have negative futures portrayed in books and movies (e.g., George Orwell's *1984, Blade Runner, Mad Max, The Matrix*). With a steady diet of these types of books and films, it is easy to get discouraged about our prospects for the future. Given the pervasiveness of negative future images, it is critically important to develop a positive view of the future that is motivating and compelling for you if you want your Life Enterprise to succeed.

Your image of the future needs to be based on what you want to have happen in your life, on your core values, and on your hopes for yourself and your family. Your Vision should draw on your deeper wellsprings of motivation. This image of the future needs to be positive and compelling enough to sustain you during the period of effort it will take to get from "here to there"—through all the setbacks you'll encounter along the way. A positive image of the future may seem unattainable now. It may be a real stretch for you to imagine a positive future, but you need one for your Life Enterprise to succeed.

A positive Vision should not be confused with specific Goals. The research on "high achievers" shows that they have a self-imposed standard of excellence (that's the Vision part) and that although they set challenging Goals, those Goals are realistic.[2] Our Vision is the broad landscape of the positive future we are headed toward in our lives. Our Goals are the many steps on the road to getting there. We talk about Goals when we introduce Steps 7 and 8, but for now we will look beyond our current horizons.

Ground Your Vision

We have found that when we have asked business clients to create a positive Vision before they have done the kind of extensive reflection and self-assessment that you have done in preparing the Annual Report and the Market Report, what we get is fantasies, not Visions. We get pie-in-the sky ideas divorced from the reality of the organization's challenges, assets, and real prospects. On the other hand, when participants have done this homework, they produce Visions that foresee positive solutions to current problems, that take into account supporting forces and assets, and that capitalize on genuine opportunities. This is why Steps 1 through 4 precede Step 5.

Be Concrete

"Life, liberty, and the pursuit of happiness" are positive directions, but they are a little vague in terms of planning your life Enterprise. A truly effective Vision may be literary in quality and inspirational in tone, but it is also specific and concrete. There has to be a "there." You need to identify what you will be doing in the future, what it will look like, what it will feel like, and what it will sound like. Remember the IRS record-keeping guidelines introduced in Step 1—who, what, where, when, and why. You will need to specify events and outcomes that will indicate success in your Life Businesses.

A positive Vision comes about through asking yourself questions like, "How do I want this to come out?" "What is the best outcome I could realistically expect in this situation?" "What would my ideal day look like in the future?" "What would success in attaining my most important life goals mean in measurable terms?"

Think Backward to the Present

Once a person has developed a positive Vision, it is necessary to get "back from the future" to the present and then determine how to move forward. In the strategic planning literature, there is a concept known as Backward Planning.[3] This involves starting from the point of achievement of a significant business goal or milestone, say 10 years out. Next we say, "Well, if that is where we are in year 10, then this is where we need to be in year 9; and for this year 9 goal to be met, here is what needs to happen in year 8," and so on, back to the present. It may take several iterations of fiddling with Goals, time lines, and activities, but when the backward planning process is completed, the corporation has a pretty realistic road map to the future. In the Life Business Program we ask participants to do a kind of backward planning for their own lives.

Once clients have established their 10-Year Vision, we ask them what "New Ventures," if any, have to be launched in order for them to get to where they want to go. We ask them how their existing Life Businesses need to change. Ultimately, in Steps 7 and 8 we work out the implications of this thinking for short-term, medium-term and long-term activities. Our future Vision is paradoxically the starting point of the planning journey. The process might be viewed as being "helicoptered up" to the top of a high wall we want to climb. We put a stake at the top—that's our future Vision in specific terms. From that stake we tie a strong rope and we carefully negotiate our way back down to base camp, and we put in steps along the way so that we can climb back up.

The key principles of Visioning in Step 5 bear repeating:

1. Make your Vision positive.
2. Make your Vision concrete and specific.
3. Think backward from your Vision to identify, in a preliminary way, what has to change for you to be successful in achieving the future you want.

Harry's Future, 10 Years On

Harry is now ready to look to the future. When Harry looks 10 years on, what does he have to consider? He is aware of the Trends and Events he identified at the end of Step 4. First and foremost, he will be 10 years older. Second, his now 15-year-old daughter will have left home and presumably gone to college, and she will be well on her way to adulthood. His wife will have finished her first novel and will possibly be working on her second or third, if things go well. An area of uncertainty is her health, given that she suffers from the aftermath of polio. The Internet will be a major factor in people's lives and businesses. No one knows where the stock market will be. Will it have recovered by 2010? The driving force of Harry's Life Enterprise is the network of relationships he has built up over the past 20 years. These people will be older; some will be retired; some will have moved on to more influential positions. There will be new faces. There are many uncertainties (e.g., will there be one or several environmental disasters?). What is the next major technological breakthrough?

Not Harry, or anyone else, can know the answers to many of these questions, but Harry can know what he wants. He can develop a preferred Vision of the future and his life and work toward that. With that Vision in mind he can develop plans, foresee obstacles, grasp opportunities, and guard against threats.

In the Life Business Program, we encourage participants to write about their life from the future perspective as if it had already happened. We suggest that you decide what publication your living biography will appear in. We've seen everything from *The Irish Lynx* to the *Scientific Australian*. Perhaps it is a story about you in the feature section of your hometown newspaper. Perhaps it is a letter you are writing to a friend, or your own diary. The important thing is that you look back on the past from the future and evoke the positive past that you are writing about. This is another one of those important "right-brain" planning activities we talked about earlier. In the next section you can read about how Harry developed his Vision.

Harry Looks Back from the Vantage Point of a Decade Ahead

Harry was glad that he had set aside time to be supportive of his daughter during her 4 years of high school. Knowing that kids in this high-achieving school often "knocked themselves out" with advanced placement courses, activities, and social life, Harry was glad that he worked to help her achieve a reasonable balance. They took several special trips together which were meaningful to both of them. Her choice of a college reflected a mature understanding of her interests, abilities, and the present level of her ambition.

Harry was also glad that he and his wife had taken time to build their relationship so as to prepare for "the empty nest." Frequent walks and talks, time away together, collaboration on a redesign of the kitchen, an increased sense of partnership in domestic relationships gave her the support she needed to focus on her writing and gave Harry the sense that this all-important connection was solid. Harry also supported his wife in her increasingly frequent writing retreats by taking care of their daughter for those times. His wife repaid Harry's efforts to partner with flexibility of her own when Harry needed to travel for business or to go on a hiking trip with the guys and with a positive and caring tone in their day-to-day relationship.

Harry stayed in close touch with his sister, mostly by phone and by e-mail. They even did a workshop together which introduced her to aspects of the consulting business that fit her experience and background. Harry also made a point of staying connected with his three first cousins and their families.

During the early years of his 10-Year Life Business Plan, Harry began to leverage his professional connections in order to become even more proactive in designing projects that met client needs, created social value, strengthened his own economic position, and gave him personal satisfaction. His increasing involvement with his professional group led to new and interesting projects around the country and also the international connections that led to some of his overseas work in the fifth and sixth years of his Plan.

Harry was able to develop new services and products that kept his consulting business vital and made him increasingly respected and sought after. Harry developed his own Web page and explored ways to transfer his special expertise via the World Wide Web.

During this period, Harry's workshops, already underway in the first couple of years of his Plan, became established to the point that he was able to hire others to offer them and to draw revenues from that activity. As part of his consulting practice

Harry developed several pilot projects that led to major social innovations, giving him the sense that he had made a major, positive contribution to society.

Harry continued his commitment to his own professional development. He feels that the time he spent with his counselors in the early years of the Plan laid a firm basis for later development. He continued to devote several days a year to attending workshops that helped him learn and grow and which paid handsome dividends for his work with clients.

By investing his time in several writing ventures, Harry gained experience in the publishing realm, Several years later this experience led to his first book, which discussed a variety of innovative approaches for improving organizations and society. In addition Harry began work on his series of articles on understanding and healing organizational conflict based on case studies of his own 30-year consulting practice.

Harry kept up his daily exercise routine but found a way to save his knees while still enjoying a workout. He contacted a personal trainer and got some advice on the particular activities that would keep him fit in an appropriate way, given the delicate condition of his knees. He found a way to take those 15 pounds off and to keep them off. He also spent the time to really figure out what he believed about diet and vitamins. As a result, despite his high cholesterol, there is still no sign of clogged arteries.

Harry also looks back with pleasure on the various hiking trips he was able to squeeze in over the past 10 years, including his regular European trips, his frequent short hiking trips to the North Carolina mountains, the western United States, and New England. These trips were also occasions to sustain friendships he developed with his good buddies over the years.

Harry made his leisure time count more and sought out books to read, museums to see, and places to visit that really gave him pleasure.

Later Harry was more known as an author, speaker, workshop leader and Internet provider than as a consultant who took on detailed projects, though he still was an active coach for a number of organizational leaders and he continued to mentor new consultants. He had several ongoing leaders' groups that he facilitated. He spent more time doing research and writing and established a non-profit corporation to support social innovations and problem solving using behavioral science approaches.

With their daughter out of the home, Harry and his wife were less tied down. During the fifth and sixth years of his Plan, Harry and his wife lived in Europe, where Harry taught and his wife wrote, while touring the Old World on weekends and holidays. It also became possible for Harry and his wife to spend long periods at the beach or in the mountains for hiking and exploring.

Marc Goes for the Gusto

While Harry took a somewhat prosaic approach to developing his Vision, Marc, who was a writer by trade, took a more literary approach. Marc decided that the article would be in the *New York Times Magazine*. He explained that "it would focus on the extraordinary success of the first two books in a series of novels set in 500 B.C. among the Anasazi. It would explore how the themes of the novels shed insight into the great issues of the time: environment, competition, spirituality, community. Like *Coldmountain*, the first of these novels was a commercial and literary success, winner of the National Book Award and a number one bestseller.

In Marc's words: "My story would go on to focus on my life, my wonderful marriage to Elana, unusual in its durability and closeness, my great relationship with my sons, my friendships and my homes in America, by the sea, and in Italy. In the article I would come through as a decent, kind, serious, beloved, creative, and successful person who took great joy in life and the people around him." An excerpt from the article is as follows:

The heavy smell of lemons intoxicates us, and we are already languid with the Southern Italian sun and the steady rhythm of the sea pounding on the craggy Mediterranean coastline. The villa with its commanding views is a hive of activity as family friends and servants prepare for a spectacular celebration in honor of the sixtieth birthday of the author whose first novel, published only a few years ago, is turning into a full fledged industry. In 2008, *Anasazi*, sold a phenomenal 3,000,000 hardcover copies, won the National Book Award, and was nominated for a Pulitzer Prize. In July of this year, the heavily promoted film will be released to coincide with the publication of *Coyote God*, sequel to *Anasazi*, in a flashback series set in North America's cradle of civilization. The paperback edition of *Anasazi* will be released with a new cover featuring artwork from the film.

The carefully controlled chaos of Marc's family life is directed by Elana, Marc's wife of 27 years, whose slender figure and palpable vitality belie her age. "This is a dream come true for Marc in so many ways," she comments, while making way for four men bearing one of the dozens of giant oak serving tables. "He spent years summoning up the courage to write *Anasazi* and many years more in the writing. Even for him its success comes as a complete surprise. To be celebrating his sixtieth birthday surrounded by his family and friends from around the world, his publishers, and even his first grandchild is literally a dream come true."

Reality Check for Your Vision

To do a reality check of your Vision, you should reflect on your work in Steps 1 through 4. In doing so, you bring together the insights and ideas for positive change that you have been gathering all along in the Life Business process. This reflection includes:

- A review of the key pieces of data that need to be taken into account for your future
- Identification and Naming of your Life Businesses to revisit the most essential themes of your life
- ROI Analysis and Value Analysis in order to find points of dissatisfaction and a need for change, as well as positive activities to be nurtured and further developed
- A review of the Voice of the Customer and Trends and Events exercises, for the current and longer-term factors that need to be taken into account when projecting your positive future

In the example that follows, we can look at the key items that served to ground Harry's future Vision. The accompanying table shows Harry's Life Businesses and the factors he thought were important to keep in mind in thinking about his future.

Harry's Vision Reality Check

Life Businesses	*Major Factors to Keep in Mind*
CONNECTIONS UNLIMITED: the business of maintaining and developing intimate relations with my wife and daughter, my close relatives, and a wide circle of longtime friends	Most expenditures are in this Business, but where it all goes isn't well understood. (R) Daughter preparing for and going off to college. (TE) Wife's unhappiness with Harry's unavailability to talk about important household matters and to partner in dealing with daughter. (VC) Wife will be finishing her novel. (TE) Harry loses a lot of energy when he is not getting along with Helen and when his daughter and wife are fighting. Harry still enjoys keeping up with his friends and colleagues. (ROI)

(continues)

Harry's Vision Reality Check (*Continued*)

Life Business	*Major Factors to Keep in Mind*
HHMO (Harry Health Maintenance Organization): the business of preventing heart disease and maintaining good physical condition	Gaining weight at rate of 2 lbs. per year, Cholesterol has been creeping up. New cholesterol-lowering drugs. Knees giving Harry trouble. (TE) Harry really gets a lot of positive energy from exercising. (ROI) Harry has felt the work he is doing with his counselor has been good for his overall mental health. (ROI)
PP&G (Personal and Professional Growth): the business of developing myself and my abilities	Many professional education opportunities will continue to be available. (TE) Harry felt that he was spending too much time in meetings which made it hard to get other things done. (R)
TGAL (Think Globally, Act Locally): contributing to the solution of problems in my community and in my state	There will be plenty of good causes to work on and contribute to. (TE) Harry's pro bono activities are satisfying, but they are still work. (R) Harry gets a lot of satisfaction from his charitable donations, feeling that he is doing his part. (ROI) Harry felt he was overcommitted to various pro bono projects. (ROI)
IGUANA (I gonna be me): doing what I like to do; having fun; recreation	Harry really enjoyed: hiking, foreign travel, visiting museums, concerts, etc. (ROI)
HEWT (Have Ear, Will Travel): Harry's consulting business	Business continues to be good, referrals increasing, more long-term projects. (TE) Too much time spent working. (ROI) Harry feels he is being very creative and constructive in his work. (VA)

(*continues*)

Harry's Vision Reality Check (*Continued*)

Life Business	Major Factors to Keep in Mind
Other	Kitchen in bad need of renovation; car is old but serviceable. (TE) Harry does not feel that he has had the amount of professional recognition he wanted. (VA) Harry and Helen still spend about 35% more than they take in yearly and cover this from sale of stock in the portfolio his wife inherited. This leads to a decline in financial assets in down market years; could be a threat to retirement income if not addressed. (R)

Sources of Ideas

R=Review (Step 1); N=Naming Life Businesses (Step 2); ROI=Evaulating ROI Analysis in Life Businesses (Step 3); VA=Value Analysis (Step 3); VC=Voice of the Customer (Step 4); TE=Trends and Events (Step 4)

Next to each of the factors we have indicated in parentheses the part of the Annual Business Planning Cycle when he became aware of this factor (i.e., R= Review, N= Naming Life Businesses, ROI= Return on Investment Analysis, VA= Value Analysis, VC= Voice of the Customer, TE= Trends and Events.). Harry reread his Vision and added to it items that seemed necessary to address any important issue uncovered earlier in this Review.

Business as Usual May Not Get You Where You Want to Go

Having done a reality check on his Vision, Harry is ready to begin putting the backward planning principle to work. We ask each participant in the Life Business Program to review his or her 10-Years-On Vision in these terms:

1. Which personal values will be more/less present in your desired future?
2. Which current Life Businesses will be important in 10 years?
3. Which current Life Businesses will seem less important in 10 years?
4. Which New Ventures need to be considered?

In terms of answering these four questions for Harry, the desired future seems to involve more of the values of fun and recognition. Whether his Vision involves more wealth is not clear. He still wants to have made some significant social contributions. He will make more investment in his relationship with his daughter while she is in high school, and that investment drops off when she is in college. He speaks of making more of a commitment to partnering with his wife in general and in supporting his wife's emerging career as a writer. Investment in health and fitness remains high. His consulting business changes somewhat radically in this projection moving Harry from being a consultant to being more of a pundit. A few new potential Businesses show their heads, around foreign travel and writing.

How does Harry "manage" to get all these goodies for himself? Stay tuned and we will see how in Steps 6 through 13. While Harry's Vision is very positive, it is anchored in current concerns and emerging possibilities. Again it is positive, but it is not pie in the sky. These things are probably within Harry's reach if he can make the right moves. The accompanying table offers a quick summary of the broad implications for Harry's Life Businesses.

Strategic Implications for Future Investments by Harry

Life Businesses	0–3 Years	4–6 Years	7–10 Years
CONNECTIONS UNLIMITED	More intensity with wife and daughter	More partnership with wife	Continued strong partnership with wife
HHMO	Continued investment	Continued investment	Continued investment
PP&G	Continued investment	Continued investment	Continued investment
TGAL	Continued investment	Continued investment	Continued investment
IGUANA	Continued investment	More investment	More investment
HEWT	Smarter investment: more training and mentoring Bigger projects	Smarter investment	Less investment

Identifying Your "New Ventures"

If you want to become a gourmet chef, as one IBM manager did in a recent Life Business Program, you probably can't wait 10 years until you retire to get started. If your goal is to have your own bed and breakfast in 10 years, you need to start preparing for that Life Business now. If you have never traveled abroad but want to make travel part of your life, you need to begin sometime. As the saying goes: "Doing what you have always done will get you the results you have always gotten." To add something new to your life, you need a Vision of how things could be different.

When we thought about where we wanted to go with the Life Business concept, we developed a Vision of the future that included the following statements:

- Life Business will become the vehicle of choice for the transformation of the organizational culture of the banking and financial services industry into more customer-meaningful organizations based on a deepening understanding of the relationship between peoples' dreams and their financial resources.
- Life Business will become a well-known framework for personal and family, Vision-anchored empowerment, in the overall culture as well as in the world of organizations.

Once we had established these Vision statements for the next 10 years, we then had to go back and look at what we were doing and to see if we were walking the walk. Guess what? We weren't! If we were going to make this Vision into a reality, we had to change the things we were doing. First, we had to develop a strategy and activities to market Life Business to the banking industry, which we did. Second, we had to do more to publicize and explain the Life Business concept, which, if you are reading this and have visited our Web site (www.lifebusiness.com), we obviously have done to some extent.

Establishing a personal Vision and comparing that Vision with how you are currently going about your Life Businesses will likely imply changes in those Businesses or even the start up of new ones. For example, if your Vision of yourself in 10 years is being a devoted grandparent but you are not on speaking terms with your son and his new wife, then you may want to consider starting a Business of "Cross-Generation Relationship Building."

Harry's Vision statement suggests several New Ventures. He describes these as:

- Writer to Pundit: Through successes in his professional writing, Harry will be more recognized as an expert in his field and more sought after for a variety of consulting and other business opportunities.

- Travelocus: While Harry still has vitality and health, he realizes his dream of spending time in some of the great Old World culture capitals and the New World natural wonders that he has missed so far.
- Home Improvement: Harry and Helen work creatively together to design the last stage of improvements for their home of the last 20 years: new kitchen, landscaping, and bigger home office for Harry.

Visions of Other Life Business Participants

Visions can include hopes for leisure, love, service, spirituality, financial gain, and a whole range of positive outcomes. You create your own Vision based on your needs, values, and hopes. Here is sampling of Visions from other Life Business participants:

- Peter and Sandy envisioned a time when they would cut loose from their U.S. base and spend 2 years or so wandering around their favorite places in the world.
- Mary saw herself happily remarried with a man she really cared about and who cared about her, and envisioned her two boys through school and away from home, but still connected to their mom.
- Brad saw himself launching first his own development firm and then writing a novel.
- George imagined a new career as a gourmet chef after retiring early from his high-tech job.
- Helen saw a successful first novel, which was parlayed into a part-time teaching opportunity in a creative writing program.
- Jena saw herself as creating a new program for leaders in the organization in which she worked that emphasized Values as much as effectiveness.
- Elaine imagined herself in her dream house.

Strategic Implications for Future Investments in Harry's Potential New Ventures

New Ventures	1–3 Years	4–6 Years	7–10 Years
Writer to Pundit	Start up	Develop	Maintain
Travelocus	Start up	Develop	Maintain
Home Improvement	Plan	Implement	Enjoy

Exercises for the Reader

1. Create your own Vision for the next 10 years. Think positive. Write it from the perspective of 10 years on.
2. Work on it until you are satisfied. Do a Reality check of your Vision against your previous work.
3. Ask yourself what New Ventures are implied by this Vision. Make a revised list of current and potential Businesses.

More information and exercises for Step 5 of the Life Business process are available on our Web site, www.lifebusiness.com.

Overcoming Your Resistance to Success

One of the reasons that a Visioning process may be problematic for some people is that their resistance to actually succeeding is very strong. While on the surface, we all want to be successful, below the surface we all have lots of reasons why we might not want to succeed. Here is a partial list. Look it over and see if any of these potential blocks fit you:

- It would be too much trouble to try for what I really want.
- If I failed, I would feel terrible about myself.
- I don't deserve it.
- I would have to give up my fantasy that there are no limits to what I can do or spend.
- I would have to really listen to what others are telling me, and I would rather "live free or die."
- There's no sense wanting what I cannot afford.

Some of these issues may be lurking if you find this Visioning exercise "stupid and boring" or if you try it and nothing specific can be written or if when you complete the exercise, instead of feeling excitement, you feel nothing or even let down. If the Visioning exercise is just too difficult for you, it may be because a significant member of your Internal Management Team has one of the above ideas and through the actions of that Management Team member, your team is being held back. This Management Team Member may need some coaching at this point. If he or she is the leader of the planning process, then you may want to replace the team pessimist with a more optimistic team member.

Business psychologists speak about "mental models,"[4] deep-seated beliefs about the corporation, its formula for success, or its markets that actually hold a company back from true success. Only by coming to understand what these mental models are and by comparing them against a more current and realistic view of the situation can the organization progress beyond its self-limiting ideas.

None of us is really immune to these antisuccess viruses, and remember they can be Life Business–specific. You may have the inner green light to be rich as Croesus, but feel hopeless about forming a truly loving relationship, or vice versa. Some of your most important accomplishments in your Life Businesses will consist of overcoming these subtle impediments to envisioning success and then following through on your Vision.

From Visions to Strategies

Successful Businesses know that it is important to move forward in a strategic way. Instead of trying to solve every problem they discover in their production, sales, or management processes, they give priority to those problems or opportunities for improvement that are most consistent with their future direction. It is because of this principle that we cautioned you in Step 3 to avoid the "quick fix." Step 3 analysis points you toward problems to be solved or managed and possible improvements. However, until your Vision is defined, you have no way of assessing the relative importance of these improvements.

For example, should Harry spend more time improving his consulting practice, doing things with his daughter, building bridges with his wife, working out at the gym, researching new cholesterol medicines, or some combination of the above? What's the priority and how do all these opportunities for improvement fit together? It is the Vision that tells us what is important and gives us our first clues as to the timing and phasing of potential improvement projects. Having completed Step 5, you are much closer to the action phase of your Life Enterprise Business Plan, but one thing is needed before you leap into the breach. This is the Strategy that will guide action for each of your current Life Businesses and New Ventures. In Step 6 you are introduced to a powerful analytical tool that will guide you in developing a winning Strategy for each of your Life Businesses.

Notes

1. Peter Senge. *The Fifth Discipline.* Currency/Doubleday, 1994, p. 139ff.

2. There is a brief discussion of the essential characteristics of the high-achieving individual in Kolb, Rubin, and McIntire, *Organizational Psychology, an Experiential Approach.* Prentice Hall, 1971, pp. 81–82.

3. Backward Planning is a concept that is related to the notion of "blue sky planning" and visioning. The idea is current in both business and policy circles. The key question is what has to happen now, if we are to achieve a certain end

by a certain time. Backward planners start with the assumption that the goal has been achieved in a certain year and then infer what had to happen in the previous year and so on down to the present. This method also provides a reality check on the goal-setting process, because if the last step is an impossible one, then you know you have overshot and must revise the goal or apply more resources

4. Peter Senge. *The Fifth Discipline. Op. cit.*, section on Mental Models, p. 274ff

PART THREE

Strategic Plan

Analysis gives rise to ideas about improving the current and the predicted, and achieving the desired.

Companies articulate their Strategies, Goals, and Projects through their Strategic Plan. Similarly, in Steps 6, 7, and 8 we address the following questions:

- Which Life Businesses do you want to maintain, build, create, or leave in order to achieve the future you desire?
- What are the specific Goals you want to accomplish in each of your current and emerging Life Businesses?
- What Projects will you develop for achieving these Goals?

STEP 6

Strategize for Success

What's a cow got to do with it?

You got to know when to hold 'em, you got to know when to fold 'em, you got to know when to walk away and you got to know when to run.

"The Gambler," sung by Kenny Rogers

LIFE BUSINESS TENET

You can create specific Strategies in your life that will lead to the successful realization of your Vision. Using a technique borrowed from the business world, you can determine which core life activities to emphasize, deemphasize, continue, or create on your journey to your positive future.

In projecting Trends and Events in Step 5, you may have been thinking about the future, but now in Step 6 you have to place a bet on it. MBA students learn that Management is about doing things right, while Strategy is about doing the right things. "Doing the right things" means providing those goods and services that people will want and pay for, now and in the future, and that will turn a good profit. Both doing things right (Management) and doing the right things (Strategy) are important, but it all starts with Strategy.

The critical Strategic question is "What business are you in?" This question is fundamental for venture capitalists trying to figure out where to put their money, for individuals starting out on their careers, and for Life Business participants. Who would have wanted to be a management trainee for a typewriter factory in 1970 or invested in LP record manufacturing facilities in 1990? No matter how well these enterprises were run, they were destined to be losers. We can let you have some rotary telephone dials cheap. They are in excellent condition. Interested?

The basic principle for successful investing is that you need to be able to predict which businesses will be vital in the near future, which are on their way out, and which will be strong over the long term. The same is true for your Life Businesses. You need to be able to understand which of your core commitments are no longer going to be satisfying in the future, which will be dependable sources of your vitality, and what new commitments can bring an increased sense of joy, meaning, and satisfaction.

Understanding the Dimensions of Strategic Choice in Your Life Businesses

Before investing in an industry, you should consider the maturity of the industry and its overall profit prospects, the position of the company in the industry, and the life cycle of the product itself. The large tonnage steel industry in the United States at this writing is past mature. It is overripe and survives only, some say, because of federal trade protection. Any investment in this industry has to be carefully calculated because the industry's underlying fundamental strengths have eroded. Biotechnology, on the other hand, is an emerging industry. However, we do not know yet which new products and companies in this industry will be the clear winners.

In addition to assessing the state of the industry, businesses also look at the life cycle of their products. Successful businesses know that at various points of a given product's life cycle they can maximize profits, at other parts of this life cycle they need to invest to make profits in the future. There comes a time in the life of most products and services when their appeal is over and they need to be phased out to make room for new products and services. Successful businesses factor in all these concerns in making their investments. Skillful understanding of the product cycle has been the salvation of the auto industry in recent decades as it introduced SUVs to the American market. Traditional station wagons are antiques, yet the Beetle is back!

In our own lives we need to consider the various cycles that will change our sense of what is satisfying and meaningful. There are at least three interdependent cycles that people have to deal with in their lives[1]:

1. The Career Cycle with its stages of preparatory education, career choice, gaining entry, building competence, renewal, and eventually retirement from the preoccupations of vocation and livelihood. Individuals may have multiple careers, and the resulting transitions will be both stressful and important times of personal growth.

2. The Family Cycle with its stages of childhood, dating, mating, child rearing, empty nesting, grandparenting, elder care, etc., sometimes with changes of partners and blending families along the way, thus introducing an additional level of pain, reward, and turbulence.
3. The Biological Cycle with childhood, adolescence, youth, adulthood, middle age, "modern maturity," and physical decline.

Each stage has its own dilemmas, developmental tasks, and associated crises that require our effort in order to negotiate it successfully. These life cycle factors may need to be considered in forecasting the profitability of your Life Business.

Identifying Your Future Life Business Strategies

How do you decide where to invest energy, time, and money to make the most of your Life Enterprise? There are a number of approaches to do this, but we have found the Strategy Matrix[2] to be among the most useful to Life Business participants. The logic behind the Strategy Matrix is simple. Each Life Business is evaluated in terms of whether its ROI is high or low in the short term (0–3 years), the medium term (4–6 years), and the long term (7–10 years). The Life Businesses are then placed on a 2 by 2 grid as shown in the accompanying figure.

Strategy Matrix Identifying Life Business Strategies

Quadrant 2: Cash Cows	**Quadrant 3: Stars**
High Present ROI	High Present ROI
Low Future ROI	High Future ROI
Strategy: Maintain/Milk	Strategy: Build
Quadrant 1: Dogs	**Quadrant 4: Rising Stars**
Low Present ROI	Low Present ROI
Low Future ROI	High Future ROI
Strategy: Shut Down	Strategy: Explore/Create

The Strategy Matrix associates a basic investment Strategy with the Life Business located in each quadrant. The Strategy Matrix will indicate whether a Business should be closed, maintained, expanded, or created as follows:

- Quadrant 1: Your Life Businesses or activities that have a low ROI today and show no signs of improving in the future are "Dogs" and should be "closed," spun-off, or sold. In your Life Enterprise this could take the form of a high-maintenance, low-producing client, relationship, or activity that has outlived its usefulness. Why is this person your client or friend now, exactly? If the thrill is gone from rock climbing, why keep doing it as the centerpiece of your "Sporting Life Business"?
- Quadrant 2: Your Life Businesses that have a high ROI today but are likely to gradually lose their competitive edge or market power are "Cash Cows" and should be "maintained" for their cash flow ("milk"). Your daughter is leaving for college in 2 years. Better reap the benefits now, despite the difficulties of hanging out with a teenager!
- Quadrant 3: Your Life Businesses that have a high ROI today and are likely to grow in profitability in the future are labeled "Stars" and should be "grown." Perhaps you're becoming a serious runner. You already love it, and it's good for you. Imagine where you could go from here. Is there a marathon in your future?
- Quadrant 4: Your Life Businesses and New Ventures which are either non-existent or have a low ROI today but show great promise are "Rising Stars" and should be "created." You have always wanted to have a garden, but you never had the right light in your yard. Your neighbor asks you if you want to go in with her and build a sunlit garden together. If you can make time for this and work things out, you can realize one of your long-term dreams. Keep in mind that Rising Stars are energy intensive, and perhaps capital intensive too. If you can't find enough energy, time, or money to invest in a Rising Star to make it successful, you may need to reconsider launching this Life Business.

Using the Strategy Matrix in your Life Businesses can give you a handle on which activities you should withdraw from, which you should continue, and which you need to start doing for your future benefit.

It is important to remember that activities in any of the quadrants will require focused attention. Businesses are not easily shut down, maintained, built, or started. Failure to execute any of these Strategies with real attention, commitment, thought, and follow-through can cause problems and incur unnecessary psychic, physical, or financial costs. More on the problems and possibilities of each of these Strategies later in this chapter, but now let's continue our example and see how the Strategy Matrix actually works in the Life Business Program.

An Example of How Businesses Use the Strategy Matrix

In its 2001 annual report, General Electric identified air craft engines, appliances, industrial products and systems, materials, NBC, power systems, technical products and services, and GE credit services as its businesses.[3] Of course, each of these businesses contains many products and services, but the leaders of GE must also think about these businesses as a whole. If GE executives were to use the Strategy Matrix to interpret the information in the annual report, their comments and questions might be as follows:

- Cash Cows. What is the profit picture for our aircraft engines in the short term, medium term, and long term? How uncertain is this? Does it depend on the level of defense spending or the quality of the European competition? How will the current contest between slower jumbo jets and super-fast, but smaller, jets affect our business? What do we need to do to hedge our bets?
- Stars. Will the financial services business remain strong as interest rates begin to climb back up? It's 40 percent of our earnings now. What will it be in the future? Where will the greater return be—in consumer financing, in industrial financing, or in insurance products?
- Dogs. Should we stay involved with NBC since it is so different from our other businesses? Is there a lack of fit that pushes this business into the Dog category for us? What about our investment in nuclear reactors in our power business—are we involved in a technology here that is on the way out or poised for a comeback?
- Rising Stars. What will be our big sources of earnings in the future? Will our digitized medical systems demonstrate their value to the U.S. health-care system? Can we extend to the huge Chinese market, and how huge is that market really?

By analogy, these are the kind of questions and concerns you would be asking about your own Life Businesses in your Strategy analysis.

Reconfiguring Your Life
Businesses for the Strategy Matrix

You may find now that the definition of the Businesses that you are in will need redefinition at this stage because of all of your analysis in Steps 1 through 5. Your first Life Businesses portfolio may no longer fully represent where you want to go in the future. Redefinition is progress!

Harry's analysis of his present Life Enterprise and desired future in Steps 1 through 5 leads him to reconfigure his Life Businesses somewhat. He comes to several very important conclusions. First, that Connections Unlimited is too big and unwieldy to be considered a single Life Business, especially in light of the messages he is getting from his wife and daughter. He thinks this Business needs to be broken up into smaller components so each can have the focus it requires. He decides to organize (in his mind) several new Businesses as follows:

* Connections Unlimited will still be the name Harry gives to the businesses of staying in touch with his wide circle of friends, relatives, and colleagues, but his relationship with his wife and daughter needs to be pulled out of the mix.
* Teen Bird will be the name he gives to the process of working with his wife to help his daughter through the difficult teenage years and onto college.
* Building Partners will be the name he gives to the business of building a closer relationship with his wife. This business is needed to launch the Teen Bird and will also prepare the way for the opportunity they will have to be together with fewer distractions after their daughter is out of the house.
* Home Improvement will be an important business, needed to oversee the major improvements required for his home sometime in the future. Harry wants to collaborate with his wife on this so it will be synergistic with his Building Partner Business. He knows this will be a stressful and expensive undertaking but ultimately satisfying if done intelligently and creatively.

Harry will still be in his HHMO (health), TGAL (community), HEWT (consulting), and IGUANA (self) Businesses. In addition, Harry will need two new Businesses, based on his preferred future.

One business will be called Writer to Pundit, which reflects Harry's goal of becoming more recognized through writing and other activities that make him more visible in his profession.

Another Business will be called Travelocus, which indicates Harry's desire to be a serious Old World "culture vulture" and a more active hiker and "enjoyer" of natural beauty.

When Harry arrays his New Ventures and continuing Life Businesses on a Strategy Matrix, as shown in the accompanying figure, the following observations stand out.

Dogs

Harry really doesn't have any Dog Businesses, but he wanted to note some things here that had been real drains on his energy even though they are just parts of several of his other Life Businesses.

In the low ROI client category Harry notes that there are several long-term client relationships that are no longer financially or psychically remunerative for him yet still take up a lot of time. Also, his monthly consultant-training group, which was very time consuming, has ceased to be so rewarding. They had all been good experiences, but Harry felt it was time to move on.

Overeating is a problem that he experiences in HHMO, because he is still gaining a few pounds a year, and that is not good for his cholesterol and overall health. He feels guilty when he has to have his pants let out, but he really likes those late night snacks and hates to diet. Harry gets enough daily exercise through his walking and exercise program. He needs to do more in the realm of cutting back on daily intake so as to stop the pounds-per-year increase in weight.

Strategy Matrix of Harry

Quadrant 2: Cash Cows	**Quadrant 3: Stars**
Teen Bird	HHMO
PP & G	Building Partners
HEWT	Connections Unlimited
TGAL	
Q1: Dogs	**Q4: Rising Stars**
Low ROI clients in HEWT	Writer to Pundit
Family spats in Teen Bird	Travelocus
Eat whatever, whenever	Home Improvement

Can Harry find a way to overcome the great pleasure he takes in eating before he develops into a blimp body type?

Another source of angst and energy drain is the recurrent and predictable spats with his daughter and wife. Can he get a better handle on those situations that seem to be chronic irritants involving the teenage daughter: starting off on trips, regulating bed time, reasonable nutrition, planning weekend activities, regulating time on Instant Messaging, etc. Part of it is the good cop/bad cop roles he and his wife tend to fall into and the way one is played against the other. This is not a Business Harry is free to leave if he hopes to make a go of partnering. He must find a way to do it better.

Cash Cows

In the Cash Cow area of Businesses that are good for the short term but may not be as profitable in the future, Harry lists: HEWT, Teen Bird, PP&G, and TGAL. The task in HEWT is to increase the relatively low ROI by raising prices so that less time need be spent in this inherently draining, if engaging, activity. (But, in order to do this, Harry may need some better-heeled clients, longer-term projects, or some other creative tactics.)

Teen Bird reflects the fact that his only child is now in high school. She is spreading her wings, and the whole family has to adjust. But after several years this is going to change—she will fly away to college. For Harry's own sense of self-respect he needs to pay attention to these developments so that he can look back on this time and say that he really made the effort to be there for his daughter and his wife.

This is probably a good time to hang in there in PP&G (Personal and Professional Growth) with Harry's personal coach and counselor even though this is time consuming and expensive. Hopefully, at some point in the future he will not require this support or incur the expense. Harry does not expect to get great joy from his pro bono work or charitable contributions that make up TGAL, but it does help him look himself in the mirror. The old saying: "If I am for myself alone, what am I?" is still a powerful driver. He needs to keep his altruism in check though so he doesn't burn out, because he has decided that charity needs to start at home, especially in regard to where his time and attention goes.

Stars

In the Star area—Businesses that are high return now *and* in the future—Harry needs to keep investing in the HHMO and continue his exercise program, regular medical checkups, deal with his weight gain, etc. The potential ROI here is in preventing the heart attack that he is at increased risk for! He also needs to invest in Connections Unlimited, the Star Business that expresses his enjoyment of family and friends. A particular area of concern are those "customers" who are getting on in years and my not be around very much longer. Harry wants to be able to have some time with them, especially with those folks who have been important to him since his younger days.

Probably most important in this area is the Building Partners Business, newly defined, to give it more focus and prominence in Harry's Life Enterprise portfolio. This is a high-gain, high-risk area. Harry needs to invest in that relationship if he expects his marriage to weather the turmoil created by the Teen Bird and the empty nest, which follows. Harry has not always done such a good job in this area in the past according to feedback from his No. 1 customer. He is resolved to make his marriage relationship more of a priority for his time and attention.

Rising Stars

In the Rising Star area (low current return but high future return), Harry has three Businesses listed: Writer to Pundit, Travelocus, and Home Improvement. If Harry wants to become a pundit as his Vision directs, he had better start mapping that out. In fact, Harry has already done a number of things to further this Life Business, but now he needs to become more serious and sharpen his focus if he is to succeed.

Relative to Travelocus, there may not be a lot of time for foreign travel and tramping around the national parks in the next few years. However, Harry is determined not to let this activity fall off the radar in the short term. Later, when his daughter is out of the home, he hopes to expand this part of his life.

Concerning Home Improvement, the house needs renovation, and it will be a big plus in Harry's life when that is completed, but it will also take a lot of work. The question for Harry here is timing. When can he and his wife best fit this in given all of their other demands and commitments?

In the table that follows on the next page, there is a complete summary of Harry's Life Businesses and their associated Strategies. Note that in the last column in the chart Harry indicates the Values (based on his Value Analysis from Step 3) that he thinks are in play in each Life Business. This is an indicator of how Harry expects to "be paid" by each Life Business.

Strategy Matrix Experiences of Other Life Business Participants

Harry's wife, Helen, had a "Dog business" in her portfolio, which she shut down recently. It was the Business of Socializing with Friends on a Regular Basis. She likes people and has many friends and a big family. She realized that if she continued to encourage going to lunch and entertaining people for dinner and

Summary of Harry's Strategic Directions

Life Businesses	*Classification*	*Investment Strategy*	*Values Sought*
Teen Bird	Cash Cow	Increase short term/ decrease long term	Being a good parent
Building Partners	Star	Increase, build the business	Intimacy and affection
Home Improvement	Rising Star	Plan short term, create business long term	Personal comfort, financial stability
Connections Unlimited	Star	Continue to build these connections	Friendship and support
Health Maintenance	Star	Continue to invest heavily	Health, fitness, and everyday good feeling; preventing illness
Personal & Professional Growth	Cash Cow	Invest short term	Sense of stretching, growing as a person
Think Global, Act Local	Cash Cow	Invest short term	Service, social responsibility
Writer to Pundit	Rising Star	Invest heavily to start this business	Recognition, financial return
Travelocus	Star	Invest medium term	Recreation and personal enrichment
HEWT (consulting business)	Cash Cow	Continue to invest; monitor returns	Financial stability, creativity, service

being invited over to other people's houses, with endless rounds of reciprocating, she would soon not have enough time left over to do what she really wanted to do, which is to write. Even though she is quite social, and can be the life of the party, she finds that it takes so much of her energy to interact in this way that she often had a serious nonalcohol-related "hangover" the next day.

She developed a Strategy to close down this Business. She got out the message partly through Harry that she was in a reclusive phase, which was nothing personal, and started turning down invitations. Harry started showing up at potlucks, etc., without his wife. Friends got the message and though some found it hard to understand, they usually did not take offense. She also softened the blow by suggesting to friends who wanted to "do lunch" that they go for a walk instead, an activity that was already on her calendar and did not detract from her writing time. She converted the investment of time from a Socializing Business into an Exercise/Friendship Business, which promised a higher payoff.

When Richard did his Strategy Matrix, he noticed that he had four Rising Star Businesses—areas in which he wanted to start things that did not presently exist in his life. These included: starting his consulting business, writing a book about modern Jewish living, relocating his family to be closer to his wife's relatives in warmer southern climes, and starting a men's group. Since he already had numerous Star and Cash Cow Businesses occupying his time, he had to look at the possibility that by trying to do too much at once, he was going to jeopardize all of his New Ventures and perhaps some of his traditional Businesses. He began to think about spacing these new Business start-ups out over the short, medium, and long term.

Betty realized that her Stars (continuing to develop her relationship with her physician husband) and Rising Stars (raising alpacas), which she was hoping would help fill the void she had felt since her children left the home, were both very risky Businesses. The alpaca Business is risky for financial reasons, and her husband, while certainly very engaged with his wife, was still locked into a very demanding medical practice for at least 5 more years. She began to think that the answer for her might lie more in cultivating her "inner garden" with the same zeal she gave to creating and maintaining her real one. She began to think about how she would go about this more subtle venture.

Mary saw that what was important in her life over the next few years were family commitments: seeing her boys through high school and taking care of her ailing grandmother, whom no one else wanted to bother about. This meant downgrading Career from the Star status it had always had in her life to a Cash Cow. While this might mean she would stop getting promotions in the big bank at which she had achieved a high rank after over 20 years of service, she accepted this as the cost of this Strategy. More important to her was the Rising Star possibility that she would once again consider finding a Life Partner, after being a single mom all these years.

Brad, coming off a year of terrible health problems, felt it was clear that he had to make physical and mental well-being the Star Business of his new configuration. Tending to family relationships after last year's harrowing time was another priority and also a Star Business. His current job was too stressful, for sure, but relatively secure. He knew how to do that job, and, by paying more attention, he could do it with less wear and tear. It would be a Cash Cow for the short term. Rising Stars in his future were the creative writing he always wanted to pursue. After the health problems of the past year, he said to himself, "If not now, when?"

Jena's major Star Business was in Home and Hearth–building with her new partner. They were not yet married but were going to take the big plunge of moving in together to see how it would work. She realized that her workplace activities had slipped from a Star Business to a Cash Cow situation in terms of her interests. She resolved to change this by taking on some new big challenges on the job, which would revitalize her excitement about work and the company.

Exercises for the Reader

1. Consider the future factors that may affect the profitability of your Businesses over time. Include family, career, and individual life cycle factors in your assessment.

2. Enter your Businesses on the Strategy Matrix. Ask yourself the following questions:

   - Do you have a good mix of Businesses that yield a good current and future return?
   - When you look at your Businesses in total, do they add up to your Vision?
   - Are there any missing important Values in your portfolio of Businesses?

For more detail on this and other Life Business exercises, go to our Web site at www.lifebusiness.com.

Tips on Guiding Your Life Business Investments in the Future

- Make sure the total portfolio of Life Businesses adds up to what you want out of your life. One way to do this is to identify what Values in your life are being realized by each of your Life Businesses as Harry did in his Life Business summary. If nothing important to you is left out, then you are okay. If something is missing, then you may want to go back to your Vision and make sure nothing has been left out there as well.

- Make sure that your Life Businesses will get you where you want to go. Look at your Vision and your Life Businesses together. If your Life Businesses are successful, will they get you to the point you raise about in your Vision statement? If not, perhaps your New Venture list is missing something.

- Check the phasing of bringing new Businesses in and phasing out old ones. Make sure you don't overreach or peak load. Schedule your investments of energy, time, and money in a way that is sustainable and effective.
- Appreciate the different challenges of each of your Strategies; devote significant attention and pick the right team leader for each initiative. For example, phasing out a relationship or an activity requires attention to timing, the ability to deal with loss and change, and a certain amount of assertiveness and discipline to stay the course of letting go. Who is the right person on your Internal Management Team to lead this effort? What skills does he or she need to learn and what attitudes does he or she need to maintain in order to be effective?
- Milking the Cash Cow requires steadiness, attention to detail, and maintaining appropriate relationships over months and years. We don't want the Inner Artist or Attention Deficit Danny handling this assignment. Is there a Gary Cooper or a Jimmy Stewart available on your Internal Management Team?
- Building the Star Business, on the other hand, requires sustained drive, energy, and creativity in pursuit of a well-developed Plan for that Business. Is there a hard charger available on the team? This might be the right assignment for that part of your personality.
- Creating a New Venture from scratch calls upon the talents of the entrepreneur: intrepid and persistent despite setbacks, willing to work long and hard to launch the new initiative, able and willing to use help, flexible enough to respond to change. If this team member does not exist, perhaps he or she will need to be invented if the New Venture is to gain a foothold.

Strategy: A Bridge to the Future

Former President Clinton was fond of talking about "building a bridge to the twenty-first century." The Strategies you develop in Step 6 really are the foundation of the bridge to your own future. They are the pillars that support the bridge and the suspension that allows it to span the future from the past. This bridge connects your current situation to your past and enables you to arrive at where you want to be in the future.

In Steps 7 and 8 we will continue to build this bridge by developing the essential Projects and Commitments that will allow you to execute your Strategies successfully. When they are completed, you will then have an actual road on that bridge to take you into your desired future.

Notes

1. Edgar Schein. *Career Dynamics.* Addison-Wesley, 1978, pp. 23–25.

2. The Strategy Matrix was developed by the Boston Consulting Group in the 1970s to help corporations assess the profitability of their current lines of business, now and in the future, and to plan for future profitability. The Strategy Matrix has been widely used by businesses and their consultants in a variety of settings ever since.

3. GE Corporation. *Annual Report 2001*, pp. 9–15, 87.

Set Heartfelt Goals and Identify Life-Changing Projects

The world is your oyster, but you will still need to open it

Our deeds determine us, as much as we determine our deeds.

George Eliot in Adam Bede

LIFE BUSINESS TENET

Success is there for you, but you will have to do your part. Each of your Strategies will require focused effort directed by the clear Goals and Projects you will define in this Step.

At this point in the Life Business process you have determined your general destination and time of arrival, but you have not yet determined your route to get there. It remains for you to flesh out your ideas about how to execute your Strategies. Step 7 begins the project planning process that is completed in Step 8. What drives your Strategic Plans are the Goals you want to achieve in your life. These Goals will be anchored in the 10-year Vision you developed in Step 5.

Know Where You Are Headed

You would be surprised how often organizations and individuals, when setting out to implement their Strategies, set Goals that are too vague. We take the idea of "beginning with the end in mind" very literally in the Life Business Program. When I say "I want to go to college," that's a very different thing from saying "I want a four-year degree in engineering from one of the top-10 ranked schools." The first Goal lacks any real specificity. The latter statement directs a person toward the Goal he or she trying to achieve.

Businesses thrive on numbers, known in MBA jargon as "metrics," to tell them how well they are doing. While we ask Life Business participants for objective measures of Goal achievement, we also challenge participants to state a Goal in terms of what it will actually feel like, sound like, and look like to achieve it. So, how will it feel to walk across that stage to get that diploma? What will people be saying to you then? What will you be saying to others?

Developing Specific Direction: The Case of the Lexus

The idea of being very specific about your destination in terms of imagining a very specific result has a venerable history in product design. *The Wall Street Journal* reported some years back that the Japanese carmaker Honda took this approach to designing the Lexus. The Lexus was seen as Honda's Rising Star in terms of future profits. To begin to form a very specific idea of the auto that would be successful, Honda took workers from their plant assembly line in Tokyo out to the parking lots of the clubhouses of exclusive golf courses. There they could look at the Porsches, the BMWs, and the Mercedeses owned by the clubs' members. The workers were unloaded from their vans and then asked to look at and touch the luxury vehicles and to note the features that they liked. They then came back and shared their impressions. Based on what they saw and felt, the beginning ideas for the Lexus took shape. Similar attention to envisioning the desired future for each of your Life Businesses will help your own direction take shape.

Understand Your Situation and What You Bring to It

Many effective businesses use an SWOT approach to plan strategy implementation. They consider their internal Strengths (S) and Weaknesses (W) as well as market Opportunities (O) and Threats (T).[1] These businesses then arrive at a plan that takes all of these factors into account. We help individuals do the same in the Life Business Program.

Identify Promising Projects

Business strategists tell us that when we marry an identified Strength with a real Opportunity, we have the basis of a promising line of action. In the Life Business

Program we encourage you to identify those lines of action, called Projects, which build on your Strengths and seize Opportunities. These Projects are the heart of the Strategic Plan, and they are the vehicles for implementing our Strategies and turning our Vision into reality.

Benefit from the Experience of Others

Effective businesses actively seek out "best practices" in their own organizations, in their industry, and in other industries so that they can solve a problem or realize an Opportunity in the most efficient way possible. In the Life Business Program you draw on the experience of others in finding the best way to achieve your objectives.

In a study of 20 companies that won awards for environmental quality, it was shown that the best environmental quality companies are constantly seeking ideas for improving environmental performance from a variety of sources and methods. These approaches included " best-practices benchmarking" with other companies, discussions with customers and vendors, and networking with external third-party resources. In this way they have a truly open systems approach. As the president of one award-winning company succinctly put it: "We are a melting pot of a lot of different ideas. We have suppliers and customers in our shop. We have open communication with our competition and our customers. We feel there is a lot more to be gained by sharing information than by not sharing it."[2]

Use All the Resources Available to You to Reach Your Destination

Many organizations are quite constrained in the way they go about implementing change; they don't take a whole-brained approach, nor do they effectively involve all of their people in the change management process. As a result they are often deprived of the resources that those individuals could bring to bear on achieving the goals of the organization. In the Life Business Program you learn to use all your mental faculties and draw on the resources of your whole Internal Management team.

The principle of drawing on the resources of all within the organization is called "The Whole Systems Approach."[3] This approach to change management is replacing the top-down model in many businesses. For example, when Ford launched its quality program, it trained as many as 1000 people in these techniques in multiple, simultaneous conferences. Recently, the mayor of Washington, DC, brought 3000 people together from various neighborhoods to give

95

input into the setting of city goals. In the Life Business Program we encourage you to use all the resources at your disposal (e.g, friends, advisers, books, articles) and to reach out for input in forming goals and plans for improving your life.

Make Sure You Have a Follow-Through Plan

A good Project in the business sense has a set of Goals, a set of activities to achieve those Goals, clear accountability for who is doing what in each step, and a system in place to monitor progress and troubleshoot problems. We use these methods in the Life Business Program to help people get on and stay on track.

Setting Goals and Identifying Projects in the Life Business Program

It has been demonstrated that athletes can "practice in their mind" (e.g., shooting the free throw, kicking the field goal). They imagine what it would look like, sound like, and feel like to hit the target. For Step 7, we recommend that you visualize in detail your desired state of affairs so that you can truly understand where it is that you want to go. In the Program we use two visualization techniques: (1) "messages" and (2) "markers."

A Message in this context is what you really want to see, hear, or feel a specific Stakeholder communicate to you. It could be your spouse saying, "You look ten years younger in your new bathing suit," or your son saying, "Dad, mom's death has been tough on all of us, and you've helped each of us learn to cope." These Stakeholders may never actually verbalize these things, but the words you are putting in their mouths are the messages they would be communicating if in fact you had realized this Goal. A Marker is a token or symbol that signifies that a Goal has been attained. Trophies, citations, letters of commendation are all Markers. But a handwritten note passed to you under the table can do as well. Say you step on the scale, and it reads 10 pounds lighter than it did a month before. That's a Marker. Your spouse looks at you approvingly as you step off the scale. That's a Message. Once Goals are stated in this vivid, concrete, and compelling way, the direction toward them becomes easier to discern.

Some Messages and Markers for Harry's Life Business

Messages and Markers for several of Harry's Life Businesses include the following.

For the Teen Bird Life Business, a Marker is that Harry's daughter graduates from high school with good enough grades to get into a college that she really wants to go to. Another Marker is that, day-to-day, she seems to be enjoying life, has friends, does things she likes to do, and doesn't get into too much trouble. The parents can identify ways that she is becoming more self-responsible and independent (e.g., is keeping up with her homework; is having fewer last-minute crises). It's likely the Messages will not be very direct from the teenager during this time. However, there will be important indirect messages—for example, is there constant complaining and fighting with parents, or are there some times of fun and good humor?

For the Partnering Business, Harry can note the times he feels he is "in the dog house." That is a bad Marker. Another bad Marker is the times he feels that Helen is not being considerate of him. On the good side are the times Harry and Helen have respectful conversations about day-to-day scheduling and longer-term plans. The times they have fun talking about a topic they both enjoy. The times they carve out to have fun together. "Time" appears to be the scarce resource here. This is not rocket science, but changes can be measured and tracked by journal entries or weekly check-in sessions between the spouses. An important Message is when Helen says to Harry "We really have been making an effort to build our relationship and I think it is really paying off." Another important Message is when Harry agrees.

In Connections Unlimited, Harry's issue is staying in touch with his far-flung network of business contacts, friends, and family members. He has friends he contacts on a weekly, monthly, yearly, or even less frequent basis. A Marker here is the dates that are on the calendar and the e-mail messages that are exchanged. A Message is that people are friendly and interested when he gets them on the phone, and a further Marker is that they reciprocate his interest by returning phone calls, visits, and e-mails.

HEWT has some obvious metrics. How much did Harry earn last year compared to the year before? Did his daily consulting rate go up or down? Less easily measured is the degree to which Harry found satisfaction in his work and how much trouble it was for him to carry it out. Yet Harry can evaluate this if he takes time to reflect. Was Harry ground down or buoyed up by his daily chores in the world of consulting? In terms of Messages, did he get good feedback from clients? Did they recommend him to others? When he checks back with them after some break in the action, did they report that the work he did with them was truly helpful? These are all important indicators of how well this Life Business is going.

In Harry's HHMO Life Business, some Markers are quantitative: weight, blood pressure, cholesterol level. But other Markers are qualitative: level of energy, experience of stomach problems, sense of well-being and alertness.

As Harry goes through his Life Businesses in this way, it becomes a lot clearer to him what he means by ROI in each of these areas of his life. Now having set out the directions he wants to go for his various Life Businesses, he still needs to figure out how to get there. This is where his Heartfelt Projects come in.

Defining Those Heartfelt Projects

As previously mentioned, the SWOT is a good tool here, along with group brainstorming, usually in that order. SWOT assessment of strengths, weaknesses, opportunities, and threats helps you understand the situation within a Life Business, and brainstorming, especially if you get ideas from friends and colleagues, also provides a wider range of approaches to choose from.

For example, in Harry's HHMO area the Strength is that he likes to exercise, and the Weakness is that he likes to eat so his weight keeps creeping up. The Threats are rising cholesterol levels despite taking medication and some recent stomach problems. The Opportunities are his wife's commitment to his increased health and the quality of human resources from whom he can get help.

When Harry talks to doctors, friends, and relatives, he identifies some of the following Projects that are required to move this Life Business along:

- Increase cholesterol medications if he can tolerate them.
- Make sure he is taking the right vitamins to help prevent heart disease.
- Change exercise routine from running, which puts pressure on the knees, to working out in some other way.
- Get some medication for his stomach.
- Go on a diet and lose weight.
- Begin meditation practice to improve stress management.
- Avoid acid-producing foods and drinks.

Harry took this potential Project list seriously and enrolled in a stress management program that involved meditation. He resolved to lose some weight, joined a health club, and changed his medications, and he swore off coffee, wine, and sodas for the sake of his stomach. After a year the results were the following: He never really took to meditation, though he did learn how to focus on his breathing and zone out at certain times, like while sitting in waiting rooms. Harry joined a health club that he really liked and began to spend time exercising more vigorously but with less knee impact. His diet efforts were half-hearted and a total failure, partly perhaps because of the increased exercise. He knows at some time that he will try to lose some weight, but for the time being he is rejoicing in the increased muscle mass brought on by the daily workouts with weights. Despite some small side effects, the new cholesterol drugs worked, and his numbers are better than ever. His stomach feels fine, though he is off coffee, diet Coke, and red wine probably forever.

Managing one's health is a continuing issue, and hopefully, for Harry the story will not end here. Harry did those things that were relatively easy for him to do on his list (take pills, change exercise routines, substitute tea for coffee or beer for wine, etc.). He did not do those things that were hard for him to do: cut down on total calories and meditate. His results have been good so far: better cholesterol numbers, higher level of fitness, good energy day to day. Not every effort you make will pan out, but hopefully the changes you do make in your Life Businesses will bring you the results you are looking for, as they appear to be doing in Harry's case.

Completing a Life Business Strategic Plan

Harry has developed Messages and Markers for each of his Life Businesses, as shown above. You also saw how he developed and then carried out a plan for his health Life Business (HHMO).

In order to have a fully developed Strategic Plan, he needs to create a series of Projects to support each of his nine other Life Businesses as well. This will take a lot of time and thought on his part, perhaps 10 hours over 2 weeks. However, at the end of that time Harry will have a very powerful and effective map to guide his Life Enterprise. Harry's completed list of Projects to implement the Strategies in each of his Life Businesses for the short term appears below. In Step 8 we discuss how Harry's Projects for the short, medium, and long term can be integrated into a full-blown Life Business Plan.

Harry's Short-Term (0–3 Years) Projects for Each of His Businesses

---

- Teen Bird (Maintain): annual family trips with daughter; monitor daughter's tendency to overcommit; continue summer camp she loves; attend daughter's performances; attend to daughter's health issues.

- Partnering (Build): support writer's retreats for spouse; weekly walking and talking; partner on domestic chores; schedule one fun trip together each year, just us.

- Connections Unlimited (Maintain): stay in touch with sister (annual beach trip); talk with cousins (by phone); have lunch with friends, colleagues, and key mentors; use business travel to visit when possible.

- HEWT (Maintain): maintain ongoing client relationships; develop Web page and Internet presence; establish workshop program.

- Pundit (Create): experience initial publishing venture; leverage book for speaking and consulting.

(*continues*)

Harry's Short-Term (0–3 Years) Projects for Each of His Businesses (*Continued*)

- PP&G (Maintain): participate in annual meeting of professional group; continue personal coaching and counseling; undertake one other development activity annually.

- IGUANA (Build): hiking trips (one per year): foreign travel.

- HHMO (Build): daily program; consider weight-training program; lose weight; continue medications for high cholesterol; monitor medical developments.

- TGAL (Maintain): charitable giving; work with socially useful organizations; pro bono consulting; give to political candidates.

Other Life Business Participants' Heartfelt Projects

Mary was originally at a loss to think about how to get started on her Life Business My Significant Other (MSO), which has the goal of finding a life partner after having been a single mother and businesswoman for a decade (and out of the dating game). She then decided, as a toe in the water, to go to her 25th high school reunion. Sure enough, she hooked up with an old boyfriend who had been recently divorced. It didn't turn out that he was the *one*, but MSO had been launched.

Sandy, who had begun a successful second career as an elementary school teacher and was devoted to improving public education, realized through her own experience, bitter at times, that school leadership made a significant difference in the children's and teachers' performance. She realized the next step in her Realizing Potential Business was to become an elementary school principal. After some investigation, she identified a 2-year fellowship program that would qualify her for that job. Completing this fellowship program became an important Short-Term Project in her Strategic Plan. In her action plan she mapped out all the steps it would take to make this happen.

Richard, the marketing consultant who felt called to deepen his spiritual life by religious study, had identified a Business called Beth Midrash. This is the Hebrew name for the House of Study where, in earlier times, learned men in the Jewish communities of Eastern Europe went to study the holy books for hours on end. One Project he chose in order to activate this Life Business was to go to Israel for a month and to learn Hebrew in an intensive study program. He had to think through how he would finance this and make this fit with his family and community obligations.

Choose When to Plan "Directionally" Rather Than with Goals and Time Lines

For some people and for some situations, a highly structured approach doesn't work. First of all they rebel against it—not everyone is a planner by nature. Also, some Goals cannot be achieved in a one, two, three, stepwise fashion. For example, finding a suitable mate, which was the focus of Mary's MSO Business, does not always lend itself to planning with Goals and time lines. Hence the pop lyric, "You can't hurry love. You just have to wait." While we can program ourselves to join hiking or book clubs where we can meet people or take a flier with match.com, we may also have inner work to do. This inner work may concern questions of selection, dealing with intimacy terrors, and the like, which have a timeline of their own that we may not control.

At these times you may need to think of yourself as planning directionally rather than planning with goals and time lines. This means you make a commitment to start off in a certain direction with very loose plans but tight support systems. You still do the main activities for Step 7: Visualize Messages and Markers, SWOT analysis, brainstorm Project ideas, and consult others who have taken similar journeys. You commit to time frames for certain steps that are under your control, but you may not always be able to set timetables for accomplishment.

Any Life Business Strategic Plan will be a mix of detailed action steps with deadlines and accountabilities that are well charted and plans with arrows pointing "this-a-way." In all cases, what is important is a clear sense of the destination and a commitment of energy, time, and money consistent with the Goal.

Use All of Your Abilities in the Planning Process

In the high-tech companies we are familiar with, especially start-ups, there can be a problem of valuing engineering over marketing, sales, finance, human resources, and other functions because these companies are concentrating on building a breakthrough product. Once the first blush of enthusiasm for a product wanes and competitors come on the market, the company stumbles because it has not made good use all of its resources to deliver a fully competitive product as the market matures.

Translating this to the level of the individual Life Business, there is a tendency to concentrate on "doing." Active and concrete elements are often favored to the exclusion of all other activities. As a result, Projects may be off the mark for what appears to be mysterious reasons. Upon analysis, we may find that we have neglected some of the inner work required to resolve ambivalence toward our

101

Using Goals or Directional Planning in the Life Business Program[4]

Planning with Goals	*Planning with Directions*
• Guided, trying to achieve external Goals	• Directional, movement toward a desired state
• Goals are specific and measurable	• Specific outcomes/intermediate steps hard to define
• Rational, often quantifiable	• Intuitive
• Focused	• Broad
• Lower need to process novel information	• Higher need to process novel information
• More efficient use of energy	• Possible duplications, false leads
• Separate planning and acting phases	• Planning and acting interviews
• People who prefer well-defined tasks	• People who prefer variety and complexity
• Relatively stable tasks	• Tasks whose nature changes rapidly
• Tightening up phase of a project	• Unfreezing phase of a project

Goal or some of the preparatory work necessary to develop sufficient self-confidence to be successful.

Those Projects that relate to matters of the heart and soul (e.g., become more appreciative of great art; communicate more intimately with my wife and children; be more at peace with my Creator) may require "actions" that are more receptive and creative, instead of proactive and tangible.

Instead of "doing" as the only way of defining action, we may also need to include reflecting, appreciating, meditating, praying, listening, encouraging, supporting, and connecting. Similarly, Goals that require the development of understanding, rather than the achievement of a specific measurable result in the outside world, may require actions such as reading, analyzing, interviewing, conversing, data gathering, and Web browsing.

We ask participants in the Life Business Program to review their planned action steps to see if they are using their diverse talents appropriately in designing their Projects. This means time spent dreaming as well as analyzing, reflecting as well as doing, feeling as well as thinking, connecting with others to get ideas as well as meditating in solitude, and so on. People's Motivated Talents are important in this regard. One person may be excellent in analysis, so he or she uses that tool for all situations, another excellent at empathy, so he or she may overuse this faculty. When the actions of an individual in carrying out his or her Projects tend to always go down the same path whatever the situation, it is a sign that the Management Team members are not being fully utilized. Sometimes, in order to grow, a person, like a corporation, has to draw on its underused and maybe (temporarily) less-skilled capacities. This may seem strange, even counterproductive at first, but harnessing underdeveloped skills may be the only way to achieve the Goal when the "tried and true" approach does not measure up to the task.

Build Additional Capacity

Effective businesses also know that they sometimes need to develop new capacities to achieve their Goals. For example, a high-tech giant we have consulted with recently realized that its "time to market" for new products was a major strategic problem. So the company purchased a much smaller company that had excellent performance in that area. The idea was they would learn from the smaller company. Purchasing is not the only way to develop new capacities, however. Sometimes companies can contract out the needed expertise or grow it from within. Similarly, you might find that in realizing a heartfelt Project, you need to develop a quality you do not now possess (e.g., empathy, assertiveness, imagination, hand-eye coordination, whatever). Then you too will be faced with the choice of purchasing that quality (hiring a helper to do it for you) or developing that capacity yourself by studying, training, or coaching.

One of Harry and Helen's joint goals was to do more fun things together, like dancing. Only Harry didn't know how to dance! As a result, dancing lessons became an important step in the fulfillment of that Project. Arlene was making a transition from one set of responsibilities to another. Because she was enthusiastic, she got a job in a new area whose demands were, in reality, a bit over her head. She closed the gap by hiring an expert to coach her. She performed well, and no one on the job was any the wiser. Like Harry and Arlene, you might find that building a new capacity is a critical action step in making one of your heartfelt Projects a success.

Acknowledge Accomplishments and Celebrate Successes

One of the major themes in the human resources literature these days is the importance of recognizing accomplishments and celebrating successes.[5] Many of your Life Business Projects will require discipline and hard work to achieve. We all need encouragement to keep at it. Acknowledging and appreciating success along the way is a good way to maintain motivation. In many manufacturing plants when work teams reach weekly quality goals in production, they receive small gifts like T-shirts, free meals, gift certificates, and the like. Larger accomplishments win trips to the beach, recognition at the annual employees' banquet, a place on the company honor roll, etc. In business, recognizing and rewarding accomplishment is a way of reinforcing values, building the group, and providing role models. Similarly, it is important to find ways, in each Life Business, to acknowledge and support progress.

So, for example, when Harry loses a pound and it stays off for a week, he gets to go to the movies (and have popcorn!—no butter, thank you). When Harry loses the first 5 pounds, he gets a day off! When he losses 15 pounds, his wife (somewhat reclusive) agrees to let him have a party (where lots of raw vegetables will be served).

Decide Who's in Charge of Your Projects

In Step 3 we discuss the importance of getting to know your Internal Management Team members, their Strengths and Weaknesses, and where they contribute or get in the way. Now is an especially good time to put that knowledge to use. Once the list of Projects has been formed, it is a useful exercise to see who is in charge of that Project, to assess whether the right Internal Management Team is in place, and to make the "personnel" changes that will strengthen the possibilities of success.

In Harry's example, Disciplined Dave must replace Friendly Frank as team leader of the lose weight Project, and Playful Paul can be in charge of the rewards component of the program. Anxious Al will take over the monitoring and recording component.

Harry has been aware that Imaginative Isadore and Anxious Al have been trading off in managing the financial side of Harry's Life Enterprise, leading to wide swings in Strategy, usually with the worst possible market timing. Maybe Disciplined Dave should step in here too, backed by some solid analysis. Perhaps a new Internal Management Team member needs to be recruited for this task. Should it be Ricky Researcher?

Exercises for the Reader

Pick one of your Businesses and work through a completed set of Projects.

1. Identify desired Messages and Markers for this Business.
2. Do a SWOT analysis of the conditions surrounding Goal achievement.
3. Brainstorm possible Projects with input from friends and helpers.
4. Choose the most promising Projects and develop a detailed action plan using the principles outlined in Step 7.

For more Step 7 exercises and a detailed discussion of the SWOT approach, go to www.lifebusiness.com.

From Projects to Commitments

Step 7 is a collection of practices that help you use the lessons that businesses have learned to achieve results and to use them to reach important milestones in your own life. It is important to have the right Strategies for your Life Businesses, but that does you no real good unless you also have well-thought-through Projects to implement those Strategies. If Strategy is the bridge between the current situation and the desired future, then your heartfelt Projects are the connection between your Life Business Strategies and the firm Commitments of energy, time, and money you must make if you are to realize your Dreams. Once you have defined those Projects, you are in a position to fully define those Commitments and organize yourself to fulfill them in a way that gives you the best chance for success. Step 8 helps you take the Projects you have chosen and begin to build them into the sequence of Commitments that are the stepping stones to achieving your life Goals.

Notes

1. David Kiel. "EQM Leadership and Management Practices: A Comparison of Small and Large Companies." North Carolina State Office of Waste Reduction, 1996, p. 21.

2. David Kiel. *Op. cit.* p. 21.

3. For one well-developed example of this approach, see Richard Axelrod. *Terms of Engagement: Changing the Way We Change Organizations.* Berrett-Koheler, 2000.

4. From John Eckblad, *Life Business Workbook*, Chapel Hill, 1978. Based on earlier work of Michael McCaskey.

5. James Kouzes and Barry Posner. *The Leadership Challenge.* Jossey-Bass, 1990, pp. 239–276.

Define Projects and Clarify Commitments

So now what are you going to do about it?

An idealist believes the short run doesn't count, the cynic believes the long run doesn't matter, the realist understands that what is attended to in the short run determines the long run.

Sydney Harris, paraphrased

LIFE BUSINESS TENET

Specific and sustained Commitment is the key ingredient in executing your Plan for success. By making specific forecasts of the energy, time, and money resources needed to realize your Dreams, you can vastly improve your chances for success and give focus and stability to your life.

Making a Commitment to your Life Business Plan involves: (1) prioritizing your Projects using whatever criteria make sense to you; (2) placing Projects in short-, medium-, and long-term time frames; and (3) forecasting energy, time, and money requirements for all Projects.

Put Future Projects in a Realistic Time Frame

Effective businesses know they cannot achieve all their goals at once. Some goals depend on the prior accomplishment of other goals. There are limited resources and time. Some problems are immediate, and some opportunities are long term. The same principle is true for your Life Businesses: You cannot achieve all of your goals all at once—you must sequence them realistically in the short, medium, and long term.

We consulted with a nonprofit organization in a large urban area that was involved in neighborhood renewal activities in a number of sections of the city. It generated its revenue by making housing rehabilitation loans to low-income residents and through foundation grants and corporate gifts. The organization knew it had an immediate problem. Because of rapid shifts in the lending market, it had been losing money over the past 2 years. Its board of directors made it a priority to correct this situation.

When it came time to write a strategic plan for this agency, it was apparent that its challenges and opportunities had clear time frames attached. In the short term (0–2 years), the organization needed to improve its financial situation and commit itself to an extensive reorganization of its lending services. The agency needed to increase its marketing and business development activities to do so. In the medium term (3–4 years), the organization plans to initiate new programs to meet emerging housing needs of immigrant groups in the city. And in the long term (5–7 years), the organization will explore ways of extending its services beyond the city limits. The organization has committed itself over 7 years to become a highly efficient, innovative, and expanding agency, which will then be a resource for its whole metropolitan area. But to be successful, the organization will need to proceed a step at a time.

Budget Project Energy, Time, and Money Requirements

In a business context, a plan without a supporting budget, and an allocation of managerial time and priority, is a wish, not a true commitment, and it isn't taken seriously. The critical point in a strategic planning process is when plans and goals are analyzed from a financial point of view, likely ROIs are calculated, and the budget is committed. In the business context, the budget is a true statement of energy, time, money, and commitments. In addition to the actual cost of labor, all personnel assignments create real "opportunity costs," that is, alternative projects that won't be "funded." Time does indeed mean money.

The budget is the true statement of what the organization is committed to, more so than the mission statement, the vision statement, or the goals statement. In well-run businesses all these documents are aligned, but in general you would be advised, when you are looking to predict corporate behavior, to "follow the money."

In the agency discussed above, it was clear from the goals, time lines and budgets that the agency was committed to reorganizing its lending services in order to cut costs and increase revenues. Money had been set aside for consultants to advise on the reorganization. Staff had been reallocated to new positions. Some positions made redundant by the reorganization had been terminated and some staff let go. A review of the manager's goals and work plans showed that activities were in place to make happen what the agency said it wanted to happen. In other words, there was a real commitment.

Life Business Projects are exactly the same. A genuine Commitment includes an estimate of the emotional effort, time, and money that a given activity is going to take and a willingness and ability to pledge those resources. In Life Businesses, as in other businesses, you should make explicit your Commitments of energy and time as well as money.

Clarifying Commitments in the Life Business Program

In Step 6 you identified the appropriate Strategy for each of your Businesses (reduce or eliminate investment, maintain investment, build investment, or start investment) depending on whether they were Dog, Cash Cow, Star, or Rising Star Businesses. When Harry looked at his potential Projects (from Step 7), he saw several Businesses crying out for attention. These included:

Potential Projects for Harry's Life Businesses and Concerns

Life Businesses and Concerns	*Potential Projects*
Home Improvement: kitchen still in the 1960s; other things need work: landscape etc.	• major renovation of kitchen, porch, and landscaping
IGUANA: would love to spend more time traveling and hiking: "You are not getting any younger, you know."	• European travel • visit national parks • local hiking trips
Teen Bird: daughter tackling high school; experiencing some problems in school; asserting teen independence causing tensions with parents	• educational testing for daughter • counseling for parents • tutoring and summer camp expenses • parental support for daughter's artistic interests

(continues)

Potential Projects for Harry's Life Businesses and Concerns (*Continued*)

Life Businesses and Concerns	Potential Projects
Building Partners: felt need for parents to work together more to support daughter and prepare for empty nest; wife needing more support for her emerging career as a writer	• set aside weekly time for parents to compare notes on how things are going, and handle business items • time alone for parents • fun things together: walks, plays, entertaining • time to support wife's residency in writer's workshops, retreats
Writer to Pundit: Harry's desire to develop an enhanced reputation, and new consulting opportunities, by becoming better known in his field	• develop book project that can give Harry more professional visibility
Harry Health Maintenance Organization: weight and cholesterol continues to creep up; knee pain makes running more difficult; ulcers have emerged	• develop new exercise routine that is not so hard on the knees • lose weight • consult with physician on cholesterol, ulcer control • work on stress management
Have Ear Will Travel: consulting business going just fine, but need to find a way to work less and earn more	• develop Web site • expand workshops • continue support for existing clients
Professional and Personal Growth: Harry's counseling is proving to be helpful; he is enjoying his work in his professional organization	• continue counseling • take on a major role in professional organization (Harry was asked to run for the board of directors)
Connections Unlimited: stay in touch with family, friends, colleagues	• continue annual trips to beach with sister's family • frequent lunches and walks with local friends • stay in touch with cousins via phone • visit with wife's family in conjunction with business travel • special effort to be with older mentors who are in ill health

Obviously Harry cannot deal with Teen Bird, travel to Europe, write a book, help Helen finish her novel, maintain his consulting business, and do a major renovation on his kitchen (which might require them to move out of the house or eat out for four months) all at the same time and still remain sane and healthy. How does he decide what to do and when to do it?

What's the Driving Force in Your Life Business Right Now?

There are a couple of business frameworks that can help you sort out what is primary and what is secondary among your Life Projects. The first is called the "Driving Force" of the Life Business in question. The concept was developed by Tregoe and Zimmerman.[1] They argued that if businesses understood where their real competitive advantage came from in the marketplace, they could build on that and continue to be successful.

McDonald's competitive advantage is in its terrific distribution system, so its future lies in developing new products and pushing them out through that system. Hewlett-Packard's advantage is in technological innovation, so its priority should be in turning out many new products each year. Weyerhaeuser's advantage lies in making the best use of all of the natural resources it controls.

Michael Porter, Harvard's Strategic Planning guru, concludes that companies should define their niche carefully and then work to create synergies within all their systems to support this niche.[2] So if you are in the organic food business, you want to find the best suppliers, improve your transportation to increase freshness, and maximize your ability to explain to the customer why he or she should buy organic. Don't divert your energies into building a secondary line of fast foods.

In determining which Life Business is most central to your Life Enterprise's Driving Force at any point in time, it would be helpful to consider the following questions:

- Is there one Business that is the critical energy supplier to all the rest?
- Which Business is in critical need of attention right now?
- Which Business embodies your Life Enterprise's most important Values?
- Which Business most clearly expresses an area of talent and motivation that is central to your sense of well-being?

What's Harry's Driving Force here? What's the niche that he needs to concentrate on if his Life Enterprise is going to be successful? To which Projects should he give priority? Perhaps the answer is obvious to the reader, but it took

Harry and Helen a little while to get it straight. It's the kid, stupid! Right now in their lives, the priority has to be getting the Teen Bird successfully through high school and to help her fly away into the next stage of life.

There are several reasons why this became their priority. First, there is the time-sensitive nature of this Life Business. Adolescence is a "big stakes" time of life and it is happening now. Second, there are the values that Harry and Helen feel as parents. If they blow this task, they might never forgive themselves, and they could "pay for it" for the rest of their lives. Third, there is synergy with other priorities. There are tremendous rewards for Harry and Helen's relationship if they can partner effectively as parents. If they fail to do so, this could spell problems for them later.

Once Harry recognizes that partnering with his wife around the teen transition is the driving force of his Life Enterprise in the short- term, then his priorities for Projects become clearer. He needs to maintain his consulting Business, but he doesn't need to be traveling all around the country just yet. While foreign travel and hiking are good things, perhaps they can be planned around the time the daughter is in camp, not during the school year. Harry can still keep up with friends and family, no conflict there. He probably needs to continue his counseling to help manage the stress of this period.

Conflicts do arise, however, with potential Projects in a couple of Harry's other Businesses. Harry was asked to run for the national board of his professional organization. He now thinks that this might be a Project for a later time, even though it would give him some of the recognition he craves, an opportunity for service, and probably as much fun as hard work.

Harry is sick to death of his 1960s tiny kitchen (it still has the original linoleum!). But, with the "Driving Force" concept in mind, he doesn't think that the stress of a major renovation, with the possibilities of moving out of the house for 3 or 4 months, or living in chaos, is something he and Helen want to take on right now. Neither do they want to inflict the confusion on their daughter who is trying to manage herself through the *Sturm und Drang* of adolescence, a highly competitive high school curriculum, and a very ambitious portfolio of extracurricular arts activities, which she really lives for.

It seems obviously impossible, but Harry originally thought he could pull all this off. That idea lasted about a week. When he got into a fight with his wife over when to schedule the meeting with the architect, he realized he was way off base and cruising for a bruising. This Project went into the medium-term category. He had also thought that he could be more active in his professional organization. After several committee meetings held in distant cities and coming back all tired and missing time with his daughter and wife, he, with some embarrassment, decided this could not be a priority and resigned from the committee.

Harry did feel that he wanted to go ahead with his book Project because while speculative, if successful, this could open up lots of opportunities in the consulting world and also bring him some of the recognition he wants. He could work on it from home base. It also drew on his creativity and Imaginative Isadore, Disciplined Dave, and Friendly Frank lobbied hard for it. In the end they over came Anxious Al's objections. It wasn't an entirely smooth process, but with the help of his counselor, Harry brought the way forward into focus. Projects in Teen Bird and Building Partners would be the short-term priorities. Extended travel is projected into the future, and any major commitment to his professional organization is also pushed forward in time. Harry's short-, medium-, and long-term Projects by time frame are displayed below.

Harry's Strategies and Projects for the Short Term

- *Teen Bird* (Invest Heavily): take family trips with daughter; monitor daughter's tendency to overcommit to things; plan enrichment experiences for daughter; attend daughter's performances; pay attention to daughter's health issues; communicate with wife about how things are going; make trips to counselor as needed

- *Partnering* (Invest Heavily): make it possible for spouse to go on writer's retreats; make time to talk about daily schedules, vacation plans, etc.; partner on domestic chores; make time for personal sharing; schedule fun trips together; gin games at night; read out loud, etc.

- *HHMO* (Invest Heavily): change jogging to walking program; consider joining spa; lose weight; continue medications for high cholesterol; monitor medical developments; explore insurance options

- *Pundit* (Build This Business): complete initial publishing venture; leverage book for speaking and consulting

- *Connections Unlimited* (Maintain Investments): stay in touch with sister and cousins; hang with friends, colleagues, mentors

- *HEWT* (Maintain Investment): maintain ongoing client relationships; develop Web page and Internet presence; establish workshop program

- *PP&G* (Maintain Investment): participate in annual meeting of professional group; continue personal coaching and counseling; undertake one other professional development activity; don't take on big responsibilities in professional association

- *IGUANA* (Maintain Investment): plan hiking trips; plan foreign travel when daughter is in camp; plan culture vulture activities; read; go to movies

- TGAL (Maintain Investment): continue pro bono consulting; give to political candidates

Harry's Strategies and Projects for the Medium Term

- *Teen Bird* (Invest Heavily for Present and Maintain for Long Term): have high school graduation party or celebration; support transition to college for daughter; make sure daughter is in right school for her; plan college viewing trips; provide tutoring support for daughter in high school (math and chemistry); formulate in-college communication plan

- *Home Improvement* (Invest Heavily): design and complete major renovation

- *IGUANA* (Build This Business): plan hiking trips (several brief each year); plan foreign travel (one extended overseas trip each year); culture vulture activities; read; go to movies

- *Partnering* (Invest for Present and Long Term): make time to talk about daily schedules, vacation plans, etc.; partner on domestic chores; make time for personal sharing; schedule fun trips together; plan trip to Italy once daughter is in college

- *Connections Unlimited* (Maintain): stay the course established; schedule more time with sister

- *HEWT* (Maintain Overall Business or Wind Down as Pundit Picks Up): maintain client relationships; use Internet as marketing tool; extend workshop program/bring in other trainers; write second and third book; develop speaking opportunities and workshops

- *PP&G* (Maintain): participate in annual meeting of professional group; plan more local involvement with professional group; undertake one other professional development activity; initiate serious exploration of temporary job in Europe

- *HHMO* (Maintain): maintain exercise program; follow professionally developed weight and strength maintenance program; keep weight off; continue medications and monitoring of medical conditions

- TGAL (Maintain): work with socially useful organizations; direct service activity working with young people; give to political candidates

Harry's Strategies and Projects for the Long Term

- *PP&G* (Invest in This Business): focus more on personal development activities

- *IGUANA* (Invest in This Business): schedule an extended stay in Europe which provides many opportunities for travel and hiking

- *TGAL* (Invest in This Business): work with socially useful organizations; take on major responsibility for professional organization; give to political candidates

(continues)

Harry's Strategies and Projects for the Long Term (*Continued*)

- *Family* (Maintain This Business): provide assistance to daughter as she launches career/graduate school; partner on domestic chores with wife; make time for personal sharing; schedule fun trips/activities together

- *Connections Unlimited* (Maintain This Business): schedule time with friends, family, colleagues

- *Pundit* (Maintain This Business): be more selective in speaking engagements; explore additional publication opportunities

- *HHMO* (Maintain This Business): maintain exercise program; follow professionally developed weight and strength maintenance program; keep weight off; continue monitoring medical conditions and taking prescribed medications

- *HEWT* (Wind This Business Down): let go of some ongoing client relationships; obtain European teaching/consulting post; continue workshop program, but rely on other trainers

---

Other Examples of Driving Force Project Priority Setting

For Brad, who had been hospitalized for a serious heart problem in the previous year, the Driving Force of his Life Enterprise was a no-brainer. Restoring his health had to be the priority. Other priorities were arranged around this.

For Mary the Driving Force became paying attention to the home front (self, children, extended family) and taking a break on professional advancement for a while.

Helen, Harry's wife, realized that with Teen Bird as the Driving Force, her novel would need to take second place and other priorities a distant third. She arranged her schedule accordingly and set aside Thursday through Saturday (when Harry would be parent in charge) for other Projects.

For Sandy, about whom you will hear a lot more in Steps 10 and 11, the Driving Force is always about identifying and developing her next important contribution.

Forecasting the Time and Money Required to Achieve Project Goals

You have done one sort of reality check on your Life Business Plan by sequencing Projects for your Life Businesses in the short, medium, and long term. Now it is time to run the numbers on what this is actually going to cost you in energy, time, and money.

115

The review of expenditures you conducted way back in Step 1 now comes in handy. You now know what things are costing you currently. Your detailed Project planning in Step 7 will also be of significant assistance here. You can go back and review your detailed Project plan and cost it out in time and money.

Harry estimates that his money costs in his HHMO diet project will be about $200 for consultation with the nutritionist and about $540 for the time he will pay his housekeeper to cook meals instead of doing other chores. His time costs will be the 4 hours consulting with the nutritionist and the 15 minutes a day to organize his meals and record his consumption.

Harry can also estimate what the Teen Bird Business will cost him during his daughter's high school years. He can add up the costs of tutors, summer camp, college visits, the "starter car," etc. There will be time expenditures for ferrying the daughter to dance lessons, etc. as well as attending recitals and performances. These expenses are familiar to almost every parent of a teenager.

In the Building Partners Business the major expenditures will be time costs:

- Daily time to touch base and talk about how the day will go and how it went
- Weekly walks with wife to talk things over
- Monthly times with the counselor
- Being available to take care of daughter so wife is able to go to a writers' colony for 2 to 3 weeks during the year
- Two weeks for a couples vacation when daughter is at camp

Harry's HHMO has a number of expenditures associated with it:

- $3000 per year for cholesterol and ulcer medicines, vitamins, etc.
- $1000 per year for health club membership
- $300 per year for running shoes and other sports equipment
- $500 per year for doctors' appointments
- $1000 per year for each of the special tests required for someone his age for a total of $5800 per year (Colonoscopy, stress test, endoscopies, etc. are not fully paid for by his major medical insurance because of his high deductible.)
- Time expenditures include an average of an hour a day for exercising and 2 days a year spent in doctors' offices.

Over the medium term, Harry can predict significant one-time financial expenses:

- Teen Bird: college expenditures of $12,000 to $40,000 depending on state vs. private school (but about $5000 of current expenditures will no longer be incurred)

116

- Home Improvement: renovation—$50,000 to $80,000
- Foreign Travel: may come to $5000 per year

You get the idea. Ultimately Harry wants to forecast the financial and time expenditures required for every one of his Life Businesses, in the short, medium, and long term. This will allow Harry to begin to do a reality test on his Life Enterprise Strategic Plan and revise the sequencing of his Commitments.

Life itself will also provide some immediate feedback. When Harry felt he could take on a major obligation with his professional association in the short term and then found that this was just not working, that Project got booted into the future. When Harry looks forward at his financial Commitments, he has to ask himself whether he can afford that renovation at the same time his daughter is attending college. Perhaps that will depend on whether she receives financial aid or a merit scholarship, or whether Harry's book is a best seller. But at least Harry is beginning to become aware of some of the potential challenges he is facing in realizing his life Goals.

Some Things to Keep in Mind About Step 8

Remember that Step 8 is about clarifying Commitments, not finalizing them. You prioritize your Projects according to whatever criteria make sense to you, and you look at what each Project will take in terms of time and money. Until you have matched your planned Commitments against your available resources, you are not truly committed. This is the process that takes place in Steps 11 and 12. At that time you will investigate all of the financial tactics that are available to you (e.g., how can Harry both renovate his house and send his daughter to a private college, if that's the choice she makes?).

Because you are not finalizing your Commitments at this stage, we urge you not to limit yourself at this point. Don't take your Dreams off the table just because the price tag seems more than you can pay at the moment. You may decide this is indeed the case at the end of Step 12, but for now "keep hope alive." This is another time for the visionary leadership that businesses require which we talked about back in Step 3. Instead of holding on to the tension between what is and what you want improved, now you are holding on to the tension between what you want for yourself and what you think might be possible. We will remind you to keep your options open at the end of Step 10 as well.

Budgeting your time Commitments to Projects on a daily, weekly, and monthly basis is as important as Budgeting your money. By asking what am I going to do every day, every week, every month, you foresee the real Commitment this Project is going to take and are able to assess whether this Commitment is realistic. Another good test of your personal motivation is to ask yourself: What am I willing to give up to have the time to take on this Project? If nothing presents itself, then perhaps you are not really motivated to be in this Business.

For example, Harry knows that his family members are late risers, which means he can usually count on the early mornings on most weekends to work on his book Project. While this plays into Harry's tendency to be a workaholic, it is feasible for him to Budget this time. If Harry had to take time out of his Monday to Friday consulting practice to work on the book Project on a regular basis, that would never happen because he needs to be available to paying clients during regular business hours. Harry also knows that late afternoons and early mornings during the week are good times for him to get in his daily exercise. This Commitment is realistic. Even when traveling, he can find an hour to walk around the hotel grounds, etc.

When you visualize your time Commitments and nail down specifically when in your busy days, weeks, and months this Commitment is going to be kept and it seems to fit with your routine, then you have a sense of confidence that this is a realistic Commitment. When this is not the case, then you need to rethink: Am I really going to be able to fit this in?

At the end of Step 8, you have a good sense of the demands on your Budget and on your daily schedule required by the heartfelt Projects you have envisioned. You have begun to build a firm foundation for your Life Businesses Plan. This is illustrated by the Strategic Plan Pyramid on page 119. Your time and money Commitments are the solid footing on which your Projects are based. These in turn support your Business development Strategies. Your Strategies drive the performance of each of your Life Businesses as they help you realize your Vision for a better life.

Exercises for the Reader

1. Sort Projects for each of your Businesses into short-, medium-, and long-term Commitments.
2. For each Project define what it will take in terms of energy, time, and money.
3. Reality test the sequencing and feasibility of your Projects in terms of whether the energy, time, and money is likely to be available, but don't shelve important Dreams because of money concerns. When you run your numbers in the Business Plan (Steps 10–13), new possibilities are likely to come to you.

The Strategic Plan Pyramid

For more detailed assistance in developing this aspect of your Life Business Plan, consult our Web site at www. lifebusiness.com.

On to the Business Plan

Congratulations. You now have a Life Enterprise strategy! At this point the Strategic Plan for your Life Enterprise is beginning to take real shape and is aimed toward the heavens but with a firm earthly foundation. Armed with the businesslike thinking of Step 9, you will complete your work with the detailed Business Plan and implementation process in Steps 10 through 13.

Notes

1. Benjamin Tregoe, John Zimmerman. *Top Management Strategy*, Simon and Schuster, 1980.

2. Michael Porter. "What is Strategy?" *Harvard Business Review*, November-December 1996.

PART FOUR

Business Plan

Analysis and planning bear fruit when resources are committed.

You know where you want to take your Life Businesses. Now you'll need energy, time, and money as resources for your Plan. You may or may not have sufficient resources to fund all the initiatives that you would like. Companies resolve conflicting resource demands and state their bottom-line resource commitments in their Business Plan. To help you do the same, Steps 9 through 13 address the following questions:

- How does a business think about and use money?
- What would change if you thought of money in a similar way?

- What energy, time, and money resources does your Plan require?
- When will these resources be required?
- Are these resources likely to be available when you'll need them?
- What can be done to provide resources when they're needed?
- What kind of help do you want to advance your Life Business Plan?

Business Thinking

What successful businesses teach us about using money to make dreams come true

Think Different.

Global advertisement, Apple Computer, Summer 2001

LIFE BUSINESS TENET

How you think about money will determine the quality of your Life Enterprise. Put your life in the center and use money to support your priorities. Businesses do!

Now you have Projects, time frames, and some sense of what each of your Projects will require in terms of energy, time, and money. Nicely done. And necessary too. You can't possibly know what to do with your money if you haven't thought through what you want to do with your life. The work you will undertake in the Business Plan section of this book will help you find the easiest, safest, and most efficient ways to provide resources for your Plan. Step 9 sets the conceptual context for the hands-on work of Steps 10–13.

Ten Business Principles

Steps 10 through 13 cover the core of the Life Business approach to personal financial planning and money management. The application of the 10 business principles presented below will put you firmly in the center of your financial life and will give you the conceptual tools you'll want to achieve your Dreams now and in future years.

To manage your resources like a successful business, you'll need to think like one. When you have completed Step 9, you will understand your financial realities in a different way. With the following critical conceptual anchors presented in this Step, you can reap the full benefits of the Life Business Program:

- A businesslike approach to your life requires business tools.
- Rediscover the true meaning of a hijacked business vocabulary.
- Businesses don't "retire," so why should you?
- It's the net worth of your life that counts, not your money's.
- Who needs profit when you have Cash flow?
- Two different kinds of "expenditures" require two different approaches.
- A Budget is the best way of demonstrating your Commitments.
- In calculating life's real Risks, market Volatility isn't one of them.
- Businesses think differently about saving, investing, and borrowing.
- Allocation, allocation, allocation is the *last* thing of importance.

Employ the Tools and Methods That Build Business Success

Principle 1: Managing your life as a business means being able to use the business mindset and adapt its processes, methods, and tools to the service of your objectives.

Over centuries businesses have developed a comprehensive array of ways to look at information, make sense of it, and act on it. Putting on a businesslike thinking cap allows you to avail yourself of this cornucopia of techniques as you implement your Life Business Plan.

Some of the business tools and methods that we have adapted for your use in Steps 1 through 8 included the Annual Business Planning Cycle, sources and applications accounting, return on investment (ROI), profit and cost centers, the customer's voice, the Boston Consulting Group's Strategy Matrix, SWOT analysis, business plans, budgets and projections, management team building, and annual reviews. In the context of offering Life Business seminars and workshops, it's been exciting to see how well these techniques and tools provide opportunities for new insights for individuals seeking to increase their life satisfaction.

One of our clients observed, "Before I got involved with the Life Business approach, I didn't truly understand the power of the Annual Business Planning Cycle . . . and I am currently responsible for the strategic planning of one of the world's largest chemical companies!" Bringing business tools and methods to bear on managing your life also sharpens your sense of how these same approaches can be used in their more usual context, back in the organization and on the job.

Use Business Terms as Businesses Use Them

Principle 2: Effectively applying the "life as business" metaphor requires understanding what business terms mean to businesses and operating consistently with this understanding.

In the few instances where financial service providers have latched onto the idea of advising their clients to think of their lives as businesses, something has been lost in the translation. Some financial advisers have adopted a business vocabulary without grasping the core ideas.

It's been suggested that if you gave a roomful of monkeys word processors and an infinite amount of time, they would eventually end up rewriting the Gettysburg Address word for word. What would happen if they could use only a business vocabulary? Looking for ways to lend legitimacy to their opinions and advice, financial planners have adopted a type of business-speak. Though they use businesslike buzzwords (cash flow, risk, return on investment), at the heart of it there is often nothing businesslike about the advice they give. It is almost as if

Key Concepts as Defined by Financial Planners and Businesses

Concepts	Financial Planners	Business
Net worth	Financial assets	Financial/nonfinancial assets
Cash flow	Useful	Essential
Risk	A threat	An opportunity
Volatility	To be avoided	To be taken advantage of
Budget	Limiting	Enabling
Saving	Set money aside	Search out efficiencies
Investment	Purchase stocks and bonds	Build the business
Borrowing	To be avoided	To be utilized
Allocation	Ratio of stocks, bonds, and cash, geared to wealth creation	Ratio is time frame contingent and geared to guaranteeing cash flow

they have taken the business vocabulary and randomly reassigned different meanings to words. Proceeding in this fashion it will take financial planners a long time to arrive at the financial equivalent of the Gettysburg Address. Can you afford to wait?

In the accompanying chart we compare a number of key business concepts, showing how they are assigned different meanings by businesses and by some financial planners.

Vision Long Term, Act Today

Principle 3: Businesses vision for the long term, plan for the medium term, and manage for the short term. They are looking to build their business's strength in all three periods. In business long-term health is built on short-term success. Invest your resources today for heartfelt returns both today and tomorrow.

In the Introduction to this book we listed a number of "people shoulds." These are the tenets of responsible money management drummed into us as a culture, parent to child, over two centuries of our national experience. When we are caught up in organizing our lives and finances in ways compatible with these fear-based cultural caveats, it's often difficult to figure out what our own Dreams and priorities really are, let alone act purposefully to achieve them. Even when we plan ahead for our Dreams, whether it's a second career or our personal version of "Margaritaville," in our culture we find it all too easy to keep stashing away money and forgetting to cash in.

Many of us take full advantage of our 401K programs and our IRAs, while, at the same time, we put away additional money to dispel our fears about having enough when the time comes for college expenses, obligations to our children, and long-term health care. This is the same money that might otherwise be employed to generate health, capability, and enthusiasm today, and thus a more vibrant and vital tomorrow.

Both the notion of hoarding and the idea of retirement defy business logic. Do you see successful businesses stashing away money to fund unclear long-term commitments while underfunding efforts that promise attractive returns today? Yet this is what most of us are actually doing when we max out our 401K or 403B contributions. Successful businesses do not guarantee their long-term profitability by amassing large cash reserves. These businesses invest today to make a profit now, and by doing so over time, they build strong corporate futures. Short-term priorities are, of course, chosen in the context of anticipated medium- and long-term events.

Fundamentally, businesses don't exist because they make money. They exist because they add value through meeting needs in society. This added value is recorded as profit. In thinking of your life as a business, your profit is your life satisfaction and that of your loved ones. While money can be an important enabler, in business terms your overriding Goal is making a satisfying life, not making money. Once this is understood, money, like time and personal energy, can be deployed very usefully in the support of identifying and achieving heartfelt Dreams.

Businesses do undertake long-term projects, but the returns and the costs, the upsides and the downsides, and the pros and cons of such projects are rigorously debated before scarce resources are committed. Personal retirement planning all too often seems to amount to stashing away valuable resources today against the hope of figuring out how to use them tomorrow.

Build Your Personal Net Worth, Not Your Money's

Principle 4: In Life Business terms high net worth is synonymous with living a full and complete life. Your life can have a high net worth regardless of the financial assets you possess. Increasing and preserving your personal and family net worth is the central Life Business challenge. How you define an increased quality of life is up to you and yours.

As consumers we often have to submit Financial Net Worth statements to obtain credit cards, higher credit limits, equity lines, and mortgages. These balance sheets, disguised as questionnaires, ask us to sum up our financial assets on one side of the page and our financial liabilities on the other. The net amount of these assets and liabilities is said to be our Net Worth. Don't you ever feel that your Personal Net Worth ought to be thought of as something more than this?

No doubt you have heard company spokespersons claim that their most important assets are their experienced management team, their employees' commitment, the loyalty of their customers, their inventory control process, or their product distribution system. Net Worth to a business, and to the markets that value that business, is indeed the sum total of all the factors making up that business's current strength: capital, inventory, employees, relationships, market position, patents, products, and products in the pipeline.

In other words a business's Net Worth is a comprehensive statement of its overall health at any given moment, not just a listing of its current financial assets and liabilities. Similarly your Personal Net Worth is at the same time something other, and something more, than your financial balance sheet; it's the sum of your Dreams, relationships, skills, Values, cares, and concerns.

Jake and Stan: A Tale of Two Investments

Jake and Stan are roughly the same age. Jake assiduously contributed the max to his 401K, working all the overtime that was available. Jake sacrificed opportunities for family outings and the social and educational experiences that would have broadened his interests. Though so far he has escaped major medical concerns and now has a great financial nest egg for retirement, Jake, now 65, has few friends or interests. Stan, for his part, voted for balance all the way through life and "invested" time and money in activities and interests both he and his family found rewarding as well as preparing for his life after his career years. Now at 65 Stan has a fulfilling part-time hobby, friends, family, numerous interests, and an active philanthropic agenda. He hasn't got a lot of extra money, but careful planning makes it all happen.

In business terms who do you think has the higher Net Worth—Jake or Stan? The, perhaps surprising, Life Business answer is "It depends." If Jake feels that he has missed out on life, his Net Worth is indeed diminished, regardless of his accumulated financial assets. If both Jake and Stan feel satisfied about where they are now, where they're likely to go, and where they've been, then they both have high Personal Net Worth. It's what they think of their lives, not what we think of their life choices or the state of their finances, that determines their respective Personal Net Worths.

A business's balance sheet reflects its overall value, not just its net financial assets. Applying this idea to your own life, clients who invest their financial assets in the development of their own and their loved ones' current experience, skills, and happiness can be seen as increasing their own value and the value of the collective family enterprise. Our personal view is that this is the way real Personal Net Worth is built.

Manage Cash Flow, and Profit Will Take Care of Itself

Principle 5: You need to have money when you need it. At the limit, you don't need to have money at any other time!

In the mid-1970s John Eckblad was a member of a panel discussion on corporate strategy at France's INSEAD School of Management. One of the other panel members represented an elite French government think tank. At some point during the discussion this fellow made the comment that "corporations never really need to make a profit as long as they can predictably maintain an adequate cash flow." John spent 15 years perplexed and bemused by this idea. Only now that he understands his own Life Enterprise and the real needs of his Life Businesses does this statement make sense.

Financial sufficiency, for that matter, financial independence, means that we are able to access the resources we require when we require them. That's *all* we need. Funding to this point is both necessary and sufficient. At the limit this could conceivably be achieved with no money in the bank. Think of it. If you knew what it was that brought you the highest satisfaction and you had the energy, time, and money to sustain this state now and in the future, what would be the value of any additional resources? Of course this argument assumes that in your Strategic Plan you have built in adequate contingencies or buffers for the unexpected. It also assumes that you will have arranged for the funding of those things that you would like to see achieved after your death. Having met these assumptions, none of us needs a penny more than our Dreams require . . . and a penny less just won't do.

If we can stay aware of what we value and continue to access sufficient resources "just in time" to fund our plans, from now until our last Dream has been achieved, we will have won. "Died with a smile" beats "Had the most toys" as an epitaph every time.

Cash flow is an entirely different animal from profit. The goal of maintaining an adequate cash flow is to increase the value of underlying assets. The goal of financial profit is to increase financial surpluses, even if it requires liquidating the enterprise's underlying assets. In line with this thinking, Life Business participants are challenged to shift their emphasis from creating financial surpluses to assuring themselves that funds will be available as they are required to support their Dream-driven Strategic Plans. You don't even have to use your own money to produce cash flow. Remember the property developers' favorite source of funding, OPM—other peoples' money.

Cash flow can be increased by taking out a loan, by selling objects we own and no longer need, or by lowering the cost of the activities we undertake and the things that we feel we must buy. In the end the surpluses we should be committed to increasing are our Life Enterprise's underlying assets: the vitality, health, enthusiasm, and life skills of ourselves, our partners, our families, and our communities, now and in the future. Seeking to secure financial surpluses for their own sake is like kicking the ball toward the wrong goal.

Distinguish Business Investment from Support Expense

Principle 6: The single most important activity in improving bottom-line Personal Net Worth is the identification of, and investment in, your key Life Businesses.

Business challenges have often attracted the attention of top-notch thinkers. One of these was Harvard's Ted Levit who, as we discuss in Step 3, challenged corporations to answer the single but central question, "What Businesses Are You In?"

Levit's point was simple. As organizations grow older they invariably become more complex. With increasingly diverse activities, organizations can lose sight of their dreams and the awareness of what it is that they do best. Levit challenged organizations to be clear about the businesses they really want to be in and to dedicate their resources to achieving their goals in these areas. This idea has been further honed by advocates of systems thinking, organization development, and reengineering.

In business thinking all line items are not created equal. Businesses make a distinction between "Business Investment" and "Support (or overhead) Expense." Both expenditures affect cash flow. The critical difference is that Business Investment builds the enterprise, while Support Expense, in effect, limits its development. Simply put, money spent on Support (e.g., heating, lighting, parking lots, security, lunchrooms) is not available for Business Investment. By distinguishing between Investment and Support expenditures, businesses are better positioned to continuously evolve by taking advantage of emerging opportunities and rejuvenating their strengths. We recommend that individuals do the same with their energy, time, and money.

Today, if it's not absolutely clear how a particular activity or line-item expense contributes to an enterprise's bottom line, then the activity is downsized, right-sized, or closed, and the resources previously dedicated to it are redirected to the company's key businesses. As individuals you need to be involved in the same process in order to give yourself the best possible chance of living most completely your desired life both now and in the future. Fortunately, as with other Life Business tools and processes, you can "download" this competency very simply and inexpensively by accessing your own business experience.

This book introduces the concept of a businesslike budget with separate entries for Life Business Investments (i.e., those activities and expenditures that build your key Life Businesses) and Support Expenses (i.e., money required to carry on activities which you consider necessary but which are not "heartfelt"). To our knowledge this is the first time that this distinction has ever been made in individual and family life and financial planning.

Budget to Enable

Principle 7: The Budget is where we sort out our priorities among the things we want to do, the things we feel we need to do, and the things we have been doing. The finished Budget captures our Commitment to a given balance among all of these activities for a specific period of time.

Budgeting is another concept financial planners and businesspeople understand differently. Budgeting, concept and practice, has a bad reputation in the personal finance marketplace. Jane Quinn Bryant is so concerned by her readers' negative reactions to the "B" word that she has renamed the activity, now calling it a "spending summary." To many of us Budgeting is what one does when money regularly runs out before the month is finished. This kind of Budgeting is meant to be punitive, limiting, and controlling—and perhaps has its cultural origins in a felt need to protect ourselves against the possible riotous exuberance of our more impulsive instincts. In classic financial planning, a successful Budget represents a victory of the super ego over the id.

To the businessperson, however, budgeting is an enabling, rather than a limiting, activity. The business budget is the place where the priorities among a number of exciting, yet often conflicting, opportunities are finally sorted out. It's where the foundations for long-term successes are laid. When the process works well, all the members of the business team have had a chance to argue their cases and the final budget is a practical and comprehensive summary of what the team is committed to achieving for the next given period of time.

In the context of businesslike personal life and financial planning, the Budget encapsulates our hopes and enthusiasms as well as our day-to-day responsibilities. The Budget combines our commitments to meeting both our highest aspirations and our most basic needs. With our Budget we are saying that we believe in these initiatives and that we want to support their achievement with the commitment of the scarce resources required to bring them about. The Budget clarifies and gives positive direction and authority to our financial investments in our Life Businesses.

To a business owner or manager "going over" budget is no less or more of a problem than ending up "underspent." If the Life Enterprise goes over budget, this is a problem because more resources have been spent than had been anticipated, and now the business may be strapped to find the resources required to do what it had hoped to do next. "Going under" Budget is a problem because the enterprise has "left opportunity on the table" by not leveraging all the resources it had available to develop the business.

Putting the "Spice" Back in Samantha's Budget and Her Life

Samantha worked long and hard hours as a real estate agent. Her financial planner had advised her to maximize her contributions to her IRA to achieve tax efficiency. The idea of paying less tax was very comforting to her because of earlier life experiences. Plugging her IRA contributions, her business expenses, the expenses for schooling and clothing her son, and food expenses for the family into her annual Budget left Samantha feeling heavy and lethargic.

131

The Budget Samantha was requiring herself to follow did not include funds for things like gifts and travel, which she thought of as the "spice" in her life. For a short time the ensuing discussion turned around whether it was better to Budget for tax efficiency or spice. Then a new possibility was hit on; by borrowing against her home equity line, both priorities could be met.

In the end carrying debt was a lesser concern to Samantha than shutting out either tax efficiency or spice. Because her IRA was earning about 9 percent a year tax-deferred and the 4.75 percent interest she was paying on her equity line was tax deductible, the decision to access her equity line also improved her cash flow. Moreover, having established a Budget that reflected her personal priorities, Samantha was now committed to making it work.

Distinguish Risk from Volatility

Principle 8: Risk is the chance that some action you take won't realize a desired outcome. Increased "Market Volatility" increases "Financial Risk" in the short term (0–3 years). *But* financial strategies designed to limit Market Volatility may create increased "Personal Risk" in the long term (7+ years). A Risk to "Personal Net Worth" may or may not have any relationship with either Financial Risk or Market Volatility.

Financial Risk is the possibility that, at any point in time, you will lose rather than gain money in the stock and bond markets. Market Volatility is the low-to-high, high-to-low, price swings stock and bond markets experience.

To hear financial planners tell it, Financial Risk is something akin to the Hong Kong flu, something to be inoculated against. In classic financial planning tolerance for Risk is seen largely as a function of your personality and the liquidity of your financial assets. It's thought that any given client either can or cannot tolerate Risk. If a client can't tolerate Risk, there isn't much that can be done about it except to try to escape it.

In the financial planner's lexicon, Risk is equated with Volatility. Because the word Volatility doesn't conjure up the angst associated with the word Risk, it is often employed as a euphemism. The term Volatility is used when it's felt that the issue of Risk really ought to be addressed, but one would prefer not to call a spade a spade.

The businessperson thinks of risk differently. In the business context risk is the possibility that one's actions (or nonactions) might not achieve one's desired outcomes. To the businessperson financial risk is, more specifically, the possibility that a given project will not result in an anticipated financial outcome. We have corporate clients who are not only used to experiencing risk but who actively go out of their way to look for it. Where there is risk, there is often the chance for disproportionate profit. Businesspeople are aware of risk factors and manage their company's risk exposure in trying to achieve their business's objectives.

At the heart of businesslike life and financial planning, Risk is related to the plans we make, not the money required to fulfill them. When you put yourself in the center of your life, as when a business manager makes the interests of his or business paramount, the real Risk is that you won't achieve your Goals, or that, when achieved, their achievement doesn't bring you the desired and hoped for satisfaction.

Risk, therefore, has nothing to do with the comfort of the ride, only the quality of the outcome. Market Volatility is a Risk to your money only if you have to cash in your stocks or bonds when their values are spiraling downward. If you don't need to cash in, the eventual, and historically predictable, upturn will start your money moving in the desired direction again.

Much more importantly, you are not your money, and a Risk to your money is only a Risk to you if it keeps you from achieving your Dreams. Traditional financial planning may in fact create a real Risk by inappropriately limiting a client's exposure to Volatility.

Volatility versus Risk: You Decide

Mary and Tom Collins put money aside for 7 years toward the Dream of a private college education for their two children. On advice from a financial planner they decided to place their college funds in a mix of bonds and CDs in order to beat inflation but minimize Volatility. Today they need the money for college but have discovered that educational costs have grown faster than both inflation and their placements. During the last 7 years the Collinses experienced low Volatility in their holdings; indeed, they slept soundly every night; but there was now the real Risk that they would have to let go of, or dilute, one of their Dreams. The Collinses's situation could be characterized as low Volatility and high Risk.

Sharon thought long and hard about her life Goals and the financial implications of trying to achieve them. She realized that she was going to have to live with some possibly significant Volatility in her interim financial placements if she was to start her own business in 6 years' time. Her portfolio would have to earn an ambitious 12 percent net annual return if her estimates were correct. Sure enough during the ensuing 6 years the markets moved up and down, down and up, sometimes swinging 25 percent annually in one direction or another. Sharon slept soundly realizing that whatever happened before 6 years was of no importance to her. All she cared about was having twice as much money as she had initially put in at the end of the time period. Six years went by, and Sharon had her grubstake. She had experienced significant Volatility, but she was able to tolerate, even ignore, that Volatility because she realized that long term, this type of placement was most likely to produce the funds she needed when she needed them.

Save by Becoming More Efficient; Invest These Savings in Your Life Businesses

Principle 9: Invest in your key Life Businesses. Save resources by running your Support activities to be as lean and efficient as possible. Invest any Savings in your key Life Businesses now.

The traditional notion of "saving" is to put money away for an undefined rainy day. "Americans don't save enough!" declare the popular financial pundits. In traditional economic thinking high citizen saving rates are a key to a robust economy. In traditional financial planning, saving is the key to a rewarding and trouble-free personal future. Now that the Japanese have Saved themselves into a 12+-year recession, the macroeconomic argument seems a bit suspect. Now that some individuals have record-level 401K and IRA holdings yet are working more hours than ever before, with many supersavers teetering on the edge of emotional "bankruptcy," the financial planning industry's invocation "to save more" needs to be questioned.

As individuals we conflate and thereby confuse the concepts of Saving and Investing. At the individual level Investing is often taken to be synonymous with stock picking. In traditional financial planning you commit to put some of your earnings away (saving), and the money you put away you place in stocks, bonds, or the money market (investing).

But businesses don't put money away for an undefined rainy day in a distant future. In fact, Saving in a business sense doesn't involve putting money away at all. Instead, businesslike Saving means doing what needs to be done more efficiently, that is, finding lower-cost alternatives that get the desired job done at least as effectively as before. These "saved" resources are then put to the service of other high-priority business development objectives.

Companies invest in the development of key businesses for short-, medium-, and long-term results. They don't expect that they will achieve desired long-term outcomes without maintaining their vitality and vibrancy in the here and now. The application of these principles is what makes corporate budgeting enabling. So it should be with individuals and families.

Peter Saves to Invest

For quite a while, Peter had been concerned with how much it was costing him to keep in touch with his far-flung family. His phone bills were running about $375 a month. Peter wasn't into penny-pinching for pinching pennies' sake, but he had Life Business Projects that were going underfunded because of insufficient cash flow. So he decided to squeeze his Support Expenses for cash. After he figured out how much he had been paying per minute for local, state, out-of-state, and international calls, Peter entered into new phone contracts. Peter ended up with a cell phone agreement giving him 3500 "free" evening and weekend minutes that he now uses for state and out-of-state calls, a local provider for in-town use, and a "phone-around" number (10 10 —) for international calls. His communications strategy now fully implemented, Peter pays about $125 a month for what was once costing him three times as much. Peter has Invested the "Saved" $250 a month in his and his wife's shared Travel 2C Kids Life Business.

As with all business management principles this principle works for the productive use of time as well as for money. Michael Eisner, Disney's CEO, is quoted as saying, "The Greek philosopher Theophrastus said, 'Time is the most valuable thing a man can spend.' My most valuable investment, and favorite splurge, is spending time with my wife and our three sons."[1] Using his business skills to manage his life, Eisner is Saving time by operating more efficiently and then Investing the saved time in the Life Businesses that bring him the returns he is seeking.

Make at Least Three Asset Allocation Decisions

Principle 10: Allocation, allocation, allocation. Allocation theory is about what's best for your money. In Life Business, the appropriate Allocation of assets is about what's best for your life. How you best allocate your assets among stocks, bonds, and cash depends on when you are planning to use the funds. Short-term (0–3 years), medium-term (4–6 years), and long-term (7+ years) payouts each requires different asset Allocations.

Allocation can be best understood by reading the following story and then considering the questions that follow.

Did Will Make the Right Decision?

In the early days of October 2000, Will reviewed his financial portfolio and decided to sell a number of his bonds and purchase a mid-cap growth fund. In his view the technology sector looked ripe to rebound from its spring drop and its summer doldrums. Furthermore, a presidential election promised to raise stock market values no matter which candidate ended up in the White House. We all know what happened. The election became a 2-month stalemate and the stock market began a 2-year swoon. Will now feels bad about his decision. Actually, he feels very bad.

Depending on which school of advisers Will listens to, he either made the right decision or the wrong one. One group of advisers tells him he did the right thing in taking a long-term perspective. Their advice is based on the fact that in every 7-year period during the last 100 years, except two, stocks have outperformed bonds. Therefore, no matter what happens today, over time Will's decision is likely be rewarded.

The other group tells Will that he should have been more concerned about balancing his allocations among stocks, bonds, and cash. In this case, such a balance would have kept more of his resources in bonds rather than overweighting his placements on the side of growth funds. This advice is based on the fact that more evenly allocated portfolios experience less price Volatility than those made up entirely of equities.

Who is right?

Whom do you think Will should listen to?

The Life Business answer to these questions is entirely different from either of the answers presented above. First of all, from the information provided in the example, we can't determine whether or not Will made a good decision. It all boils down to when Will wanted to use his money. If, to meet his objectives in the time frame of 7+ years, Will needed a current and steady 6 percent total return on his financial assets and had been getting a good deal more than that over the previous 5 years, then there was really no reason why he should be concerned about market Volatility at all. Under this scenario Will was already "fireproof." Whether he put his money in CDs, bonds, or the stock market, he was still likely to be able to fund his Plan. In this case, Will had already achieved independence from his finances. When you can see that your Dreams can be funded now and in the likely future, we say you've made your "nut." If your Dreams are already funded, more is not better, just more complicated.

If, on the other hand, Will hadn't yet made his "nut" and his concerns were about whether or not he would have the financial resources to enable his long-term (7+ years) Dreams, he still probably made the right decision by keeping his funds in equities. Just any return on his placements simply wasn't going to be enough. In this case Will needed a return that he was likely to get only in the stock market. The first group of advisers is correct that over the long term equities have almost always outperformed bonds.

The only wrong decision Will made was concerning himself about the short-term market Volatility his portfolio was experiencing. In the short term, the prices of good technology stocks will move up and down; in the long term, good technology stocks will outperform bonds.

Finally, if Will's concerns were about whether or not he would have the financial resources to enable his short- (0–3 years) to medium-term (4–6 years)

Dreams, he did indeed do the wrong thing. Mid-cap growth is a more volatile placement than bonds every time out, and market Volatility is an enemy of the reliable short-term availability of funds.

Will's example suggests that he is still thinking of his finances as something separate from his life. If Will knows what he needs to have and when he needs to have it, and these plans are not threatened by goings-on in the financial markets, then what's happening in the financial markets is really of no importance to him. Will needs to pursue his work in Steps 10 through 13 to gain this perspective.

The Business Metaphor

Looking at personal finance from a business perspective started out as an anchor for us and soon became a continuously accessible metaphor. We began to, consistently and methodically, ask ourselves, "Given this specific financial planning opportunity or challenge, how would a businessperson look at this situation and what would he or she do?"

The great thing about a metaphor is that it keeps on giving; it continues to shine new light on new problems. We have come to think of it as having our own personal guru whom we can turn to when addressing a life planning or resourcing challenge. "What would I do if this was happening in my business?"

People need to identify and find ways to get into the center of their lives. Resources—energy, time, and money—should be used to support agendas arising from this awareness. This is what successful businesses do. The comprehensive and systemic qualities of a businesslike approach to life and financial planning can deliver increased individual and family vitality and strength. When in doubt, ask yourself how a successful businessperson would address an analogous business challenge. In this way the business metaphor becomes a tool for acting on any situation you might face.

Blocks to Applying Business Thinking

Why, if we already know how to think and act like a business, haven't we been doing it when it comes to our own and our family's self-interest?

For starters, we're all ambivalent about being in business. We have come to associate being businesslike with being ruthless or unethical, hardheaded or unfeeling. When we acknowledge these feelings in ourselves and reflect on them, we often find their origin in one or more situations where we wish we had had the courage to have challenged someone or done something differently. As we discuss in the Introduction, businesslike thinking and planning are no guarantee that we will be "good" or courageous people in either our jobs or our lives.

137

Likewise, there is no reason to conclude that being businesslike has to lead to being less good or courageous than would any other approach.

In developing your Life Businesses, you will thoroughly examine your life through the filter of your own Values. If you are an ethical person, your life will be more effectively so; if you are not, then your life will not be. The choice is yours.

Exercise for the Reader

Thinking of yourself as an Enterprise and your most important life agendas as Businesses will radically change the way you use various financial planning terms and concepts. By applying Life Business concepts to your financial planning, you can arrive at more life-affirming and serviceable definitions of concepts such as Net Worth, Cash Flow, Risk, Savings/Investment, and Allocation. Our quiz, which you will find in Appendix B, is designed to highlight and reinforce some of these new perspectives. Give it a go.

Visit our Web site at www.lifebusiness.com for additional Step 9 exercises.

The Bottom Line

By applying businesslike approaches to Net Worth, Cash Flow, Business Investment and Support Expenses, Risk, Budgeting, Saving and Investing, and Asset Allocation in our personal lives, we can harness the real power of these concepts to realize our Dreams. For those of us already in business it's a matter of sweeping aside the meanings the financial planning industry has affixed to key planning concepts and reintroducing what we already know from our own work experience. There's no new jargon to learn. You've got the language, you've got the tools, and you've got the experience. Those readers not experienced in business can improve their personal planning and business acumen by mastering these few key concepts discussed above.

An integrated philosophy and practice of life and financial planning is now possible, and the model comes from the experience of businesses. Only with a comprehensive conceptual and practical framework can client and planner make sense out of seemingly conflicting strategies such as those proposed by Internet brokers like Discover Brokerage, discount brokers like Charles Schwab, market makers like Merrill Lynch, asset managers like First Union Bank, contrarians such as the brothers Motley Fool, lifestyle downsizers like the authors of *Your Money or Your Life,* and lay philosophers like the authors of *Die Broke.*

Moving on From Here

In Step 10 we concentrate on showing you how to clarify your future financial situation by first developing a meaningful and enabling Plan-Ahead Budget.

Step 11 demonstrates how to determine how much funding you'll need and when you'll need it by projecting and assessing your likely financial situation over the next 0 to 10 years utilizing short-, medium-, and long-term Projections. At the end of Step 11 you will know what it's going to take to "float your boat" or "make your nut." This is the magic moment we promised. There is an almost indescribable feeling of freedom that will flow over you when you know the number that will enable your Dreams.

Finally in Steps 12 and 13 we introduce ways to increase the financial productivity or efficiency of your Life Enterprise and look at the money management implications of your Projections.

Note

1. *USA Weekend,* April 9–11, 1999.

Budget to Enable Your Dreams

Business investments, support expenses . . . and just plain fudge

It's unwise to pay too much, but it's worse to pay too little.

John Ruskin

LIFE BUSINESS TENET

The Budget is the key to executing a successful business strategy. A comprehensive personal and family Budget process will support a focused and satisfying life. By learning how to create the "Historical," "Look-Ahead," and "Plan-Ahead" Life Business Budgets, you gain the critical financial tools you'll need to connect your life Goals and your finances.

The objective of our work in Steps 10 through 13 is to help you line up your money in support of your emerging Strategic Plan. In this chapter (Step 10) we show you how to clarify your next year's priorities and Commitments through developing a meaningful and enabling Budget. In Step 11 you will learn to determine how much funding you'll need and when you'll need it, by projecting and assessing your likely financial situation over the next 0 to 10 years utilizing short-, medium- and long-term Projections. When completed, your Life Business Plan will answer the questions: What Life Businesses are you in? How are these Businesses to be developed? How much investment is required and when? and What are the resource management implications of these decisions?

In Step 10 readers work toward living "independent of their finances" by discovering how to commit to their Dreams in a world of trade-offs, limitations, and confusions. The centerpiece of this work is the Life Business Budgeting process.

The Goal of the Life Business Approach Is Financial Independence

Becoming financially independent in the Life Business sense has nothing to do with having a lot of money. It also has little to do with whether the money you do have comes from working, Social Security, your portfolio, a pension, loans, gifts, a lottery, or an inheritance. Being financially independent is, instead, a state of mind. It's feeling confident that you will be able to live the life you want with the resources that you are likely to have.

Gaining financial independence depends on achieving three things:

1. Knowledge of how much money you need now to live a satisfying life, a good estimate of how much you are likely to need in the future, and knowing when you'll need it.
2. Knowledge of how much money you either have or can access now and a good estimate of how much you are likely to earn and/or receive in the future.
3. A Plan, in which you have confidence, for producing the funds you require, when you require them.

The clever bit is how you organize this information and what you do about what you learn from the process. With the focus, knowledge, and confidence that result from this discipline, money worries—as most of us experience them—are banished. When you have "arrived," you will have stopped worrying about, and being preoccupied with, money and its place in your life. In other words, you will feel independent of your finances no matter how much or how little money you actually have or whether or not you earn income! Enabling you to achieve your chosen Dreams while experiencing independence from your finances is the essential Goal of Life Business work.

Create a Solid Foundation: Know What Your Money Is Doing Today

An important aspect of effectively planning for the development of your Life Enterprise is organizing your personal resources (e.g., energy, time, and money) so that they can be fully employed in the service of your most important personal Goals. You can arrive at financial independence only by fully understanding where your money comes from, where your money goes, and how it can best be committed. Unless you're a CPA, there is some tedious work ahead. Our promise is that, once invested, this time will pay off exponentially in peace of mind. Financial "planning" begins with a summary, or accounting, of what is already happening. This is necessary because only by truly understanding your current expenditures, that is, how much is being spent and for what, can you make meaningful decisions about how to use your resources more effectively in the future.

Budgeting Short Term and Projecting Long Term

Budgets and Projections go hand in hand. Budgets gain much of their meaning when they enable us to Project seamlessly from now through a distant tomorrow, and it's impossible to build a future Projection without the anchor of today's Budget.

In order to know what energy, time, and money resources you will require at any given moment, you will need to have developed a quantitative picture of the life you want to lead over that time. We call this long-term view a *Life Projection*. Of course your ideas will change. What's important is that you take a view. Once a good working model has been constructed, you can entertain any number of what-if scenarios.

A fully developed Life Business Projection emphasizes what "you want to do," reminds you of what "you have to do," and indicates the resources you are likely to have available to make these things happen from now until anytime you select in the future.

The Projection's bottom line is a statement by time period, Short Term (0–3 years), Medium Term (4–6 years) and Long Term (7+ years), of how much money will be required and available to fund your Life Business Plan, assuming conservative assumptions about inflation, income, and asset growth. As we promise above, the Projection's bottom line will tell you what kind of "nut" you'll have to crack in each of these time frames and will give you the information you'll need to determine the likelihood of getting it cracked.

Distinguish Investments from Expenses

We think of resources invested in Life Businesses as Investments, and resources required to maintain or Support our lives as Expenses. Your most heartfelt Goals and essential Dreams about how you want your life to be are expressed in your Life Business Investments. In general, your Support activities are those things you need to do to maintain a basic existence (food, clothing, transportation, etc.). Of course, what's basic to some of us is "living large" for others.

As you will see, making this distinction between Investments and Expenses leads to a very different kind of Budget—one designed to take the Enterprise forward rather than one held hostage by past obligations.

Three Kinds of Budgets

As individuals, we have been taught by our experience and the feedback of others that Budgets are constraints on living our lives. What does the Business metaphor tell us about how businesses understand and use budgeting? Businesses budget so that they can know where they are, clarify and clear up past entanglements, align their resources in order to achieve their chosen goals, redistribute money to get more "bang for their buck," and lay a foundation for their projected futures.

In the Life Business Program we use three different levels of budgeting. In order of their increasing enabling power they are:

- 12-month Historical Budgets—a comprehensive listing of expenses by line item over the past 12 months
- 12-month Look-Ahead Budgets—an extrapolation of next year's expenditures from an analysis of last year's experience
- 12-month Plan-Ahead Budgets—Business Project and Support line items and line item funding levels, in accordance with your Life Business Plan.

To help you develop your own Budgets, the following pages offer a worked through example featuring Sandy, a real-life Life Business participant, and the wife of Peter, another Life Business participant.

Sandy's Story

Sandy and Peter are a second-marriage couple, each with three children from their previous marriages. Sandy has shared custody of her three children (Joseph, Beth, and Anna), and Peter's children (Nicholas, Gabriel, and Marie-Laure) have graduated from college and started their independent lives. Sandy and Peter's relationship is a blended odyssey, replete with complications, frustrations, and frequent delights. Peter and Sandy decided that it would be best to develop their separate Life Business Plans before looking at the interrelationship of their respective Plans. Our work with couples, blended or not, has taught us that this approach yields the most constructive results.

Sandy has identified her Life Businesses. She has also decided on Projects she wants to pursue in the Short Term, Medium Term, and Long Term to meet her Goals for the development of these Businesses. In reality Sandy has 10 active Businesses, but for illustrative purposes we have selected the 5 that have the most implications for her financial resources. We look at Sandy's 12-month Historical, Look-Ahead and Plan-Ahead Budgets in this chapter and her short-, medium-, and long-term Projections in Step 11.

How Peter and Sandy Arrange Their Finances

Sandy and Peter were married in 1993 after several years of courtship. While Sandy and her daughters do the cooking and Peter maintains the house, the couple splits the costs of food and a cleaning service. Sandy purchased and maintains her car, pays her professional and medical expenses, and covers half (joint custody) of her children's education, travel, and holiday expenses. Peter has been picking up the tab for most airline and rail travel when it's Sandy and Peter traveling without the children. Sandy has an employer-sponsored medical plan covering herself and her children. The couple is living in a house owned by Peter.

In her relationship with Peter, Sandy has, from the beginning, taken responsibility for her car expenses and meeting her children's needs. With a good deal of trepidation she now wants to build on these achievements and challenge issues that she has always found just plain too tough to face.

Sandy's Big Dream

Sandy is 12 years younger than Peter and, in large part, as a result of Life Business work, has chosen to begin a new professional career in educational administration. Sandy has entered a 2-year master's degree program at her local university and has received a fellowship paying approximately $20,000 per year that helps her cover the cost of her studies and her other expenses.

Now with her professional and financial horizons widening, Sandy has set out to achieve a broad spectrum of Goals and Dreams. She is well on her way to living independent of her finances because of the thought she has put into determining what is fundamentally important to her and her efforts to develop a long-term perspective.

Sandy's Quandary

Getting to this point with her "life and financial planning" has not been easy for Sandy. Before she began Life Business work, both goal setting and money management caused her considerable anxiety. Acute money problems experienced in her first marriage, a tendency to seek short-term rewards, and a sinking feeling that she really couldn't count on others all contributed to difficulties. Sandy has

145

had problems both in allowing herself to aspire to things that were important to her, that is, to Dream, and in having confidence that she could achieve her Dreams, if she were ever to commit herself and her resources. More than anything, Sandy hates the thought of investing herself and risk failing to achieve what she has set out to do. After all, she could just be setting herself up for a broken heart.

At the same time Sandy has a good deal of hard-won confidence in her professional abilities and feels that she can and should expect more from herself. In the past, these conflicting pressures have stranded Sandy somewhere between wanting someone else to take care of her and a desire to stand on her own two feet.

She finds herself in a planning quandary. Whereas she keeps meticulous records of her expenses, she rarely uses this information to inform her future buying decisions. When Sandy's annual expenditures are added up and her income is shown, you'll see why Sandy has historically found it hard to make ends meet.

Sandy's approach to planning is made even more problematic by the way she has always thought of Dreams. To her, a Dream is a view of a future way of life that has to be taken absolutely literally and specifically. In her idea of a farm, there is a screened sitting porch, several goats, a '52 Chevy pick-up, and two dogs to be named Willi and Nilli; not an open porch, several pigs, a '60 Ford pick-up, and one dog to be named later.

Now let's see how, using the Life Business Budgeting process, Sandy finds a way forward despite financial challenges, some personal ambivalence, and a complex history in dealing with money and finances.

Creating Sandy's 12-Month Historical Budget

To prepare the foundation for future planning, Sandy first has to get a handle on what activities she is involved in now and how much it is currently costing her. To do this, Sandy generates a complete listing of her expenses over the past 12 months (using a format similar to that found in Appendix A). She lists only those expenses she paid herself from her own resources. See Sandy's 12-Month Historical Budget on page 147.

Creating Sandy's Look-Ahead Budget

Next Sandy develops a Look-Ahead Budget. She first reviews her past year's costs and gives some thought to the next year. Sandy asks herself how known changes in what she'll be doing, what others will be doing, her age and the ages of significant others, others' emerging needs, the changes in her work and family situation will

Sandy's 12-Month Historical Budget

Type of Expenditure	$ Amount	Remarks
Personal		
• Clothing	1,000	
• Other	1,200	Includes contribution to her travel costs with Peter
Professional	600	When you teach, there are constant pressures for gifts, donations, etc.
Food	3,600	Half of household food expense
Medical		
• Medical/dental	250	$250 deductible
• Prescriptions	600	Employee health insurance doesn't cover prescriptions
Car		
• Payments	0	1989 car paid for
• Maintenance	1,200	1989 car needs increasing maintenance
• Gas, oil, taxes, license, insurance	905	Thank goodness for decent gas mileage
Utilities	1,320	Sandy contributes to utilities; Peter covers the rest of housing
Children		
• College	3,200	Half of in-state tuition, room and board—joint custody agreement
• Clothing	750	Half of costs—joint custody agreement
• Skiing vacation	900	One child per year—not subject to joint custody agreement
Other	0	
IRA	2,000	Build financial strength
Total Funds Required	17,525	
Type of Funding		
Income		
• Earnings (net)*	21,600	Last year as a teacher before entering graduate school
• Investments	0	
Total Funds Available	21,600	
End-of-Year Finances	4,075	Having 20% of her income left feels good

*After deductions for federal and state taxes, FICA, and state retirement program.

affect line-item funding for the next year. Sandy's Look-Ahead Budget reflects her feelings and thoughts about the year to come:

- Sandy has projected a 4 percent across-the-board increase in her expenditures to account for inflation.
- Changes in the reimbursement policies of her health-care program will lead to higher costs.
- Her costs for college education will rise sharply as both she and her daughter Beth join her son Joseph at college.
- She plans on taking all three of her children on the family's ski vacation for next year.
- With Beth away at college food costs should go down but higher house cleaning costs will more than offset any financial gain.

With her Look-Ahead Budget Sandy has extended the areas in which she is willing to take personal responsibility. In addition to the everyday feeding and care of her children and the maintenance of her car, Sandy's Look-Ahead Budget covers another child at college (Sandy and her ex-husband split college costs 50/50 for in-state tuition, living costs, books, and fees), a big commitment to a special family holiday, and half of the cost of cleaning the family home.

Now that Sandy has done the essential preparation by creating her Historical and Look-Ahead Budgets, she is ready for the big step of tackling her Plan-Ahead Budget, the Budget that will form the basis for Projecting her future plans and their financial implications.

Sandy's 12-Month Look-Ahead Budget

Type of Expenditure	$ Amount	Remarks
Personal		
• Clothing	260	Don't need new clothes as a student!
• Other	624	Better count on the same as last year
Sandy's College	1,352	In-state tuition and books for master's in education administration
Food	3,744	
Medical		
• Medical/dental	806	Responsible for health insurance premiums during educational leave
• Prescriptions	624	Employee health insurance doesn't cover prescriptions

(continued)

Sandy's 12-Month Look-Ahead Budget (*Continued*)

Type of Expenditure	$ Amount	Remarks
Car		
• Payments	0	1989 car paid for
• Maintenance	1,248	1989 car needs increasing maintenance
• Gas, oil, taxes, license, insurance	921	Thank goodness for decent gas mileage!
Utilities	1,373	Sandy contributes to utilities; Peter covers the rest of housing
Children		
• College	6,656	2 children: half of in-state tuition, room and board—joint custody agreement
• Clothing	780	Half of costs—joint custody agreement
• Skiing vacation	2,808	3 children: not subject to joint custody agreement
Other	0	
IRA	2,000	
Total Funds Fequired*	23,196	
Type of Funding		
Income		
• Earnings (net)[†]	0	
• Investments	0	
Carryover	4,075	Last year's surplus comes in handy, assume no earned interest
Fellowship	20,000	First of two-year award
Loans	0	
Total Funds Available	24,075	
End-of-Year Finances	879	Tight going into the second year as a student!

*All line items carried over from 12-Month Historical Budget increased by 4% for inflation.

[†]After deductions for federal and state taxes, FICA, and state retirement program.

Constructing Sandy's Plan-Ahead Budget

Life Business Projects are the vehicles for bringing Dreams into reality. Plan-Ahead Budgets differ from Look-Ahead Budgets in that they show a complete division between Business Investments and Support Expenses. Every Plan-Ahead Business line item will represent a planned Investment in current and proposed Projects. Every Plan-Ahead Support line item will have been scrutinized to ensure maximum time and money efficiency. In other words, fine-tuned Support line item entries will reflect the expectation of getting a required value for the minimum possible outlay of resources. (In Step 12 on money management, we talk about how funds squeezed out of Support line items can be "invested" to make Life Business Projects happen.)

Let's see how Sandy started to build a Plan-Ahead Budget using her Look-Ahead Budget as a starting point. To get things rolling, Sandy restated her five most finance-dependent Businesses:

Sandy's Five Most Finance-Dependent Life Businesses

- Being & Becoming: The quest to continually identify and exercise the essential me professionally and personally.
- Call Me Mom: Continue in the manner I've begun to be a mother and stepmother to all my children.
- Realizing Potential: More than being a Mom in a day-to-day sense, being there as the children in turn seek support on their own journeys.
- Mrs. P. Wife & Partner: To balance on a day-to-day basis my marriage commitments and hopes with the rest of my life.
- Roaming: A special time sometime in the future for Peter and me to live out our shared Dreams.

Sandy next summarized her most important short-term Projects (0–3 years) and the likely resource requirements for each of these five Businesses. While some of these line items will be new Investments (i.e., her new car and medical expense), a few Business Investment line items will replace previous Support Expenses (i.e., Sandy's old food budget).

Sandy's Life Business Project List for the Short Term (0–3 Years)

Being & Becoming

- Exercise regularly: Running shoes, plus time and energy. (Annual total $80)

- Consider purchase of a home treadmill. (Annual total $1000)
- Cooking *en famille:* Afford the groceries that I buy—approximately $350 monthly over and above Peter's contribution. (Annual total $4200)
- Dressing the part: Construct a professional wardrobe. (Annual total $1000)
- Moments of whimsy: Personal allowance of $100 monthly. (Annual total $1200)
- Entertaining family, friends, neighbors, and colleagues: Quarterly small dinner parties $75 every 3 months except summer. (Annual total $225); Christmas party $225 (Peter will probably agree to pick up half of this "investment.") (Annual total $113)
- A new "Career Car" to kick off new career: 4-year lease on new, economical, 4-door sedan, $226 monthly, 1st to 4th year +$250 once. (Annual total $2962)

Call Me Mom

- Surprise mailings and supportive gestures for the older children: Establish a Gift Fund. (Annual total $200)
- Keep the skiing alive: Take one child skiing out west every year while kids are in school. (Annual total $1000 2nd to 6th year). Take three children skiing next year for a special occasion. (Annual total $3000)
- Find and fund opportunities to do special things: Establish an Occasion Fund for doing things with children including Graduation Celebrations 1st year for Beth, Nicholas, Marie-Laure, and Sandy herself. (Annual total $1000)

Realizing Potential

- All: Make old car available to children on oldest first, needs-arising basis. (Forgo $1500 trade-in)
- $250 required to maintain the old car to be paid by whoever drives it. (Annual total 0)
- Establish Opportunity Fund for children's emerging opportunities while in school/college: $500 year × 3, 1st to 2nd year; $500 × 2, 3rd to 4th year; $500 × 1, 5th to 6th year. (1st year total $1500)
- Joseph: Contribution to tuition, board, books, living. (Annual total $3600 1st to 2nd year) Clothing allowance while in school. (Annual total $250 1st to 2nd year) Car insurance, pays own. (Annual total $0) Gifts. (Annual total $200)
- Beth: Help her find a college/university that meets her needs. (Annual total $500 once) Contribution to tuition, board, books, living. (Annual

151

total $3600 1st to 4th year) Clothing allowance while in school. (Annual total $250 1st to 4th year) Car insurance. (Annual total $250 1st to 4th year) Gifts. (Annual total $200)

- Anna: Tennis lessons $65 per month x 12. (Annual total $780 1st to 2nd year) Help her find a college/university that meets her needs. (Annual total $500 once) Contribution to tuition, board, books, living. (Annual total $3600 2nd to 5th year) Clothing allowance while in school. (Annual total $250 1st to 5th year) Car insurance. (Annual total $250 1st to 5th year) Gifts. (Annual total $200)

Mrs. P. Wife & Partner

- Be available to my family: Leave school by 5:30 p.m. every night; no more than one night meeting per week. Help pay for someone to clean the house (annual total $900). Contribute to utilities ($117 monthly). (Annual total $2204)
- Contribute to family expenses: Utilities ($1404), pay for my own transportation on holidays and my own ski rental/lift ticket on annual ski holiday. ($2750; annual total $4154)

Roaming

- Plan the 4-year new car lease to end at the point when the 2-year Roaming period begins. (Annual total $0)

When looking at Sandy's Plan-Ahead Budget below, you will find a couple of things that may seem a bit peculiar: There are no entries for income. Also, we are not talking about any particular 12-month period. We begin the Plan-Ahead Budgeting process this way because we want you to be clear about what it is that you want to achieve before you give any consideration to whether or not you'll have enough funding available, and before you decide how to array your Projects over the next 3 years. This approach gives you the best possible chance of enabling the key Projects that you have decided you want to achieve, when you want to achieve them.

In business thinking, Dreams drive resourcing, not vice versa! It doesn't look like Sandy will be able to fund all her initiatives in any one year, but, in order to determine her priorities, she needs to first identify all her Dreams. The Plan-Ahead Budget is, in the first instance, a statement of all these options. In Step 11, Sandy will consider her priorities, evaluate her trade-offs, study her financing, and make her Commitments.

When you look at Sandy's Project list, what strikes you? What do you think is most important to her? What, perhaps, is becoming less so? One of the themes running through Sandy's list appears to be "increasing and broadening responsibility."

Sandy is identifying more priorities and earmarking more funds for the financial needs of herself and her children. At the same time she is setting out to play a larger role in building her joint life with Peter by covering more of her own travel expenses and an increasing share of household expenses.

Progressing from a "living from payday to payday" mentality to an awakening sense of her professional worth, and now onto "Being & Becoming," we are seeing Sandy's increasingly confident and optimistic stance in the world. She's taking overt responsibility for more aspects of her life and setting out to do this over the longer term. Sandy's growing confidence is a direct outgrowth of her Life Business work. She realizes that having a written and considered Plan makes dreaming feel much less risky.

Sandy's 12-Month Plan-Ahead Budget

Type of Expense	*$ Amount*
Support Expenses	
Medical	
• Medical/dental	806
• Prescriptions	624
Subtotal	1,430
Car	
• Payments	0
• Maintenance	0
• Gas, oil, taxes, license, insurance	921
Subtotal	921
Total Support Expense[*]	2,351
Type of Investment	
Business Investments	
Being & Becoming	
• Complete M.S. degree	1,352
• Exercise regularly	1,080
• Cooking *en famille*	4,200
• Dressing the part	1,000
• Moments of whimsy	1,200
• Entertaining	338
• New career car	2,962
• Continue IRA	2,000
Subtotal	14,132

(*continues*)

Sandy's 12-Month Plan-Ahead Budget (*Continued*)

Type of Investment	$ Amount
Call Me Mom	
• Gift fund	200
• Keep skiing alive	3,000
• Occasion fund	1,000
Subtotal	4,200
Realizing Potential	
• All	
• Old car subsidy	1,500
• Opportunity fund	1,500
• Joseph	4,050
• Beth	4,800
• Anna	1,980
Subtotal	13,830
Mrs. P. Wife and Partner	
• Available at home	900
• Home contribution	4,154
Subtotal	5,054
Roaming	
• Financial commitments	0
Subtotal	0
Total Business Investment	37,216
Total Funds Required	39,567

*All line items carried over from 12-Month Historical Budget have been increased by 4% to account for inflation.

    With her Plan-Ahead Budget worked out, Sandy is ready to begin thinking (1) how to fund her Budget and (2) how to project this year's situation into the future. Both of these challenges are covered in Step 11, Projecting Your Future in Dollars and Sense.

Lessons from Sandy's Plan-Ahead Budget

Completing a Plan-Ahead Budget is meant to be an empowering, not a constraining, experience. There are several Life Business "lessons" to be learned from Sandy's example:

- To get the most out of your opportunities, it's important to allow yourself to recognize all that you'd like to achieve.
- When your Budget becomes your Projection in Step 11, there will be time enough to weigh the relative priorities of various initiatives in an environment of scarce resources.
- When you cost out your Dreams, you are taking a big step toward turning them into reality.
- Articulating a Dream will often make you more aware of possible funding sources.

Remember, thousands of Life Business participants have shown that you can get more out of life than you ever thought possible.

Tips for Constructing a User-Friendly Budget

1. When it comes to developing your own Plan-ahead Budget, be patient with yourself. The experience of Life Business participants suggests that, working from a comprehensive 12-month Historical Budget, it takes 3 years (i.e., three annual planning cycles) to build a Plan-Ahead Budget that reflects a comfortable confidence in your entries and estimates. While 3 years may seem like a long time to get the full effect, you begin to get benefits from the process on day one as actual spending and your Budgets converge. We have repeatedly found that years of continuing reward more than justify these 3 years of investment.

2. Beware of Fudge. One place to look for extra funds is in Commitments that you may have been making to activities that are neither Business nor Support. For example, if you drive a flashy and pricey German sports car and you can't see how this expenditure supports any significant Business development Project, then the chances are that you are either (a) not owning up to some significant Business need, (b) out of touch with what basic Support-level transportation would cost you, or (c) willfully throwing away money. We call these misallocated or unconsciously allocated funds Fudge. Either find the Business need behind the expenditure or free up the funds for other Projects that are in need.

155

3. It's worth the effort! A fully operational Plan-Ahead Budget is worth working toward because, once completed, the confidence it generates will move you yet another big step closer to living your Dreams with true financial independence. At this point you will also have earned another reward. You will have internalized the Budget process, and from then on you may not even need to commit your Budget to paper!

Where You've Been and
Where You're Going

In Step 10 we started you on the road to clarifying your future financial situation by developing a meaningful and enabling Plan-Ahead Budget.

In Step 11 we demonstrate how to determine how much funding you'll need over time and when you'll need it, by projecting and assessing your likely financial situation over the next 0 to 10 years utilizing Short-, Medium- and Long-Term Projections.

At the end of Step 11 you will know what it's going to take to "float your boat" or "make your nut." This is the magic moment we promised.

In Step 12 we introduce ways to increase the financial productivity or efficiency of your Life Enterprise, find the funds that you'll need for your Plan, and look at the money management implications of your short-, medium- and long-term Projections.

Finally, in Step 13 you'll learn how to use your Life Business Plan progressively in a financial services world not always prepared to deal with those who chose to live their Dreams throughout their lives.

Please remember to consult our Web site, www.lifebusiness.com, for additional exercises related to Step 10.

Projecting Your Future in Dollars and Sense

The clearest statement you've ever made about your future

Take a full comprehensive view of the Path of Life.

Book of Luke, New Testament

LIFE BUSINESS TENET

You can make money your servant and not your master. By projecting your planned expenditures and revenues forward through time, you can determine how much money you'll need to fund your Dreams and when you'll need it.

Companies think ahead, and then they look hard at the financial implications of their thoughts. In their own way companies can be said to dream. And when they decide on the dream they want to commit to, corporations bring everything they can to bear to making these dreams come true. Dreams are wonderful guides to possible futures; resourced dreams are powerful predictors of future realities.

One of the most important corporate strategic planning tools is the forward projection of business investments, support expenses, and likely corporate revenues. Once companies have seen how they can finance (i.e., provide resources for) their business development projects, the pursuit of these dreams is translated into job content and becomes the everyday corporate agenda. The business principle here is plan ahead to achieve your chosen Dreams; don't just wish for them to happen.

The Life Business Projection

In the Life Business Program participants are challenged to identify their most significant Businesses, their Strategies for the development of these Businesses over time, and the Projects they plan to undertake to carry out these Strategies. The implementation of each of these Projects will require some kind of Resource (energy, time, and money). Life Business participants state their Resource requirements for the next year in their 12-month Plan-Ahead Budgets.

The fully formed Plan-Ahead Budget becomes the single most comprehensive statement of what an individual, a couple, or a family values right now, today. A fully articulated Plan-Ahead Budget is a prerequisite for constructing a forward-looking financial Projection. This Projection will, in turn, showcase the financial implications of living your Dreams over time. Understanding and achieving these financial objectives will enable readers to live their Dreams independently of their finances.

As we proceed through this Step, we introduce a number of businesslike Guidelines for constructing and reviewing your Projections. These include:

- Set Limiting Conditions, that is, default levels,[1] for likely rates of inflation, borrowing, and returns on your financial placements.
- Plan Positively; what you can envision you can achieve.
- Look for Trade-offs, or choices, among possible uses of funds.
- Provide for Commitments already made and Contingencies that may arise.
- Take advantage of the "Planning Bonus"—the ability to fund more Projects by thinking in multiple-year planning periods.
- Strive to increase your Ratio of Business Investment to Support Expense.
- See Borrowing as Income.
- Learn to use what-if analyses to increase returns in personal satisfaction.
- Let Business considerations drive money decisions, not vice versa.
- Question standard financial planning advice; for example, think emergency credit line, not emergency cash fund.
- Bring Dreams forward in time; don't wait for retirement or death.

Build a Short-Term (0–3 Year) Projection of Your Expenditures and Income

From Step 10, we have Sandy's 0- to 3-year Life Business Project list and her Dream-driven 12-month, Plan-Ahead Budget. Now we can build a 3-year Projection if we add information on Sandy's Income and Financial Assets. To complete

Sandy's financial asset picture, we include balances for IRAs and pensions even though these assets are usually not thought of as being accessible until age 59½. If your Life Business Plan necessitates it, you can find ways to access these resources, in most cases, without penalty.

In creating your own 0- to 3-year Projection, you'll need to reconsider which line items you most want to fund after you've taken a hard look at the money you will have available. The first year of your Projection will tell you a lot about what you value and can lead you to a more complete understanding of what's really important to you and why.

Plan Positively

In considering revenue, plan for what you fully expect, not for what you may have to end up accepting. Life Business planning is an exercise in positive thinking. There will always be time to make adjustments if things don't turn out the way you have every reason to expect them to. For example, Sandy is preparing to be an education administrator. The job outlook for the education administration market in her state is positive, so she'll use her likely income after graduation in her 0- to 3-Year Projection.

Identify Trade-offs

When you think of all the things you'd like to accomplish this next year, it quickly becomes apparent that you live in a world of "scarce resources" and "opportunity costs." Because you do not have infinite energy, time, or money, a choice to invest your resources in one thing can often mean a choice not to invest in something else. In the end all choices reflect preferences among possible opportunities. We call these alternate choices *Trade-offs*.

Alternatives are often posed in the form of a question. For example: Does it make better sense to lease a new car rather than buy and use the extra monthly cash flow to fund the rental of a larger, more convenient apartment? Or should you stay where you are, buy a new car now, plan to keep it at least 3 years after all your payments have been made, and use the last 3 years' extra cash flow to establish a down payment for your own home? Both plans take the same amount of funding, and both plans are feasible. What's not feasible is to have a nearly new car every year, a larger more convenient apartment now and still come up with a down payment on a house in 3 to 4 years. Only when you can see the trade-off opportunities that your specific situation presents, can you make informed decisions about how to commit your resources.

Remember Already Committed Funds and the Likelihood of Surprises

Decisions made yesterday and surprises that can occur tomorrow will have an impact on resources available for your Plan. At certain periods in your life your available resources will be constrained by previously planned or contracted expenditures such as those for college, home improvements, or entrance into a retirement community. Additionally, you need to have in hand a contingency plan for accessing emergency funds to cover unpredicted or surprise expenses (e.g., medical, accident, loss, or theft) as they occur. When you make your 0- to 3-Year Projection, you will want to include line items that cover these Commitments and Contingencies.

Plan over a 3-Year Period and Gain a Bonus

Planning in multiple-year periods can lessen the impact of scarce resources. In order to stretch the amount of resources available for planning purposes, we like to work in 3- to 4-year planning chunks—short term 0–3 years, medium term 4–6 years, and long term 7 plus years. Taking a multiyear view, each planning period contains 3 to 4 years of resources rather than representing only the resources available during the next year. Thus there is the potential to carry out three to four times as many Projects as would normally be considered in a One-Year Plan-Ahead Budget. Some Projects may get funded the first year, others the fourth. The key is to commit funds to as many heartfelt Projects as is both possible and manageable. A specific planning period may now also include a "free" year or more of resources as funds previously dedicated to long-term Commitments are freed up as those Projects are completed (e.g., in Sandy's case, Joseph's college education).

Money Decisions Need to Support Life Business Decisions

Feed the Business when the Business needs the money, not when it's easiest to come up with the money. For decision-making purposes the short term needs to be considered in the context of longer-term probabilities. Often short-term difficulties can hide longer-term potential, and we may find ourselves acting inappropriately out of short-term concerns. For example, here is how Sandy solves her children's transportation problem:

Children are only 16 to 22 for six years! Because of joint custody and the resulting fact that they have two homes in neighboring towns, Sandy's children need transportation support in the 0- to 3-year period. This need won't wait until later when a second car could be more affordable either because Sandy's cash flow picture might have improved or because her children could have paid for it themselves. Sandy had her old car, and the children needed it now. Even though she could have conceivably traded her old car in on the lease of her new car and used the car's book value of $1500 to help balance her Budget in the short term, an important Realizing Potential Business opportunity would have been missed—an opportunity to help one or more of her children reach their potential. In the first instance, this opportunity took the form of an internship for Joseph that promised to provide a potential jump start to his career but which required reliable everyday transport.

The flip side of this situation is interesting as well. Note that Sandy is currently committing 35 percent of her Plan-Ahead Budget to supporting her Realizing Potential Business. If Sandy decides that her financial involvement with this Business finishes when all three children complete college, significant resources will then be available for other Life Business priorities.

Sandy's Short-Term Review

We will now see how Sandy uses the above guidelines to create her 0- to 3-Year Projection, which will help her understand her short-term cash flow situation. Basically, this first Projection tells her whether or not her boat will float in the short term. Sandy's Projected Expenses, Investments, Revenues, and Assets are shown in the accompanying chart.

Let's review Sandy's first draft 0- to 3-Year Projection. According to these numbers, Sandy's Net Financial Situation ends up in negative territory in each of the next 3 years. Bottom line, her boat won't float without access to significant credit. Confronting this situation, Sandy decides that she'd prefer to begin her postgraduation career with as small loan obligation as possible. Sandy next reviews both her Support and Business line items to decide which Expenses or Investments can be postponed to coincide with her expected increase in income once she is working full time in education administration.

Sandy's Short-Term Support Expenses Review

After reviewing her Support Expenses, Sandy realizes that she will have full medical coverage in her new job. This allows her to cut her projected medical costs in the third year to the cost of her deductible, i.e., $200. The same will be true for prescriptions, so Sandy replaces her forecast amount with $200 to start in the third year.

Sandy's First Draft 0–3 Year Projection

	Sandy's Planning Year/Age		
Type of Expenditure	*Year 1/44*	*Year 2/45*	*Year 3/46*
Support Expenses			
Medical			
• Medical/dental	806	838	872
• Prescriptions	624	649	675
Subtotal first year	1,430		
Percentage of total first year	4%		
Car			
• Payments	0	0	0
• Maintenance	0	0	0
• Gas, oil, taxes, license, insurance	921	958	996
Subtotal first year	921		
Percentage of total first year	2%		
Total Support Expense*	2,351	2,445	2,543
Business Investments			
Being & Becoming			
• Complete M.S. degree	1,352	1,406	0
• Exercise regularly	1,080	83	87
• Cooking *en famille*	4,200	4,368	4,543
• Dressing the part	1,000	1,040	1,082
• Moments of whimsy	1,200	1,248	1,298
• Entertaining	338	352	366
• New career car	2,962	2,712	2,712
• Continue IRA	2,000	3,000	3,000
Subtotal first year	14,132		
Percentage of total first year	36%		

(continues)

Sandy's First Draft 0–3 Year Projection (*Continued*)

	Sandy's Planning Year/Age		
Type of Expenditure	*Year 1/44*	*Year 2/45*	*Year 3/46*
Call Me Mom			
• Gift fund	200	208	216
• Keep skiing alive	3,000	1,040	1,082
• Occasion fund	1,000	1,040	1,082
Subtotal first year	4,200		
Percentage of total first year	11%		
Realizing Potential			
• All			
• Old car subsidy	1,500	0	0
• Opportunity fund	1,500	1,560	1,622
• Joseph	4,050	208	216
• Beth	4,800	4,472	4,651
• Anna	1,980	4,472	4,651
Subtotal first year	13,830		
Percentage of total first year	35%		
Mrs. P. Wife & Partner			
• Available at home	900	936	973
• Home contribution	4,154	4,320	4,493
Subtotal first year	5,054		
Percentage of total first year	13%		
Roaming			
• Financial commitments	0	0	0
Subtotal first year	0		
Percentage of total first year	0%		
Total Business Investment[†]	37,216	32,465	32,073
Total Funds Required	39,567	34,910	34,616
Ratio of Investment to Expense	16:1	13:1	13:1

(*continues*)

163

Sandy's First Draft 0–3 Year Projection (*Continued*)

Type of Funding	Sandy's Planning Year/Age		
	Year 1/44	Year 2/45	Year 3/46
Income			
• From job (net[‡])	0	0	37,080
• From current assets (net[‡])	4,075	0	0
• From fellowships/grants (net[‡])	20,000	20,000	0
• From borrowing	0	0	0
Total Current Funds	24,075	20,000	37,080
Assets at START of Budget Year			
• *Taxable*			
• Equities	0	0	0
• Bonds	0	0	0
• Cash	4,075	0	0
• *Other*			
• Home equity	0	0	0
• Car equity	0	0	0
• Possessions	0	0	0
Total Current Assets	4,075	0	0
Finances at END of Budget Year[**]	-15,492	-30,402	-27,938
Tax-Deferred Assets			
• IRA at 5%	4,250	6,463	9,786
• 403b	0	0	0
• State pension—Sandy's contribution	26,000	26,000	28,225
• Annuities	0	0	0
Total Tax-Deferred Assets	30,250	32,463	38,010

[*]All line items carried over from 12-month Historical Budget increased by 4% annually to account for inflation.

[†]All Business Investment line items increased by 4% in years 2 and 3 to account for inflation.

[‡]After any deductions for federal and state taxes, FICA, and state retirement contributions.

[**]Aggregate year over year, excludes tax-deferred assets. Spreadsheet subtotals and totals subject to rounding error in units place.

Upon reflection, Sandy observes that the real reason she needs a new car is because she wants to make the old one available to her children (Sandy's "Old Car Subsidy" Project in her Realizing Potential Business). Because she has no real love of cars, Sandy sees transportation as a Support Expense, not a Business Investment. To replace her old car, Sandy decides that she wants the least expensive car that she can find. A new car promises fewer repair surprises. Her 0- to 3-Year Projection will be revised to show her new car as an expense item. Sandy also realizes that she currently depends on public transportation to go to and from school and that Peter's car can almost certainly be made available in a pinch. Peter agrees. As a result, Sandy decides that she can postpone her new car purchase until her first year of employment. The funds projected for gas, oil, taxes, license, and insurance are no longer required but will need to be replaced by a figure for public transportation.

Sandy's Short-Term Business Investment Review

How does Sandy's financial review of her draft 0- to 3-Year Projection affect her plans for the development of her Life Businesses?

Being & Becoming

Sandy decides to keep her commitment to Cooking *en famille*. After all, she and Peter won't be *en famille* very much longer. In thinking about her IRA contribution, Sandy reasons that her new job will take care of tomorrow. Right now current cash flow is more important than future cash flow. Sandy decides to postpone any IRA contribution until Year 3 and then make a larger contribution taking advantage of the more generous provisions of the new tax law.

Sandy decides that she doesn't really need an Emergency Fund. What she now feels she needs is an Emergency Credit Line. She plans to talk this idea over with Peter hoping that he might be able to help with any surprise emergency expenses. With this plan of action in mind, Sandy renames her Emergency Fund, now calling it her Uncommitted Fund. You might think that the Emergency Fund issue would be more appropriately discussed under Support Expense. Remember, whether a line item is Support or Business is determined not by the nature of the item but instead by the significance you attach to it. Because of her strong desire to take full responsibility for the choices in her personal financial situation, Sandy considers all money-related issues as being part and parcel of her Being & Becoming Business.

165

Call Me Mom

Here Sandy would like not to have to make any changes. She feels that she'll get a higher return from keeping the "Occasion Fund" and cutting the children's "Opportunity Fund" (a Realizing Potential Project). The kids are getting college support; they don't have to have Cancun too! More to the point, if they want Cancun, then they can get out and earn it. The Occasion Fund is for Sandy to be able to interact with her children, not for the children to interact with themselves. After she runs her numbers again, Sandy will decide if she has to make a decision about "downsizing" either Keep Skiing Alive or the Occasion Fund. In order to be clear about all of her options or Trade-offs, Sandy wants to wait and run her numbers after completing her Support and Business Review.

Realizing Potential

As mentioned above, the Opportunity Fund has been axed. Sandy remains committed to her other Projects in this Business.

Mrs. P. Wife & Partner

Talking over her situation with Peter, he suggests that Sandy allow him to "subsidize" their annual ski holiday until her income allows her to take over this responsibility. Skiing is a shared Dream. When two people hold a Dream in common, it's less important where the funding comes from than that the Dream be realized. In other words, shared Dreams invite shared funding—each party contributing to the extent each is able. Rather than combine their finances and not explore their mutual Dreams, we counsel couples to find their shared Dreams and continue to keep separate accounts.

Sandy's Business Investment to Support Expense ratio is a high 5:1. This is what you want to be achieving, more investment in your Businesses with less taken up by Support Expense. It's never possible to say what this percentage ought to be in the abstract, but anything over 2:1 has proved to be a good start. The challenge is to continually increase your Investment to Expense ratio over time. As this ratio increases, so will your life satisfaction. Remember it's the success of your Businesses that drives your life satisfaction. At the limit, get your Businesses the funding they need even if you have to starve your overhead commitments.

Sandy is pleased with her "Revisited" 0- to 3-Year Projection (see below). It shows that she can advance a number of her important Business Development Projects (e.g., Complete M.S. degree, Cooking *en Famille*, Dressing the Part, all of Realizing Potential) while keeping her financial head above water. Although Sandy decided to postpone her contributions to Peter's and her annual ski

Sandy's "Revisited" 0–3 Year Projection

	Sandy's Planning Year/Age		
Type of Expenditure	*Year 1/44*	*Year 2/45*	*Year 3/46*
Support Expenses			
Medical			
• Medical/dental	806	838	200
• Prescriptions	624	649	200
Subtotal first year	1,430		
Percentage of total first year	5%		
Car			
• Transportation	225	234	0
• Payments	0	0	2,792
• Maintenance	0	0	0
• Gas, oil, taxes, license, insurance	0	0	996
Subtotal first year	225		
Percentage of total first year	0%		
Taxes	0	0	0
Total Support Expense[*]	1,655	1,721	4,188
Business Investments			
Being & Becoming			
• Complete M.S. degree	1,352	1,406	0
• Exercise regularly	1,080	83	87
• Cooking *en famille*	4,200	4,368	4,543
• Dressing the part	1,000	1,040	1,082
• Moments of whimsy	1,200	1,248	1,298
• Entertaining	338	352	366
• Continue IRA	0	0	3,000
Subtotal first year	9,170		
Percentage of total first year	31%		

(continues)

Sandy's "Revisited" 0–3 Year Projection (*Continued*)

	Sandy's Planning Year/Age		
Type of Expenditure	*Year 1/44*	*Year 2/45*	*Year 3/46*
Call Me Mom			
• Gift fund	200	208	216
• Keep skiing alive	3,000	1,040	1,082
• Occasion fund	1,000	1,040	1,082
Subtotal first year	4,200		
Percentage of total first year	14%		
Realizing Potential			
• All			
• Old car subsidy	1,500	0	0
• Opportunity fund	0	0	0
• Joseph	4,050	208	216
• Beth	4,800	4,472	4,651
• Anna	1,980	4,472	4,651
Subtotal first year	12,330		
Percentage of total first year	42%		
Mrs. P. Wife & Partner			
• Available at home	900	936	973
• Home contribution	1,404	1,460	4,379
Subtotal first year	2,304		
Percentage of total first year	8%		
Roaming			
• Financial commitments	0	0	0
Subtotal first year	0		
Percentage of total first year	0%		
Total Business Investment[†]	28,004	22,333	27,626
Total Funds Required	29,659	24,054	31,814
Ratio of Investment to Expense	17:1	13:1	7:1
Type of Funding			
Income			
• From job (net[‡])	0	0	43,260
• From current assets (net[‡])	4,075	416	822

(*continues*)

Sandy's "Revisited" 0–3 Year Projection (*Continued*)

	Sandy's Planning Year/Age		
Type of Funding	*Year 1/44*	*Year 2/45*	*Year 3/46*
• From fellowship grants (net‡)	20,000	20,000	0
• From borrowing	6,000	5,000	0
Total Current Funds	30,075	25,416	44,082
Current Assets at START of Budget Year			
• *Taxable*			
• Equities	0	0	0
• Bonds	0	0	0
• Cash	4,075	416	822
• *Other*			
• Home equity	0	0	0
• Car equity	0	0	0
• Possessions	0	0	0
Total Current Assets	4,075	416	822
Finances at END of Budget Year**	416	822	278
• Loan cost—first year of loan, $6,000 at 9%; second year of loan, $11,000 at 9%	0	540	990
• Repayment of principal	0	0	11,000
Tax-Deferred Assets			
• IRA at 5%	4,250	4,463	4,686
• 403b	0	0	0
• State pension—Sandy's contribution 6% of salary	26,000	26,000	28,596
• Annuities	0	0	0
Total Tax-Deferred Assets	30,250	30,463	33,282

*All line items carried over from 12-month Historical Budget increased by 4% annually to account for inflation.

†All Business Investment line items increased by 4% in years 2 and 3 to account for inflation.

‡After any deductions for federal and state taxes, FICA, and state retirement contributions.

**Aggregate year over year, excludes tax-deferred assets. Spreadsheet subtotals and totals subject to rounding error in units place.

holiday, she will be able to take all her children on the special occasion trip and cover the costs of taking one child skiing a year in each of the 2 years that follow. Sandy was also pleased to know that she would be able to fund her IRA to the max in the third year of her Plan.

In Life Business planning we recommend using borrowed money to fund important Dream-driven Projects as long as either (1) interest costs are less than the returns you can reasonably expect to get on a conservative financial place-ment, or (2) you can figure out how to bring your books back into balance by the end of the current planning period. Here that means by the end of the third year. If you can meet the first "test," continue to borrow as long as the borrowed funds support your Life Business priorities. The second test is a way of making sure that you continue to be aware of the role of borrowed money in the context of your Life Business planning. If you haven't planned to pay off any debt within a 3- to 4-year period, you will be more vulnerable to surprise events and the pos-sibility of an increased dependence on borrowed money. Borrowed money is income, but it is not a benign source of income and needs to be treated with respect.

Sandy's Life Business Project List for the Medium Term (4–6 Years)

We've found that if Life Business participants can "vision it," they can "achieve it." Solid preparation won out, and Sandy, who had been hoping for a job as an assistant principal in her first year out of graduate school, landed her ideal job in a school close to home. With the resulting increase in financial resources Sandy felt she now had what she needed to "think outside the envelope" which had con-strained her previous planning efforts. As with her Short-Term Projection we'll need Sandy's Business Project List in order to set up her Medium-Term Projec-tion. Below we include only investments or expenses not mentioned above.

- Being & Becoming: Complete the 4 years of service to the state required by my fellowship. Get on a work schedule that allows our family to have time and holidays together.
- Call Me Mom: Visit kids and hold family gatherings. Continue the Occa-sion Fund to achieve this goal. (Annual total $1000)
- Realizing Potential: Install Anna in college. (Annual total $3600 4th to 5th year)
- Mrs. P. Wife & Partner: Get a dog?
- Roaming: Prepare and plan Peter's and my 2-year Roaming Project in years 5 and 6. (Annual total ?)

Sandy's 4–6 Year Projection

Type of Expenditure	Sandy's Planning Year/Age			
	Year 3/46	Year 4/47	Year 5/48	Year 6/49
Support Expenses				
Medical				
• Medical/dental	200	208	216	225
• Prescriptions	200	208	216	225
Subtotal first year	400			
Percentage of total first year	1%			
Car				
• Transportation	0	0	0	0
• Payments/ 4-year lease	2,792	2,792	2,792	2,792
• Maintenance	0	0	0	0
• Gas, oil, taxes, license, insurance	996	1,036	1,077	1,120
Subtotal first year	3,788			
Percentage of total first year	12%			
Taxes	0	0	0	168
Total Support Expense[*]	4,188	4,244	4,302	4,530
Business Investments				
Being & Becoming				
• Exercise regularly	87	90	94	98
• Cooking *en famille*	4,543	4,725	4,914	5,110
• Dressing the part	1,082	1,125	1,170	1,217
• Moments of whimsy	1,298	1,350	1,404	1,460
• Entertaining	366	381	396	412
• Continue IRA	3,000	3,000	3,000	3,000
• Emergency fund	0	7,000	7,000	7,000
Subtotal first year	10,376			
Percentage of total first year	33%			

(*continues*)

171

Sandy's 4–6 Year Projection (*Continued*)

	Sandy's Planning Year/Age			
Type of Expenditure	*Year 3/46*	*Year 4/47*	*Year 5/48*	*Year 6/49*
Call Me Mom				
• Gift fund	216	225	234	243
• Keep skiing alive	1,082	1,125	1,170	1,217
• Occasion fund	1,082	1,125	1,170	1,217
Subtotal first year	2,380			
Percentage of total first year	7%			
Realizing Potential				
• All				
• Old car subsidy	0	0	0	0
• Opportunity fund	0	0	0	0
• Joseph	216	225	234	243
• Beth	4,651	4,837	234	234
• Anna	4,651	4,837	5,031	234
Subtotal first year	9,518			
Percentage of total first year	30%			
Mrs. P. Wife & Partner				
• Available at home	973	1,012	1,052	1,094
• Home contribution	4,379	4,554	4,736	4,926
Subtotal first year	5,352			
Percentage of total first year	17%			
Roaming				
• Financial commitments	0	0	0	0
Subtotal first year	0			
Percentage of total first year	0%			
Total Business Investment[†]	27,626	35,611	31,839	27,705
Total Funds Required	31,814	39,855	36,141	32,235
Ratio of Investment to Expense	7:1	8:1	7:1	6:1
Type of Funding				
Income				
• From job (net[‡])	43,260	44,558	45,895	47,271
• From current assets earning 5% from fifth year (net[‡])	822	278	11,981	29,334

(*continues*)

Sandy's 4–6 Year Projection (*Continued*)

Type of Funding	*Sandy's Planning Year/Age*			
	Year 3/46	*Year 4/47*	*Year 5/48*	*Year 6/49*
• From borrowing	0	0	0	0
Total Current Funds	44,082	44,836	57,875	76,605
Current Assets at START of Budget Year				
• *Taxable*				
• Equities	0	0	0	0
• Bonds	0	0	0	0
• Cash	822	278	11,981	28,735
• *Other*				
• Home equity	0	0	0	0
• Car equity	0	0	0	0
• Possessions	0	0	0	0
Total Current Assets	822	278	11,981	28,735
Finances at END of Budget Year**	278	4,981	21,735	44,370
• Loan cost	990			
• Repayment of principal	11,000			
Tax-Deferred Assets				
• IRA at 5%	4,686	7,920	11,316	14,882
• 403b	0	0	0	0
• State pension—Sandy's contributionv 6% of salary	28,596	31,192	33,865	36,619
• Annuities	0	0	0	0
Total Tax-Deferred Assets	33,282	39,112	45,181	51,501

*All line items carried over from 12-month Historical Budget increased by 4% annually to account for inflation.

†All Business Investment line items increased by 4% in last 3 years to account for inflation.

‡After any deductions for federal and state taxes, FICA, and state retirement contributions.

**Aggregate year over year, excludes tax-deferred assets. Spreadsheet subtotals and totals subject to rounding error in units place.

Sandy's Medium-Term Review

If Sandy was happy with her 0-to 3-Year Projection, she was ecstatic about her 4-to 6-Year outlook. In this time frame it looks as if Sandy can fund all her priorities. Now that she sees that it is possible to achieve it, Sandy admits to herself how important it is to her to begin building a sense of financial well-being. In the 4-to 6-Year Projection Sandy will be able to fund her IRA at the maximum allowable amount all years. She will also have her newly named Uncommitted Fund (equivalent to 6 months net salary) fully funded at the end of year 6. In fact, toward the end of this planning window Sandy's taxable financial resources seem to be growing nearly exponentially.

"What could be better?" Sandy wonders. She sees a way forward where she can live her Dreams, do the work she loves, become more financially secure, and meet the obligations of the fellowship she has accepted. Sandy likes what's happening to her Life Businesses and is beginning to "feel financially free." Her Projections are central to her new feelings of confidence. Prior to this work Sandy was always fearful of committing to, or even owning up to, her Dreams. The confidence that Sandy is gaining through seeing how her Dreams can actually be "made whole" is lighting up her life.

Sandy's Long-Term Projection

Roaming

Roaming is a joint venture that Sandy and Peter have been envisioning since before they married. The idea is that they are going to spend 2 years doing whatever it is they decide they want to do wherever that turns out to be. Parenting a joint family has been challenging, and the Roaming period is part of the reward. Because of the 12-year difference in their ages, Peter and Sandy want to roam earlier rather than later so that they can both enjoy an active and challenging experience. While the Vision is still embryonic, the 2 years are likely to encompass some travel, some skiing, a considerable amount of time in Paris, and possibly, either an overseas professional assignment or doctoral level studies for Sandy. Roaming is scheduled to take place during the Long-Term Projection, probably during the seventh and eighth years.

What If?

We are going to look at two different versions of Sandy's 7+ Year Projection so that we can test the effects of two different scenarios. The first scenario assumes all of Sandy's Business Projects for the long term except the last Roaming. The second scenario gives us an opportunity to explore the implications of adding the Roaming project.

Here again we need Sandy's Life Business Project List in order to construct her 7- to10-Year (Long-Term) Projection:

- Being & Becoming: Continue skiing and resume swimming. (Annual total $1250)
- Call Me Mom (and just maybe Grandmother). Weddings? (possible $4500 once); continue visiting kids and holding family gatherings.
- Realizing Potential: Grandchildren? Reinstate Opportunity Fund. (Annual total $2000) Family foundation. ($?)
- Mrs. P. Wife & Partner: Travel together—determine scope and cost.
- Make a decision about remodeling or selling and building or buying a new home. ($?) Get the dog(s)! (Annual total $500)

Do you see any additional changes in Sandy's stated priorities? Looks like continuing progress on the same and similar themes. Before her first Plan-Ahead Budget Sandy had just started to project, with any confidence, the everyday needs of herself and her children. She next added major Commitments to both her children's education and her own professional development. Later she took on larger responsibilities in line with "paying her own way." Only once she believed that she had a good chance of success in these areas was Sandy willing to put her Dreams on the line.

One of Sandy's big Dreams is sharing the responsibility 50/50 with Peter for the Roaming period. Another Dream is her hope for a "farmlike" existence some day, some time, in the future when she can achieve a better balance among all the important elements in her life. Far from a state of retirement this Dream will probably include continuing to work and/or volunteer in some capacity with children. It may even include something like a family foundation—a way to "give back" in a thoughtful, organized fashion. If you bring your Dreams forward, what is left to retire? Hopefully this new phase in Sandy's life will begin around age 57. The Projection shown below goes out 10 years, or until Sandy is 54.

As to leaving a financial estate to her children and Peter, Sandy prefers to give her loved ones the living benefit of her long and joyful presence in their lives. She figures that money spent now on achieving her satisfaction today will put everyone on a better and healthier track for tomorrow. Certainly a businesslike position. We challenge Life Business participants to plan "a zero in the last bottom-line cell" of their Life Projections. King Lear's experience aside, why not get all the satisfaction that your contributions and bequests can bring while you can still enjoy it—that is, while you are still alive? Similar to our question above about retirement, if you have brought *all* your Dreams forward, what would you need to bequeath? On all these longer-term issues Sandy will gain a better understanding of what she really wants to do as she lives through the first years of her Projection and gains more confidence in both the skills and the rewards of Life Business planning.

Sandy's Long-Term Review

When Sandy projects her likely situation out the full 10 years without including Roaming, she sees her mounting financial assets. It begins to feel to her almost as if she is being forced to eat more and more of something that she loves while getting less and less satisfaction from doing so. The marginal returns from the idea of accumulating larger and increasing financial reserves are starting to diminish. Sandy asks herself, "Going forward will I still be getting the most life that I can from my money?"

A Long-Term Projection with Roaming helps explore the real planning power that constructing Projections gives us. Sandy knows that she wants to undertake the Roaming Project as a 50/50 partner. By plotting the Support Expenses and Business Investments that she wants to continue funding during this period, and an estimate of her half of Roaming costs, Sandy can ballpark the figure that she will either need to earn or find through alternative means of funding.

In today's dollars Peter and Sandy estimate that each of the 2 years of the Roaming Project will cost them together additionally something like $18,000 for lodging, $12,000 for food, and another $20,000 for transportation and matters arising. That makes $50,000 in today's dollars per year or $25,000 for each of them. Plugging this figure (and adding a factor for inflation) into her Projection shows Sandy that she'll need to find additional funding of $29,500 net of taxes during the Roaming period in order to recoup this Project's extra costs within 2 years after Roaming is over. Sandy now feels confident that if she can be out of debt in this time frame, she won't jeopardize her other Long-term Projects like building a house together with Peter. We arrive at the figure of $29,500 by trial and error—substituting numbers until we find the lowest number that will give Sandy a positive annual cash flow 2 years after they return.

There are, of course, a number of ways in which these funds might be acquired. These include remunerative work in one or both Roaming years; increased pay for work before, after, or before and after the Roaming period; borrowing during the Roaming period against an increased earnings potential later; doing something during the 2 years that enhances her likely "market value" when she returns; receiving an inheritance or even an "early inheritance" from Peter. With the help of her Projection, Sandy knows exactly what her "nut" is and now she can get on with figuring out how to acquire it. Sandy's Business-to-Support ratio reaches an all-time high for the two-year Roaming period, an indication that she is more fully living her Dreams.

Sandy's 7–10 Year Projection Without Roaming

	Sandy's Planning Year/Age				
Type of Expenditure	Year 6/49	Year 7/50	Year 8/51	Year 9/52	Year 10/53
Support Expenses					
Medical					
• Medical/dental	225	234	243	253	263
• Prescriptions	225	234	243	253	263
Subtotal first year	450				
Percentage of total first year	1%				
Car					
• Transportation	0	0	0	0	0
• Payments/4-year lease	2,792	2,792	2,792	2,792	2,792
• Maintenance	0	0	0	0	0
• Gas, oil, taxes, license, insurance	1,120	1,165	1,211	1,260	1,310
Subtotal first year	3,912				
Percentage of total first year	12%				
Taxes	168	503	899	1,180	1,558
Total Support Expense*	4,530	4,928	5,389	5,738	6,187
Business Investments					
Being & Becoming					
• Exercise regularly (+ swimming in years 7–10)	98	352	366	381	396
• Cooking *en famille*	5,110	5,314	5,527	5,748	5,978
• Dressing the part	1,217	1,266	1,316	1,369	1,424
• Moments of whimsy	1,460	1,518	1,579	1,642	1,708
• Entertaining	412	428	446	463	482
• Continue IRA	3,000	3,500	3,500	3,500	3,500
• Emergency fund	7,000	7,000	7,000	7,000	7,000
Subtotal first year	11,297				
Percentage of total first year	35%				

(continues)

Sandy's 7–10 Year Projection Without Roaming (*Continued*)

	Sandy's Planning Year/Age				
Type of Expenditure	*Year 6/49*	*Year 7/50*	*Year 8/51*	*Year 9/52*	*Year 10/53*
Call Me Mom					
• Gift fund	243	253	263	273	284
• Keep skiing alive	1,217	1,266	1,316	1,369	1,424
• Occasion fund + wedding(s) in year 7	1,217	5,766	1,496	1,556	1,618
Subtotal first year	2,677				
Percentage of total first year	8%				
Realizing Potential					
• All					
• Old car subsidy	0	0	0	0	0
• Opportunity fund	0	2,000	2,080	2,163	2,250
• Joseph	243	253	263	273	284
• Beth	234	243	253	263	274
• Anna	234	243	253	263	274
Subtotal first year	711				
Percentage of total first year	2%				
Mrs. P. Wife & Partner					
• Available at home	1,094	1,138	1,183	1,231	1,280
• Home and travel contribution + dog in years 7–10	4,926	5,623	5,848	6,082	6,325
Subtotal first year	6,020				
Percentage of total first year	19%				
Roaming					
• Financial commitments	0	0	0	0	0
Subtotal first year	0				
Percentage of total first year	0%				
Total Business Investment[†]	27,705	36,163	32,690	33,577	34,500

(*continues*)

Sandy's 7–10 Year Projection Without Roaming (*Continued*)

	Sandy's Planning Year/Age				
Type of Expenditure	Year 6/49	Year 7/50	Year 8/51	Year 9/52	Year 10/53
Total Funds Required	32,235	41,091	38,079	39,315	40,687
Ratio of Investment to Expense	6:1	7:1	6:1	6:1	6:1
Type of Funding					
Income					
• From job (net[‡])	47,271	48,689	50,150	51,654	53,204
• From current assets at 5% (net[‡])	29,334	52,806	69,974	92,415	116,206
• From carryover	0	0	0	0	0
• From fellowships/grants (net[‡])	0	0	0	0	0
• From borrowing	0	0	0	0	0
Total Current Funds	76,605	101,496	120,123	144,069	169,410
Current Assets at START of Budget Year					
• *Taxable*					
• Equities	0	0	0	0	0
• Bonds	0	0	0	0	0
• Cash	28,735	51,370	67,405	89,045	111,754
• *Other*					
• Home equity	0	0	0	0	0
• Car equity	0	0	0	0	0
• Possessions	0	0	0	0	0
Total Current Assets	28,735	51,370	67,405	89,045	111,754
Finances at END of Budget Year[**]	44,370	60,405	82,045	104,754	128,723
• Loan cost	0	0	0	0	0
• Repayment of principal	0	0	0	0	0

(*continues*)

Sandy's 7–10 Year Projection Without Roaming (*Continued*)

	Sandy's Planning Year/Age				
Type of Expenditure	*Year 6/49*	*Year 7/50*	*Year 8/51*	*Year 9/52*	*Year 10/53*
Tax-Deferred Assets					
• IRA at 5%	14,882	18,626	22,557	26,685	31,020
• 403b	0	0	0	0	0
• State pension—Sandy's con-tribution 6% of salary	36,619	39,455	42,377	45,386	48,485
• Annuities	0	0	0	0	0
Total Tax-Deferred Assets	51,501	58,081	64,934	72,071	79,504

*All line items carried over from 12-month Historical Budget increased by 4% annually to account for inflation.

†All Business Investment line items increased by 4% in years 7–10 to account for inflation.

‡After any deductions for federal and state taxes, FICA, and state retirement contributions.

**Aggregate year over year, excludes tax-deferred assets. Spreadsheet subtotals and totals subject to rounding error in units place.

Sandy's 7–10 Year Projection with Roaming

	Sandy's Planning Year/Age				
Type of Expenditure	*Year 6/49*	*Year 7/50*	*Year 8/51*	*Year 9/52*	*Year 10/53*
Support Expenses					
Medical					
• Medical/dental	225	234	243	253	263
• Prescriptions	225	234	243	253	263
Subtotal first year	450				
Percentage of total first year	1%				
Car					
• Transportation	0	0	0	0	0
• Payments/4-year lease	2,792	0	0	3,000	3,000

(*continues*)

Sandy's 7–10 Year Projection with Roaming (*Continued*)

Type of Expenditure	Sandy's Planning Year/Age				
	Year 6/49	Year 7/50	Year 8/51	Year 9/52	Year 10/53
• Maintenance	0	0	0	0	0
• Gas, oil, taxes, license, insurance	1,120	0	0	1,254	1,304
Subtotal first year	3,912				
Percentage of total first year	12%				
Taxes	168	503	899	163	0
Total Support Expense[*]	4,530	971	1,386	4,923	4,831
Business Investments					
Being & Becoming					
• Exercise regularly (+ swimming in years 7–10)	98	0	0	110	114
• Cooking *en famille*	5,110	0	0	5,723	5,952
• Dressing the part	1,217	1,266	1,316	1,369	1,424
• Moments of whimsy	1,460	1,518	1,579	1,642	1,708
• Entertaining	412	0	0	461	479
• Continue IRA	3,000	0	0	3,500	3,500
• Emergency fund	7,000	0	0	0	0
Subtotal first year	11,297				
Percentage of total first year	35%				
Call Me Mom					
• Gift fund	243	253	263	273	284
• Keep skiing alive	1,217	1,266	1,316	1,369	1,424
• Occasion fund + wedding(s) in year 7	1,217	5,766	1,496	1,556	1,618
Subtotal first year	2,677				
Percentage of total first year	8%				
Realizing Potential					
• All					
• Old car subsidy	0	0	0	0	0
• Opportunity fund	0	2,000	2,080	2,163	2,250

(*continues*)

Sandy's 7–10 Year Projection with Roaming (*Continued*)

	Sandy's Planning Year/Age				
Type of Expenditure	*Year 6/49*	*Year 7/50*	*Year 8/51*	*Year 9/52*	*Year 10/53*
• Joseph	243	253	263	273	284
• Beth	234	243	253	263	274
• Anna	234	243	253	263	274
Subtotal first year	711				
Percentage of total first year	2%				
Mrs. P. Wife & Partner					
• Available at home	1,094	0	0	1,225	1,274
• Home and travel contribution + dog in years 7–10	4,926	0	0	6,077	6,320
Subtotal first year	6,020				
Percentage of total first year	19%				
Roaming					
• Financial commitments	0	30,000	31,200	0	0
Subtotal first year	0				
Percentage of total first year	0%				
Total Business Investment[†]	27,705	42,807	40,020	26,269	27,179
Total Funds Required	32,235	43,778	41,406	31,192	32,010
Ratio of Investment to Expense	6:1	44:1	29:1	5:1	6:1
Type of Funding					
Income					
• From job (net[‡])	47,271	0	0	48,689	50,150
• From current assets at 5% (net[‡])	29,334	53,094	12,398	1,051	1,923
• From carryover	0	0	0	0	0
• From fellowships/grants (net[‡])	0	0	0	0	0
• From borrowing	0	0	29,500	0	0
Total Current Funds	76,605	53,094	41,898	49,740	52,073

(*continues*)

Sandy's 7–10 Year Projection with Roaming (*Continued*)

Type of Expenditure	Sandy's Planning Year/Age				
	Year 6/49	Year 7/50	Year 8/51	Year 9/52	Year 10/53
Current Assets at START of Budget Year					
• *Taxable*					
• Equities	0	0	0	0	0
• Bonds	0	0	0	0	0
• Cash	28,735	51,370	9,316	492	1,893
• *Other*					
• Home equity	0	0	0	0	0
• Car equity	0	0	0	0	0
• Possessions	0	0	0	0	0
Total Current Assets	28,735	51,370	9,316	492	1,893
Finances at END of Budget Year[**]	44,370	9,316	492	1893	3,167
• Loan cost at 9% on outstanding balance	0	0	0	2,655	1,395
• Repayment of principal				14,000	15,500
Tax-Deferred Assets					
• IRA at 5%	14,882	18,626	22,557	26,685	31,020
• 403b	0	0	0	0	0
• State pension—Sandy's contribution 6% of salary	36,619	39,455	39,455	39,455	42,377
• Annuities	0	0	0	0	0
Total Tax-Deferred Assets	51,501	58,081	62,013	66,141	73,396

[*]All line items carried over from 12-month Historical Budget increased by 4% annually to account for inflation.

[†]All Business Investment line items increased by 4% in years 7–10 to account for inflation.

[‡]After any deductions for federal and state taxes, FICA, and state retirement contributions.

[**]Aggregate year over year, excludes tax-deferred assets. Spreadsheet subtotals and totals subject to rounding error in units place.

Going for one of her biggest Dreams and feeling that she can really bring it off is a life experience that Sandy had never expected to have. Sandy is now experiencing truly living independent of her finances. Sandy is pleased that even while undertaking Roaming, she will be able to fund one child joining her and Peter to ski (Occasion Fund) and the others to at least visit them during her and Peter's travels (Opportunity Fund). And if during this time one or more weddings should occur, Sandy is ready.

Tips for Creating Your Life Business Projection

- If you have a fixed rate mortgage on your home and/or a fixed car payment give yourself a gift! When you are calculating the effect of a 4 percent inflation rate on future Support Expenses and Business Investments, remember fixed commitments don't increase with inflation. For example, if 40 percent of your Support Expenses and Business Investments are for a home mortgage and car payments, then a 4 percent annual inflation rate adds only 2.4 percent to your costs.
- Add up your expenditures for each of your Life Businesses and divide the resulting figure by (1) your total Life Business Investment and (2) your total Support and Business Expenditure. Comparing Business Investment percentages across Businesses gives you an idea of whether or not your resources are going where you want and need them to go. If the ratio of Investment to Support is less than 2:1, then you may want to review your Commitments.
- Plan heading year columns with your age. Nothing evokes a future time like how old you will be at that point. Some Life Business participants also enter the ages of their key customers and/or suppliers. In Sandy's case she might well have entered the age of her youngest child to remind her of the very significant change in expenditure that will occur when Anna graduates from her Ivy League college.

Exercises for the Reader

1. Estimate your Support Expenses for the next 3 years.
2. Estimate your Business Investments for the next 3 years.
3. Estimate your current financial assets and your income from all sources for the next 3 years
4. Identify one financial challenge you expect to be facing in the next 3 years and, using the businesslike planning guidelines in this chapter see if you can come up with one or more possible solutions.

More information on Step 11 exercises can be found on our Web site, www.lifebusiness.com.

Moving On from Here

Next, Step 12 will help you think through what to do in case your Projection results show that you have "more life than money," that is, your planned Investments in your Life Businesses exceed the income you are likely to have available.

Note

1. Our "default settings" on the spreadsheets found in this chapter are a 5 percent average annual return on assets placed in the money, bond, and stock markets, a 9 percent cost of borrowing (using collateral-based vehicles such as equity lines), and a 4 percent inflation rate on expenditures.

Managing the Way Forward

Achieving the magic number that will free you financially

We don't work for the economy, the economy is supposed to work for us.

Robert Reich from Market Place radio interview, October 11, 2001

LIFE BUSINESS TENET

There is a way to live independent of your finances! You may already be there. Using the seven levels of financial analysis introduced in this Step, you will find out if it is possible to never have to worry about money again! When you achieve freedom from your finances, you will then be able to focus on what gives meaning and value to your life.

There is a logical conundrum implicit in our work. We challenge you to live a Dream-driven life while working to achieve independence from your finances. Yet in the Life Business approach, life and money are inextricably connected. Simply put, a Dream-driven life is necessarily sustained by energy, time, and money resources. How can you live independent of your finances while your Dreams depend in part on money?

In our Vision, money supports life, not the inverse. The Dream is the horse, money is the cart, and we strive to keep the horse before the cart. Still it is all too easy to get caught up in worrying about whether or not you'll have enough money to fund your Dreams. It's not good enough just to be able to find the money you need. The state of mind that we are seeking is a fundamental and abiding confidence that the money you need will be there when you need it. When you have achieved this sense of the place of money in your life, you will be living "independent of your finances" even though you may well need money to support the achievement of your Dreams.

One of the keys to feeling independent of your finances is understanding the various funding strategies available to you and knowing when it's appropriate to use one rather than another. Some of the possible ways of funding your Life Business Plans will seem more attractive than others, but each strategy has its time and place. Basically it boils down to making the things we want to achieve happen by employing whatever resources are available to us.

Having said that, there is a hierarchy of funding strategies. Businesses fund their Plans in ways very similar to those we use. For businesses "internal" or "revenue stream" funding has the best impact on the corporate balance sheet. If a company can fund its plans from it's current revenues, then the costs of "issuing" corporate paper (shares and bonds) or borrowing are held to a minimum. But make no mistake about it. Corporations can dig deep when they have to. We have all heard of downsizing and rightsizing. And of course corporations also borrow funds. When really pushed, corporations also carry out strategies like "capital recovery." *Capital recovery* is a fancy way of saying to sell anything that's not nailed down in order to support changing corporate priorities. A capital recovery strategy usually entails selling off nonessential corporate assets such as slow-moving inventory or obsolete goods.

Financing your Life Business Plan from your revenue stream is a long way from funding Projects by selling the living room furniture. Yet any of these strategies can make sense depending on your particular situation. We have identified "seven levels" of funding strategy to help you decide how to go about funding your Plan. In thinking through the resourcing of your Plan, it will pay big dividends to be familiar with each of these levels.

The Seven Levels of Financial Strategy

Managing your financial realities will be easier the closer your situation is to the first, or top, of our seven levels. The deeper you need to go into these levels, the more preparation you will want to undertake, and the more you may also want to involve outside assistance. Our seven levels are:

1. Recognize that you are already living your Plan independent of serious financial challenges.
   Have you already achieved independence from your finances and don't yet realize it?
2. Achieve independence from your finances by freeing up assets.
   Can you free up sufficient assets to "float your boat"?

3. Achieve financial independence by squeezing your Support Expenses.
   Does aggressively tightening your Support Expenses "make your nut"?
4. Achieve financial freedom by reprioritizing/rescheduling/rightsizing your Dreams.
   If you restructure your Dreams, do your funds meet your requirements?
5. Achieve financial freedom by substituting time for money.
   Does substituting other resources for money balance the books?
6. Achieve independence from your finances by earning more money or accepting higher portfolio Volatility.
   Would additional "remunerative employment" get the job done?
7. Achieve financial independence by cutting your Business Investment program.
   What are the fewest, lowest-priority Projects, which, if cut, make it work?

How do you figure out which level you are on? The process begins the same way it began in Sandy's case. You first have to know what you want money for, how much you'll need, and when you'll need it.

The goal of this Step is to enable you to adopt a practical, businesslike approach to the financial planning challenges you are facing. While you will find that much of the advice you read here is contrary to that usually given by the financial planning industry, it is all consistent with the business analogy that underlies every aspect of the Life Business approach and the specific concepts presented in Step 9, Business Thinking.

Level 1—Did You Just Go Past GO or What?

What is the lowest annual return on investment (ROI)—and here we're talking about ROI in the traditional, purely financial sense—at which your current income and liquid assets, plus likely future income, will provide the funds your Dreams require? Is this ROI probable? Yes or no? Over the period of any of your three Projections (0–3 years, 4–6 years and 7+ years), an ROI higher than 8 percent on funds placed in the stock market is not probable. On the other hand, the probability of an overall return of at least 5 percent is highly likely.

Sandy is lucky. Her Dreams can be achieved by her making conservative assumptions about continued employment and achievable rates of return on her financial placements. In year 1 Sandy has no taxable financial assets and owns mutual funds only in her IRA and state employee's pension fund. In the 0– to 3–year period Sandy will begin investing in her Life Business Projects and will require a 2-year loan for $11,000. This debt will be repaid during year 3. At the end of year 3 Sandy will have implemented all of her 0– to 3–Year Life Business Projects and will have covered all of her Support Expenses. In Sandy's 4– to 6–Year Medium-Term Projection (see Step 11) she will be accumulating considerable taxable cash reserves. In her 7+ year Long-Term Projection Sandy's Investment in Roaming will require a loan. She should be able to repay it within 2 years of her returning to work

By investing her energies in making a Plan-Ahead Budget and Short-, Medium- and Long-Term Projections, Sandy has done all the heavy lifting herself, and now simple answers to simple questions will enable her to achieve her Dreams. She could have been in a different situation. What if her Dreams and resources didn't come out even? The next six levels deal with the situation where your Projections indicate that you have more Dream than resources. But first a word about the previously unthinkable.

Oops! What Do I Do with the Leftovers?

After doing your Projections some of you will have a new concern. Perhaps even more challenging than not having enough money is having "leftovers." What if, by using conservative assumptions, you end up with more, even far more, resources than Dream? Any time you have more resources than Dream, you are in effect "leaving opportunity on the table." Life is hard enough without squandering opportunities for increased satisfaction! If this is happening to you, review your current Life Businesses and reflect on whether more money invested sooner wouldn't return more satisfaction sooner. If investing more earlier in your current Businesses absorbs your overflowing capital, so be it. If not, stretch farther. Consider thinking of yourself as a kind of "venture capital" resource for those most important to you. Which of their Life Business Projects need funding? Which, if any, would you be interested in funding? If you exhaust your list of fund recipients close to home, raise your horizon, and think about what you can effectively aid and support in your community.

Here's an example of how personal assets can be leveraged for greater satisfaction. Through an innovative use of his home equity line, Bill joined four of his friends to help another mutual friend come up with the cash she needed for her own house purchase. Bill's friend in need, Janet, had credit challenges and is a single parent. The builder's mortgage lender ended up demanding a lot more up-front cash than Janet had been told to expect. Things were at an impasse, and Janet was on the verge of letting go of her Dream of owning her own home. Then Bill's wife Gloria suggested that she and Bill tap their home equity line to help. Running with the idea, Bill called several of his friends and asked them if they were interested in joining in. Each friend contributed at the level to which they were comfortable, and the group gift ended up totaling $1800. That's all it took for Janet to qualify. The economy gained a homeowner and a Dream believer. Bill and Gloria gained the satisfaction of using their money to live their values now, today.

Another example is a relative of one of our Life Business participants, who struck it rich during the Tech Boom and who sold at the right time. She set up a fund, which provided $10,000 toward the first year of college for each of her 13 nieces and nephews. In this way she advanced two of her most important life values: family connection and continuing education.

Sandy leaves the process at Level 1 because she's gotten a big yes to the big question. She has a nut that she can crack. In other words, she knows what she wants to achieve in her life, has identified the Projects she thinks will realize these Dreams, has estimated how much resource these Projects are likely to require, and has calculated that she'll have enough to make it all happen. She is right now, believe it or not, independent of her finances, and well ensconced in life's catbird seat. Sandy is both financially independent and earning a salary. No conflict here. Sandy's employment represents the achievement of a heartfelt Project. She isn't working for a living; she's working for a life.

Level 2—The Hidden Asset Tree

If your answer to the Level 1 question (Is the cash flow your Dreams require probable?) is no, you'll next need to determine whether or not there is any place you can find or free up sufficient additional funds to invest in your Dreams.

Do you still have a "rainy day" fund? Do you have money tied up in retirement or estate planning funds for which you have made no concrete plans? Do you have marketable possessions no longer associated with prized personal Dreams (extra cars, antiques, old coins, paintings, furniture, etc.)? Do you have available credit in your home equity lines? How about the possibility of liberating capital by refinancing your mortgage at an attractive rate? Maybe you have loans made to others that could be called in? If shaking the "hidden asset tree" turns up the funds that maintain your Plan, you can exit our seven-level Path to Financial Freedom process here at Level 2.

If the way forward is not immediately clear, let's look again. Consider liquidating hidden capital for cash flow. We can't count the number of clients who've come to us worried that they won't be able to get through the next 10 years who, at the same time, have significant IRA and/or 401K retirement portfolios, paid-up "whole-life" life insurance policies, trust funds for their kids, and/or equity in their home or homes. Each of these assets can be liquidated or leveraged to provide funds today. And—here is the important point—often the purposes to which these funds are currently dedicated can be met more effectively by other means! Why, for example, pile up whole dollars now, to be distributed to others at your death, when term life insurance could pay out the same benefit at a cost to you of a good deal less than "dollar for dollar"? Why lock up half the value of your house in equity when you could still earn appreciation on the house's total market value and have a good deal of that equity available to fund important Projects now? Why squirrel away 15 to 20 percent of your current income for retirement if you then can't afford to Invest in building the skills and experiences today that will give your retirement meaning tomorrow?

Projects whose financial requirements haven't been estimated, can't be efficiently funded. Unconscious commitments are truly understandable in terms of our cultural heritage, but they are not businesslike. You want your financial assets available to you to fund Dreams you know that you want to achieve today, in 4 years, and in 7 years. You don't want to sabotage your Dreams because you feel some cultural imperative to finance college, illness, retirement, and inheritance the old-fashioned way. Unless you decide what you want to "feed" these asset-devouring cultural imperatives, you'll be left with crumbs to fund your Life Business Plan. When thinking about funding your Life Business Plan, remember that income, capital, borrowing, or inheritances are just different kinds of money. You don't need to live on earned income alone, and it's really no sin to liquidate some of your capital.

Cy Dares to Dip into His IRA Cookie Jar

The cash requirements of Cy's Life Business Plan challenged him to make an about-face and stop making payments to his retirement accounts. In fact, his Plan called for him to partially disassemble his IRA. With his businessman's hat on Cy

Not Living Your Dream Could Be as Bad as Outliving Your Money

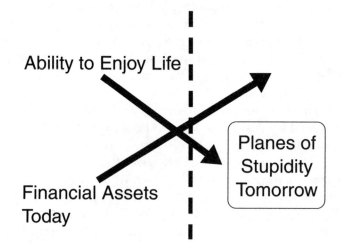

couldn't see any sense in overinvesting for a distant tomorrow when today was coming unglued. This thought was also reinforced by his changing domestic situation. Cy was about to marry a woman some 15 years younger than him. The impact of this marriage on his retirement planning meant that when he was $59\frac{1}{2}$ and ready to start withdrawing, without penalty, taxable funds from his retirement accounts, his wife would likely be in her peak earning years. Thus the core gimmick of retirement planning—that one shelters today's income from high peak earnings tax rates to take it out later at lower retirement income tax rates didn't apply at all in their case. Cy arranged to start taking actuarially computed "72T" (thus no penalty) annual distributions from his IRA retirement account. Cy uses this new "income" to fund the Projects he and his new wife want to undertake together to give their life meaning today while continuing to ensure that adequate funding will be available for tomorrow's priorities.

This decision made Cy a pariah to his financial adviser. Cy got the courage to undertake this somewhat unchartered approach because as a businessman he knew that he wasn't alone. Successful businesses employ similar creative money management strategies every day to build stronger and more resilient companies. Taking our thinking a step further, it's important to recognize that cash flow doesn't even have to be your own money!

Save or Borrow?

Without your telling us what you value and when you value it, we can't competently advise you as to whether it makes sense for you to save or borrow to realize your Goals. Despite plenty of cultural noise to the contrary, there is no inherent virtue or vice in either course of action. What we can tell you is that it doesn't make much sense to save if important Dreams are not being funded, and it doesn't make sense to borrow if you don't truly value that which borrowing will enable you to purchase.

Saving or borrowing is often a simple trade-off. If you borrow, you pay an interest premium for so doing, but you get the thing or experience now when you can be relatively sure that you can use it. If you save, you "pay" the opportunity cost of not having the thing or experience now but pay no interest and possibly earn a "compound interest" bonus.

An examined life is not necessarily a less expensive life. Sure, most of us could get by with fewer things, but might we not all benefit from more and richer experiences? Experience is an Investment in our future capacities. People met today, skills and knowledge acquired now, and perspectives and appreciations arrived at sooner, all set the table for a deeper, fuller existence from this point on. In the example above, in terms of his own personal value system, Cy's motto might well read, "Live the experience now." Interest on a loan can be a small price to pay for acting on something today that may not be available tomorrow. Your kids won't always want to go to Disney World, you won't always be able to enjoy your diving suit, and people graduate and marry relatively few times in their lives. Make the money do what you and your life require of it, when you require it.

There are also no good or bad things to purchase. We can imagine a situation in which it could make real good sense to borrow money at the prime rate (currently 4.5 percent) or below to finance a daily mocha cappuccino even while one is unemployed. If the grog is what helps you feel confident as you pore over the help wanted ads, it could be an excellent investment. You might want to ask yourself what a double almond latte would do. The way to decide whether debt is a good or bad thing for you is to first of all determine the importance to you of that which it can make possible.

Good and Bad Debt

Of course, even if all your debt meets the criteria of being a Business Investment in your life, there are more and less intelligent ways to arrange for it. For example, an 18 percent credit card debt is not an attractive option, but a 4 percent subsidized student loan is. If you have certain kinds of life insurance or own your own home, you can often borrow from yourself, the lender of first resort. While it's almost a cultural imperative to pay off your mortgage, this often makes no economic sense. You own your house and receive any capital appreciation on its market value whether or not you have a penny of equity in it. Why have a bundle of money earning no return sitting in the middle of your living room floor? If you can get your equity out of your house at an interest rate equal to or lower than what you could earn by placing that sum in the financial markets, and you have underfunded Life Business projects, do it and do it today. Now there is even a more efficient opportunity to create liquidity. Consider the following discussion.

Interest-Only Mortgages

An interest-only mortgage is one way of freeing up assets for the development of your Life Businesses. Why build equity at all if you're going to liquidate it once you have it? Instead, from day one pay only the interest you owe on the equity you are borrowing from yourself. That's right, don't repay any of the principal. Interest-only loans based on an overnight index like the London Interbank Offering Rate (LIBOR) enable you to borrow money at the lowest possible rate and pay back only the interest. Today's LIBOR-based rate of about 3.35 percent (including the mortgage broker's commission) makes your monthly payment on a $150,000 mortgage about $450 versus $970 for an ordinary 30-year mortgage at the fixed rate of 6.75 percent. Could your Life Business priorities effectively utilize an extra $520 a month? $6100 a year? What Business development projects waiting in the pipeline could be brought forward to make use of this funding? If you don't know of any, then your life may not be big enough to need the money you already have. In this case your most important challenge is to create a bigger life, not find more funding.

When the Dow recently dropped from almost 12,000 to below 8,000, Harry and Helen's financial plan took a big hit. Could they now find the funds for both their kitchen renovation and the expenditures associated with an elite college experience for their daughter over the next 5 years? The housing market came to their rescue. With mortgage rates at close to historical lows and housing prices at historical highs, they were able to refinance their home and cash out enough equity to keep both Dreams alive.

There are at least four significantly different types of mortgages on the market today; the Interest-only alternative we've just been discussing, the 1-year ARM, the 30-year fixed, and the 15-year fixed. We advise choosing a mortgage type based on when you need the cash flow advantages each option offers. The Interest-only mortgage gives you the lowest current monthly payment but will require a balloon payment for the entire principal somewhere down the line. The 1-year ARM can be the next lowest current monthly payment, but your payments will increase or decrease with changes in interest rate policy. The 30-year fixed mortgage locks in your monthly payments for 30 years so you know what your monthly nut is going to be. Finally the 15-year fixed mortgage gives you the fixed payment advantages of the 30-year plan, but since your payments are only for 15 years, they are higher, dropping to 0 in the sixteenth year.

At the limit the economy is us and should be evaluated on the extent to which it meets our needs. The same is true for the ways in which money can be used. And saving and borrowing are two important ways in which money can be manipulated. Life is uncertain. You don't want to be in a situation where you have postponed an important experience or purchase beyond the point of its usefulness to you. You also don't want to be in a situation where you have purchased something that is of no real use to you.

Consumer durables like the largest SUVs are often ciphers for wealth accumulation. The same advice applies to both. SUVs and large bank accounts seem to say, "Look at me. I'm strong (if not entirely invincible)." Sometimes it's hard to see that. more stuff or more money is not necessarily more life. The Life Business Program doesn't make that call for you. Your life, your decision. We think that you will get closer and closer to where you need to be by increasingly accurate iterations of our process. The Life Business question is what will the luxury SUV bring you that can't be gotten with a smaller Commitment of energy, time, and money?

It can make sense to save and it can make sense to borrow, depending on when you need the money, when you can pay it back, and what happens in your life as the result of whichever action you take.

Level 3—Do the Tighten-Up

If you couldn't find the funding your Business Plan requires at Level 2, is there any possibility that you have not reviewed and arrived at the very leanest Support Expense Budget that still gets the job done? In Step 9 we state that the best-run businesses believe Support Budgets should be continually challenged in order to free up resources for important investments. Here is where we bring that business principle into play. Money squeezed out of Support Budgets and reallocated to Business Development Projects can often make your Plan viable. In the accompanying figure, you see a few of the things that Peter did to tighten up his Support Expenses by more than 25 percent to increase funding for Business Investment.

Opportunities to cut Support Expenses are out there, but you have to keep your eyes open. Cellular companies are just waiting for you to negotiate or renegotiate with them. Grocery stores run 10-week promotions. You can now compare auto, home, liability, and health insurance costs on the Internet. The same is true for mortgages, used cars, and even cookie jars. But, as with selecting stocks, you want to be careful how much time and energy you commit to saving or making money. If getting the best price is a "Motivated Talent," then it's a fun game to play. If you need the cash flow, then it's a necessity. In Harry and Helen's case above, they funded the increase in their monthly mortgage payment by reducing the payment Harry had been making for whole-life life insurance. This trade-off had the added value of moving funds from an after-tax placement to a tax-deferred placement.

Creative Family Finance

In *Open Book Management,* John Schuster shows how companies that train their employees in financial literacy create channels for participation, and award incentives tied to the bottom line both reduce costs and generate a real sense of employee ownership.[1] Similarly, you might make "increased domestic efficiency" a family Project and by so doing not only better fund your Life Businesses but also build family unity and responsibility. Keep in mind that even if there is a family member or a member of your own Internal Management Team who enjoys this work for its own sake, the only Business reason for saving on Support Expenses is to fund valued individual and/or family Life Business development Projects.

Life Program Participant Peter Does the Tighten-Up

Actions	*Effect on Support Expenses*	
Got bids and renegotiated		
	• Mortgage	lowered
	• Insurance	lowered
Professional "reengineering"		
	• Closed office	lowered
	• Replaced outside contractors with family	lowered
Family "reengineering"		
	Children	
	• Replaced open checkbook with line-item contracts	lowered
	Whole Family	
	• Each person responsible for own long-distance calls	lowered
	Car	
	• Replaced new lease car with quality 10-year-old car	lowered
	• Ran one car rather than two	lowered
Review holiday policy		
	• Limited to 1 major winter, 1 major summer	lowered
	• If air ticket had to be purchased, drove instead	lowered
	• Consider only those options favored by a majority of family members	lowered

(continues)

Life Program Participant Peter Does the Tighten-Up (*Continued*)

Actions	Effect on Support Expenses	
Review Food Budget		
	• Purchased from comprehensive checklist after doing inventory of what was on hand	lowered
	• Limited to $120 per week	lowered
	• Restaurant meals that replace eating at home counted against home food budget	lowered
Review Housing Expenses		
	• Did only required maintenance, inspections, etc.	lowered
	• Put all work out for competitive bid	lowered
	• We purchased all materials for contractors' use	lowered
Monitor Budget		
	• Reviewed Budgeted and Actual expenditures monthly for first 6 months, then quarterly	lowered

Careful with That Knife

About 10 years ago IBM, in the pre-Gerstner era, was in big trouble. Its response was to "decimate" the company, that is, literally cut 10 percent across the board, every business, every department, every cost. The problem is that this approach throws out 10 percent of the baby with 10 percent of the bath water. Cuts should be made in Support Expenses when and where there is real fat, and the funds that are freed up can immediately be invested in Stars, Rising Stars, or Cash Cows.

Anna Takes on the Ivy League

Sandy's youngest child, Anna, is off to the Ivy League this fall. In financing her education, Anna's parents would like to achieve a couple of their Life Business Goals: (1) help Anna develop her growing independence and accountability and (2) find the least expensive (read cheapest) overall means of paying their part of Anna's college costs (thus freeing up funds for other ventures).

Throughout the college selection process Sandy and Peter have helped Anna to get "in the center" of the decisions that were being made. Sandy has agreed to pay the costs of Anna's going to any school she wanted to attend, and could get into, to the tune of what it would cost them to send her to an in-state, state-supported university. Because of Anna's academic record and national examination results, a number of southern and western universities sent her unsolicited offers of full tuition, room and board, and research stipends. Peter "spreadsheeted" the comparative costs of Anna's short list of schools. There were even college situations where, after adding in her parents agreed-upon contribution, Anna could attend for free and also pocket several thousand dollars a year. While to be "spreadsheeted" has become a household term of derision, the process did empower Anna, and her brothers and sisters before her, to choose their own directions.

In the end Anna went for her Dream, a big city, Ivy League experience. While the school of her choice gave her a significant grant, even after applying her parents' contribution, Anna had to commit to eventually repay some $16,000 in loans. In order to achieve the above goals, the following action steps were taken. They are grouped by the Projects they enable:

GOAL 1 PROJECTS—HELP ANNA DEVELOP HER GROWING INDEPENDENCE AND ACCOUNTABILITY

- Help Anna set up her own checking account in her hometown and a second at her college. The hometown account is to be jointly held with her parents. All college expenses are to be paid from one of these two accounts, and the college account is to be funded from her hometown account and her work–study earnings.
- Honor the school's estimate of the student's own financial responsibility, in this case $1600 per year.
- Provide Anna with "home work" (i.e., paid work at home) sufficient enough to fund her $1600 obligation.
- Accept the college's offer of a $20,000 per year grant and $4000 per year in student loans.
- Accept the college's offer of a work–study job, in this case valued at $2350 a year before taxes.
- Accept the college's estimate of Anna's yearly on-campus financial needs as $2030.
- Sandy to deposit the remaining amount Anna will require for a semester's worth of tuition, room, and board, travel to and from school, clothes, and room setup funds in her account.

- Set up a debit card (not a credit card) in conjunction with each of Anna's bank accounts (hometown and college). Anna to pay all bills by check or debit card from her checking accounts.

GOAL 2 PROJECTS—FIND THE CHEAPEST METHOD OF PAYING SANDY'S CONTRIBUTION TO ANNA'S COLLEGE COSTS

- Sandy deposits her contribution to one of Anna's accounts from Peter's equity line, which is currently charging a 4.75 percent interest rate.
- Peter then transfers his equity line balance to a credit card offering a 6-month, 0 percent interest rate, no transfer fees, low airline mileage requirements, and a mileage bonus on transfers.
- When the introductory deal on this card is about to expire, Peter writes a check on his equity line to pay off the card's balance or transfers the balance to a new 0 percent introductory rate card. Sandy figures she gains about $200 on this transaction and $400 for the year by doing the same thing the second semester.
- With the mileage they earn for tuition, room and board, and bonuses, they can get at least one airline ticket with a value of approximately $350 each year.
- Altogether this is an annual savings of about $750, or 15 percent of their Federal Application for Student Aid determined parental contribution.

You might ask why Sandy didn't pay the college's bill directly with a credit card. The answer is threefold: (1) Anna needs to be in the center of the process, and, by writing her own check, she is; (2) the college charges $126 to accept a credit card payment; and (3) Peter would lose the 5000-mile mileage bonus for transferring funds from his equity line to a mileage-earning credit card.

You might also ask why not pay cash instead of borrowing. The answer is simple but not culturally easy to accept. Our forefathers instructed us to "never a borrower be." It is better money management to borrow at 0 percent and let your cash keep earning 4 to 6 percent in a money market account. Often borrowing, strangely enough, will give you a better figure on the bottom line than not borrowing. Companies know this and act on it. We should too.

Level 4—Review Your Life Businesses

Still shy of your nut? You may need to reschedule, reprioritize, or "rightsize" your Dreams.

If you couldn't raise the funds your Plan requires at Level 3, is there any possibility that you are not concentrating your Business development efforts on your highest priority Businesses? Below is an example of how John reviewed his Business portfolio and some of the productivity-improving actions that he took.

Business Review: Identifying Your Highest-Priority Businesses

In reviewing his Life Businesses, John found that:

- There was little or no money going into his "Personal" Business.
- There was nothing at all going into "Professional Development."
- A very high percentage of his disposable funds was going into "Savingslike" Projects (e.g., buying antiques and paintings), a Business not even represented in his initial portfolio!

Discussing these findings with his wife Susie brought more insight. Comparing his energy, time, and money behavior, it gradually became clear that John's use of energy and time reflected short-term objectives, even though frequently frustrated, to establish solid foundations with both his family and his profession. On the other hand, John's use of money was predominantly geared to the long term and, until now, nearly unconscious concerns with security and besting his father's financial and material achievements. The result was that highly significant Businesses were being literally "undercapitalized" (resource-starved)! And there were other "a-has." John had always spent a high percentage of his time on family holidays. Now he could see that because these were done on the cheap, these holidays weren't really satisfying and thus contributed little to achieving his strongly held objective of fostering "family identity and commitment." As John's awareness increased, he began to see that the large "stolen" and "lost" entries on his Where Gone ledger could be seen as energy wasted on Projects where he had hoped for too much and invested too little in material resources. Then it became really clear to him—his hobby "collecting stuff" was actually suffering from exactly the opposite problem—too much money invested and not enough energy or time.

John decided to create more psychological liquidity through supporting his key energy investments with more money. Curtailing his collecting until he could decide whether or not to spend more time on it freed up about $5000 in the first year. One year after having done his first Business Review, John was able to report that his slightly more expensive skiing holiday had paid off a good deal more energy than it had cost. It will often be possible to phase or schedule your Business Development Projects in a different way to take advantage of available funding. For example, postpone implementing the money-intensive "Backyard Pool" Project until year 3 when you know that you'll receive a bonus that will cover your required investment; and bring forward into year 2, the time-intensive "Elysian Gardens" Project.

Level 5—Increase Project Productivity

If your analysis at Level 4 hasn't produced the funds necessary for the achievement of your Plan, reflect on whether any of your critical Business Projects can be accomplished by substituting a less scarce resource for a more scarce one, that is, time or energy for money.

This is kind of a "paper, scissors, rock" thing. Substitute time for money when you are "motivated" and "talented" in terms of the activity that needs to take place. Be aware of the potential problems of just being either motivated or talented. When you are motivated and perhaps not talented, things can take longer to do than they otherwise might. You'll enjoy the learning (you're motivated, right?), but you may be surprised by the time commitment. Worse is being talented and not motivated. Too many of us have spent too long doing tasks and jobs that we are good at and get well paid for but no longer care much about. Don't substitute time for money if you are talented yet not motivated—your life's load will only increase. Certainly in John's case, time (because it was motivated time) invested in his Art Business turned out to be a much more effective investment than more money.

In considering how to finance college tuition without having to liquidate their inherited nest egg, which was already committed to funding their Retirement, Harry and Helen realized that with their daughter out of the home and with Helen's novel near completion, they could do without the $7000 of household help that they had invested in over the last 2 years. Thinking about their trade-offs, Harry and Helen reached a new agreement about who would do the dishes, cooking, laundry etc. Substituting their own time for money spent on domestic services, they took a big step toward protecting their financial assets for the future while recommitting to their home life together. While household chores were not necessarily their motivated talents, Harry and Helen were motivated to find a less money-intensive way forward.

Level 6—Get a Job

If Level 5 thinking hasn't done the trick, can you see any possibility that additional funds could be earned (e.g., turning time and/or energy into money)? Remember, being financially independent is not necessarily in conflict with receiving money for time invested, that is, having a job. The Life Business proviso is that any job must call on your Motivated Talents in order to coexist with financial independence. Bottom line, you can't be working primarily for money and be financially independent.

Anna needed to earn money at college to cover her out-of-pocket needs. She also needed not to get sidetracked from her main Goals. Fortunately Anna loves working with children, and America Reads offered her an opportunity to serve elementary school students in Harlem and earn enough money to, ever so occasionally, trip the light fandango.

Helen, who has always been a homemaker and a writer, wants to work outside the home once her daughter leaves to go to college. Helen is very interested in, and knowledgeable about, creative writing. In writing her own novel, Helen developed her own perspective on what constitutes good fiction. She wants to share this with the world. She believes that by getting a job in the writing field, she will be leveraging a motivated talent. Even if her eventual job is not a great money-maker, Helen will be increasing her life satisfaction and in so doing will be advancing her own and her family's Life Business Plans.

Level 7—First Things First

Finally, if your answer at Level 6 was "still no nut," you will need to consider which Business Projects can be postponed with the least detriment to your short-term personal profit, in other words, your life satisfaction.

It's not enough to have a Dream. The Dream has got to be implemented. And often Dreams are anchored in a person, a time, and a place. In this sense postponing a Dream can sometimes render the Dream unreal. The bottom-line criterion here is that we give up "anchored" Dreams only when we are up against an insurmountable wall.

Jack ran his numbers after the recent market decline. After a thoughtful financial review, he realized that overall things would work out more smoothly if he stayed in his current job another 2 years before devoting himself full time to golf and his grandchildren.

Mark, an adult student, felt that if he attended a private college, he would be so saddled with debt when he graduated that it would limit his career choices to those jobs that would pay him enough so that he could clear his loans. In the end he decided to concentrate on getting good grades at a local commuter college and keep his money to put toward an eventual M.B.A. or an M.F.A. as his career goals became more clear.

Sometimes postponing or changing the nature of your Investment in a Dream will do the trick. In John's example above, investing more time and less money in his Art Business helped that Business become more profitable.

Other Tips for Finding Effective and Efficient Funding

- If you are thinking about liquidating some of your assets, be careful that you are aware of all the consequences. Even if you can get out of any penalties associated with dissolving, say, a 401K, think twice about doing it. Your employer is probably making a significant contribution to your portfolio. This is free money. Don't give it up without exhausting less expensive alternatives. Because of the 72T provision, IRAs are usually a better bet for liquidation.

- Procrastination could be one of your Life Enterprise's biggest Risks. If it feels as though you've got a problem, you've got one. The sooner you attack the cause, the sooner you'll have one less time- and energy-intensive drain on your resources.

Exercises for the Reader

1. Scan your assets by making a list of those that are not now leveraged.
2. Review your Support Expenses by identifying those things you could cut back on or fund more cheaply.
3. Shore up your Business Investments by reviewing which Life Businesses could use more resources and return more satisfaction.
4. What would you give up? Review your expenditures and rank them in order of what you would be willing to let go of in order to achieve financial independence.

Additional Step 12 exercises can be accessed at our Web site. Go to www.lifebusiness.com.

Money Management

In Steps 10 and 11 we have shown how knowing what you want to achieve, how much it will cost, and when Investment is required will enable you to effectively commit your resources to your life priorities both today and in whatever distant future you care to contemplate. This done, you will know exactly what your financial planning challenges are. Once these challenges are mapped out, you will find both a new clarity and a new ease concerning your financial situation. This clarity and ease can grow into a true sense of independence from your finances. When your personal financial situation is truly understood, it loses the power it might once have had over you.

In Step 12 we've looked at how you can find the funds you require to "make your nut," that is, live life independent of your finances. Finally, in Step 13 we discuss how you can best progress your cash-flow–based Life Business Plan in a financial services world that is just itching to help you create wealth.

Note

1. John Schuster, et. al. *The Open Management Fieldbook.* Wiley, 1997.

Getting the Help You Need When You Need It

Advancing a cash-flow agenda in a wealth-creation world

Customs are made for customary circumstances . . . and customary characters.

John Stuart Mill

LIFE BUSINESS TENET

You already know how much money you need, when you need it, how much money you have, and how much you are likely to have in the future. Now you need to decide what kind of help you want as you manage your finances and how to deal with the challenges you are going to face in trying to get it.

We had a client, the young CEO of a large coatings and resins company, who had retained the company's previous owner as an adviser. When we asked our client if he was getting what he needed from this relationship, he told us that he was indeed. He elaborated by telling us how he worked with this adviser. Our client would pose a specific company management concern and ask his adviser what should be done. Having heard the older fellow's advice, our client would then proceed to do something entirely different. Our client's rationale was that it was the adviser's way of thinking that had cost him his company in the first place. As you progress forward with your Life Business Plan, you will want to limit the amount of energy and time you spend rethinking inappropriate advice.

In organizing your finances to support your Plan, you will probably want some help. Getting that help from the financial services industry could prove to be problematic. This is because people there think that they already know what

205

you want, and what they think you want is ever-increasing wealth. Having decided that wealth creation is the name of the game, the financial services industry has structured its processes and products to help you do just that. The best way to prepare yourself to get what you really need in this environment is to: (1) have a good idea of why financial consultants and planners think the way they do, (2) know exactly what help you want, and (3) know the role that you want to play in the client-adviser relationship.

Wealth Creation versus Cash Flow

The financial services industry has values, a vision, goals, a strategy, and a set of tools much as you do. The essential problem is that the industry's objective is wealth creation and yours is having the cash flow required to fund your Life Business Plan. What follows is a critique, or comparison, of the two sets of objectives.

Values and Reward Systems

While the "life as business" idea is new to those actually offering financial services, it is not new to the creative talent at their leading advertising agencies. These folks are fervently running the "life as business" banner up their respective

Comparing the Objectives of the Financial Services Industry with the Life Business Approach

	The Financial Services Industry	**The Life Business Approach**
Objective	**Wealth creation**	**Cash flow**
Values	Self-protection	Self-empowerment
Vision	Become materially rich	Live a "rich," full life
Goals	Retirement; a significant estate	Short, medium, long term per your Plan
Strategy	Save to create future wealth	Guarantee cash flow for your Plan
Tools	IRA, 401K, and saving	Borrowing and cash-flow allocation
Rewards	Wealth-creation–based pay	Time invested or transaction-based pay

flagpoles because their focus groups, surveys, and polls have concluded that a businesslike approach will bring up-market consumers into the offices, and onto the Web sites, of their financial industry clients.

In the autumn of 1997 billboards throughout New York City touted Fleet Bank's message—"Be the President of Your Life." In the autumn of 1998, the polished pages of weeklies targeting the sophisticated professional man and woman trumpeted, "You are the CEO of Your Life" for Morgan Stanley. In the spring of 1999 Merrill Lynch entered the foray with "Managing the business that's most important to you, Your Life, Incorporated." Unfortunately, there is very little support for clients behind these come-ons. If you were to go into any financial service-firm today and ask to see someone who could help you manage your life like a business, you would be handed over to the first available "financial consultant." This financial consultant would, in turn, ask: (1) How much money do you have to invest as a lump sum today, and how much additional will you have each month? (2) What are your goals? and (3) How much "risk" (read Volatility) are you willing to take?

Depending on your answers to these three questions, you will receive a recommended portfolio of money managers (if you have big bucks) or mutual funds (if you have fewer bucks), "allocated" and "diversified" across different investment strategies. You will also receive lectures on the "Big 3": (1) the rising costs of your children's or grandchildren's eventual college education; (2) how you aren't saving enough for your retirement; and, somewhat incongruously since you are not supposed to have been saving enough, (3) the big tax bite that could be a disadvantage to the beneficiaries of your estate. In other words, once you are in the door, you're likely to find that it's business as usual. So why is the usual usual?

The problem is that while a great deal of resource, and effort has gone into trying to build up the expertise and credibility of financial planning, the profession continues to suffer from having grown up in the same culture as the rest of us.

There are aspects of the American experience that inhibit us in our quest to identify our Dreams and to think holistically about managing our energy, time, and money. These are the "shoulds" of responsible money management. We discussed these "shoulds" in the Introduction and ascribed their origin to the challenges faced by our ancestors as they carved out a new existence while rolling back an often unwelcoming frontier. Nurtured in this environment, professional financial advisers tell us that Americans should: (1) own their own homes; (2) pay off their mortgages as soon as possible; (3) stay out of debt—debt is bad; (4) save as much as they can—saving is good—and prepare for a retirement income equal to 65 to 80 percent of their last 3 years' employment earnings.

Trapped in these metavalues of the American way of life, the financial planning profession lacks a comprehensive structure and strategy for enabling its clients to do anything but accumulate wealth. Now these values have become institutionalized through changes in financial consultant pay and rewards.

There is a cultural revolution going on in the financial planning industry, and it began well before the Enron, Arthur Andersen, and Merrill Lynch debacles. Unfortunately the changes are not bringing the industry closer to the values we would hope to see. Now the industry has consciously decided to be in the "wealth creation" rather than the "transaction" business, and it's working hard to realign it's reward systems to bring this about. Perhaps the single most significant change that has already been engineered is the way in which client account managers are being paid.

Increasingly brokers, advisers, money managers, and the like are being paid a percentage of the funds "under management" rather than a per transaction fee. (A transaction takes place every time a financial placement, a bond, stock, mutual fund, is bought or sold.) The significance of this change is that the person you are likely to approach for financial advice and assistance now has a vested interest in the dollar value of your "wealth" rather than the number of transactions he or she can generate (at its worst, "churn") from your account.

Even though the industry's core values are different from ours, this change is in part good news for the cash-flow–motivated client. Now, at least for your long-term (7+ years) planning period your best interests will be in your adviser's best interests as well. This is revolutionary. Whereas before you might have found an adviser who took an interest in your personal situation and its money-management implications, even though it could well have cost him or her transaction-based income, now that adviser gets paid to grow your money. However, this change might not help you achieve the performance you require in the short term (0–3 years) and here's why.

In the Short term your first priority is not to grow your money. Instead, for these funds, you want the highest possible guarantee that money will be available on the dates when you will be requiring it. For Short-term funds you would probably choose a money market deposit, a certificate of deposit, a treasury bond, or a corporate bond over a value or growth stock or a stock mutual fund. Emphasizing liquidity could lead to a lower overall asset base than a strategy where you place your money in equities. In this scenario your adviser could be paid less than he or she would receive if you had been in equities. The ideal reward structure might combine a percentage fee for "assets under management" Long term and transaction fees for Short-term placements.

The Savings Industry

Many financial advisers have been classically conditioned to talk with you primarily about retirement, college expenses, home purchases, estate planning, and long-term care insurance. Be careful. Tell them your age, and these advisers already know what your major life priorities should be. Their priorities for you all involve saving and then saving some more. Of course a savings-based money-management strategy goes hand in hand with a wealth-creation–based remuneration system. Remember, financial advisers have bosses, and their bosses, like yours, expect them to produce.

If it hadn't already existed, financial planners would have had to invent the idea of Retirement. Think about it. The easily hyped anxiety of never being able to prepare enough for an eventuality that we haven't clearly envisioned has convinced large numbers of people that they need to "save" ever-increasing amounts of their current income. Because businesses aren't planning for their Retirements, they can focus their energies on meeting today's challenges in ways that improve tomorrow's strength. Businesses do undertake long-term projects, but the returns and the costs, the upsides and the downsides, and the pros and cons of such projects are rigorously debated before scarce resources are committed. Money manager VALIC has come up with a simple way to think through how much money you're going to need for Retirement (available on its interactive Retire Net Web site www.valic.com). Its "easy gap calculator" projects current retirement Investments and compares them to future income needs. As VALIC states, "the results can be astonishing:" Assuming a 5 percent annual pay hike, a 40-year-old currently earning $75,000 will be earning about $250,000 by retirement. To retire comfortably, the VALIC calculator assumes that our young executive will need between 70 and 80 percent of his or her final working income and thus estimates that he or she will require between $175,000 and $200,000 each year.

Much of what currently passes for retirement planning seems akin to launching a vaguely defined business venture, in a not very well-understood market, the funding of which will require an investment of something like 20 percent of every year's projected cash flow for the rest of the business's working life. When was the last time you proposed to your boss or the members of board that they go forward with such a project? In the business world, making long-term investments without regard for short-term cash flow (in the Life Business sense, both personal and family energy, as well as money) is a guaranteed strategy for losing those 5 percent annual increases and, perhaps, even your whole salary. In the Life Business world, its an effective strategy for ending up burned out, "unmerged" (i.e., divorced), or emotionally bankrupt. Clearly the businesslike approach to this challenge lies somewhere else.

By looking at Retirement planning from a businesslike perspective, we see that real Retirement costs don't go up or down depending on your current income. Costs go up or down depending on what you want to experience and achieve and how you want to spend your money to make these things happen.

What is your Vision of your "Retirement Business?" How much will it cost in constant dollars to fund this Vision? What things can you do now to test the validity of this Vision? What can you do now to build the skills and networks necessary to be successful in this Business? Moreover, what can you do now to lower the eventual energy, time, and money costs of implementing this Vision and get more Retirement for your resource Investment? This is a businesslike thought process.

The focus on Retirement is only the visible edge of the financial services underlying strategy, which is to get you to save more. The rallying cry goes something like this—Americans ought to save more because it's good for our futures, it's good for our character, and it's good for our country. This obsession with saving (or feeling guilty about not saving) is now being challenged by popular and academic business writers.

In an article entitled "Are You Saving Too Much," in *Money* magazine, Jean Sherman Chatzky talks about her readers increasingly feeling "retirement poor."[1] Chatzky says that money-management advisers and pundits are always congratulating their clients and readers for "maxing out" their contributions to their retirement plans. Maximum 401K contributions often bring with them the "opportunity cost" of postponing important life-enhancing decisions such as the purchase of a better home in a better school district. Feeling somewhat guilty about her own role in pushing people to save more, Chatzky's rather New Age advice is "to be as deliberate about spending as you are about saving." She advises her readers to set life goals as well as retirement goals. She reminds them not to shortchange the bar mitzvahs and the kitchen renovations. She ends by quoting one repentant planner as saying, "What difference does a nice retirement make if you've been on austerity for 30 years?"

Looking at the issue of saving from a more macroeconomic level, *Business Week* columnist Margaret Popper argues that contrary to perceived wisdom, a country's "ability to fund investment doesn't depend on it's own savings."[2] Popper observes that despite the fact that the U.S. household savings rate averaged 3.1 percent from 1996 to 2001, the lowest among major industrialized economies, our domestic product grew at an average rate of 3.6 percent, the highest of all of our country's major economic competitors.

Financial markets are becoming global, and the attractiveness of our economy and stock market pulls money in from all around the world. Increased financial market deregulation, freer international trade, and the improved quantity and quality of information ensure that quality investment opportunities will attract international capital. In this environment there is no necessary connection between a country's savings rate and its economic growth. Witness Japan's 1 percent a year growth rate as compared to its average household savings rate of 11.4 percent in the years between 1996 and 2001. The cultural imperative to save appears to have outlived its reason for existence. Today the act of household saving appears to be neither patriotic nor unpatriotic; rather it now seems to be "apatriotic."

For those of us with a cash-flow agenda, the most important challenge to the cult of saving comes from three academic economists, Laurence Kotlikoff, Douglas Bernheim, and Jagadeesh Gokhale. They advocate attaining, as young as you can, "the highest possible standard of living that you will be able to maintain for the rest of your life."[3] These economists call this idea "life-cycle smoothing." They argue that "really good times never make up for really bad times." Smoother from start to finish is better. The implication of this proposed economic principle, supported by an ungainly array of regression equations and reams of statistical analysis, is that you should neither shortchange today for tomorrow nor tomorrow for today. In this perspective saving is worthwhile as long as it helps you to even out your standard of living over a lifetime. On the other hand, if you live to save, then spending becomes contingent on what you have left after saving. This is antithetical to good economics wherein "spending is the main event, not an afterthought." The real purpose of both saving and borrowing is to underwrite a higher level of Investing in yourself over a lifetime.

Life-cycle smoothing is a difficult act to pull off for young people who run up against significant borrowing constraints. They most often don't have a means of securing loans that would allow them to borrow against the future to raise their current standards of living. By implication younger people should be saving less than they are currently being advised to by popular software packages like Quicken Financial Planner. And what they don't save they should spend according to some kind of overall life plan, (e.g., the Life Business Program). Life-cycle smoothing is a new idea in financial management discourse and has yet to have any significant impact on the thinking or behavior of financial planners. However life-cycle smoothing has recently received the endorsement of such heavy lifters as economist Stephen Ross (MIT) and economics Nobel Laureate Franco Modigliani.

A New Look at Allocation

Allocation theory holds that, up to certain levels of return, you are going to experience less Volatility (up and down market movement) and earn higher returns on your placements, if you divide your holdings among stocks, bonds, and cash than if you keep all your money in any one of the three. Financial planners equate Volatility with Risk and don't like their customers to experience a lot of the "V" word. The Risk they may be thinking about is the Risk to themselves, because portfolio Volatility can translate into persistently angry and often hostile clients. Life Business thinking holds that people are never at Risk financially unless they find that they don't have the money they need when they need it, no matter how much Volatility they experience in the meantime. Do you care if your money moves up or down or all around if it is very likely to be there when you need it? Financial planners care. They have seen too many clients who haven't thought enough about what they want money for and when they want it. It's a sure thing that if you don't yet know what it is that you want to do or how much it will cost or when you'll need the money, financial Volatility is indeed a scary ride.

The Life Business concept of Allocation differs from that of the financial service industry. Theirs is a top-down concept built on empirical data telling you what's best for a wealth-creation strategy. Ours is a bottom-up concept built on your understanding of how much money you'll need and when you'll need it. You should only be concerned about Volatility when it has a good chance of upsetting your well-laid plans. The farther out in time your need to access your funds, the less significant Volatility is as an issue. Since financial performance records have been kept, over the long term, stocks have nearly always outperformed every other type of placement. Who cares what's happening to our stash today if we aren't planning to access it for the next 7 years? Choose the placement that is going to give you the highest possible chance of having the money you need ready when you need it. The Allocation you want for your long-term needs is going to be something like stocks (100%), bonds (0%), and cash (0%).

But you also have Medium- and Short-term needs for returns from your placements. The closer to today your planning horizon, the more Volatility becomes an issue. You don't want to have to cash in part of your portfolio when it is in the process of diving lower. Money required in 0 to 3 years should largely be in cash or a cash equivalent such as a certificate of deposit. This would give you a 0- to 3-year Allocation of stocks (0%), bonds (0%), and cash (100%). For money needed from your placements in 4 to 6 years, you can afford a little more Volatility for a little higher return, say, stocks (50%), bonds (30%), and cash (20%). Remember these are rolling periods. Each year some funds will move forward into the next nearest planning cycle.

Following the Life Business approach you will have a different Allocation of resources for each of the three time periods in your 10-year plan. In this way you will have the best chance of having the funds you require in each planning period.

Allocation in Action

When your Life Businesses need money depends on what you want to achieve and when you want to achieve it. Your 10-year Projection is the source for knowing what you need and when you need it.

Let's look at Sandy's financial summary, or financial planning database, gleaned from her projections in Step 11. It shows when Sandy needs money, how much she needs, and how much she has.

Sandy's Financial Summary

What can we tell from Sandy's financial summary? First of all we see that with fairly conservative assumptions Sandy is going to be able to "make her nut." These assumptions include being able to return to a job after 2 years of "Roaming" similar to the one she left; earning 6 percent on her surplus funds from year 7 on; being able to put aside $21,000 ("Funds accrued") during the Medium term; being able to contribute the maximum annually to her IRA when she's not Roaming ("Tax-deferred funds"); and being able to borrow $29,500 at 9 percent to make Roaming possible ("Borrowed funds").

Sandy's Financial Planning Database, Showing When Funds Are Needed, How Much Is Needed, and How Much Is Available

Time Frame for Funding	0–3 Years	4–6 Years	7–10 Years
• Support expense	7,564	13,076	12,111
• Business investments	77,963	95,155	136,276
• Loan: interest/principal	12,530	0	33,550
Total Funds Required	98,057	108,231	181,937
• Income	83,260	137,724	98,839
• Funds at start	4,075	278	44,370
• Funds accrued from revenue	0	14,000	7,000
• Placement income*	0	599	5,395
• Borrowed funds	11,000	0	29,500
Total Funds Available	98,335	152,601	185,104
Finances at END of Budget Period†	278	44,370	3,167
Tax-deferred funds at START of budget period (not including employer pension)	4,250	4,686	14,882

*From funds held in stocks, bonds, and/or cash
†Spreadsheet subtotals and totals subject to rounding error in units place.

What does Sandy want? First, Sandy wants to decide how to Allocate her funds effectively. Later she will need to choose specific stock, bond, and money market vehicles within the Allocations she decides are right for her. She knows that she has to choose her own preferred Allocations because she's the one who best understands how much money she needs to have and when she needs to have it.

Sandy will be choosing two different Allocations because she has different financial requirements for her taxable funds and nontaxable (IRA) funds: a Short- and Medium-term time frame for her taxable funds and a Long-term time frame for her tax-deferred funds. Sandy will consider specific placements when we discuss role clarification below. For Sandy her immediate decision about Allocations is largely academic. She doesn't really expect to have any surplus funds ($278!) in the current planning period. Her Projection assures her that she won't need to tap her IRA account, and so she wants these funds placed for the Long term. The chart below represents Sandy's Allocation decisions for the taxable and tax-deferred assets she has today, not those she expects to have later.

Sandy's real challenge is not how to Allocate her assets but, instead, how to find the best way of borrowing the funds she needs to "make her nut." She's considering taking out low-interest student loans, switching to low to zero percent interest rate credit cards, and asking Peter if she can tap his prime rate equity line for a specific period of time. Saving any of the 9 percent interest that equity line loans might cost her improves her already tenable situation. Borrowing, not Allocating, is Sandy's most important financial planning challenge.

Sandy's Current Allocations

	0–3 Years		4–6 Years		7–10 Years	
Allocations	*%*	*$*	*%*	*$*	*%*	*$*
Stocks	0	0	0	0	100	4250
Bonds	0	0	0	0	0	0
Cash	100	4075	0	0	0	0

Cy's Financial Summary

You may remember from Step 12 that Cy receives nearly all of his current income from an annual IRA payout without penalty (the "72T" disbursement protocol). Cy has calculated that he needs about $60,000 per year to cover his Support

Life Program Participant Cy's Financial Planning Database, Showing When He Needs Money, How Much He Needs, and How Much He Has

Time Frame for Funding	0–3 Years	4–6 Years	7–10 Years
Total Funds Required	180,000	201,600	301,056
Placement income*	225,000	231,750	315,030
Total Funds Available	225,000	231,750	315,030
Net +/-	45,000	30,150	13,974
Tax-deferred funds (IRA) at start	1,500,000	1,545,000	1,575,150

*From funds held in stocks, bonds, and/or cash

Expenses and Business Investments. Cy guesses that because of inflation his expenditures will increase about 12 percent moving from one 3-year planning period to the next. Cy expects to spend about 5 percent of his tax-deferred reserves annually. Cy's biggest Life Business concern is how to get more "life" from his assets, not how to build a larger bottom-line Financial Net Worth figure. This having been said, Cy wants to manage his funds carefully while he comes to grips with the possible futures his assets might afford him.

To cover his 0- to 3-year expenditures, Cy decides to keep $30,000 in his money market checking account; put $30,000 in a certificate of deposit that will mature (pay out) in 6 months; and buy two $60,000 Treasury bonds, the first maturing 1 year from today and the second maturing 2 years from today. Cy is

Cy's Current Allocation of $1,500,000

Allocations	0–3 Years %	0–3 Years $	4–6 Years %	4–6 Years $	7–10 Years %	7–10 Years $
Stocks	0	0	50	100,800	100	1,118,400
Bonds	100	180,000	50	100,800	0	0
Cash	0	0	0	0	0	0

employing a similar "bond ladder" strategy for 50 percent of his cash needs in years 4 to 6. Each year he will take the next year's required cash out of his Medium-term stock holdings and use it to replenish his bond fund. Cy can make these arrangements either through his broker or through a mutual fund.

As they move through the financial planning process, Sandy and Cy need to increase their understanding of Diversification and Risk.

Diversify within Your Equity Portfolio

Businesses pay attention to their dependence on various suppliers and try to make sure they have alternative sources should there be a disruption in a part of their supply chain. This is to ensure that production and, by implication, revenues and profits are not disrupted by any sudden changes. Your financial assets are suppliers of cash flow to your Life Businesses, so you need to make sure those assets are adequately diversified to protect your Life Enterprise against changes in the financial markets.

Of course, equally attractive stocks can have different profiles. There are companies that are attractive because of how fast they are growing their revenues and others that are attractive because of the value they represent in terms of the cost of the stock relative to its underlying assets. Some of these growth and value stocks are large companies, others are medium and small. Some are headquartered in the United States (domestic/global), and some outside (international). Some of these companies are involved in the new economy; others are stalwarts in the old. And remember here we are talking about only good, attractive, alternate placements.

Once you have determined your preferred balance among placements in stocks, bonds, and cash for each of your three planning periods—Short, Medium, and Long term—you need to diversify your stock portfolio within these time frames in order to protect yourself against fluctuations in the value of your holdings.

In your Medium-term time planning period you need a balance of these different orientations within your stock holdings. To leave one group out is to put yourself at the mercy of an inconsiderate market. Despite what you might have been told, no one knows who tomorrow's winners or losers are going to be among today's quality stocks. Better to cover the bases.

These considerations go out the window for Long-term planning. Over a 10-year period there is almost no difference in the relative performance of growth or value stocks! This also holds true between international (no U.S. stocks) and domestic (only U.S. stocks) portfolios.

Manage Your Risks

One of our medical industry clients gave us the following idea when he commented that most otherwise healthy people can survive a significant problem involving one of their major organs, skin, heart, lungs, kidneys, or liver, but things start getting real tricky when two major organs are compromised.

The recent downward spiral of world stock markets reminds us that it's not always going to be "business as usual." What happens to your Short-, Medium-, and Long-term Projections when you assume a 30 percent drop in equity values? This collapse has just occurred for most of us. Now what happens when you add another significant problem on top of this? Say you or your wife experiences a major illness, one of you loses your job, you have to relocate because you have been transferred, or one of your older children needs a helping hand or returns home to live for an indefinite period.

If, under these conditions, your "boat still floats" (i.e., your Dreams are still realizable assuming probable future returns on your placements and continued earnings), you indeed have achieved independence from your finances. One way to protect your Life Business Plan against a "double organ" contingency would be to fund it at 70 percent of your most likely funding capacity so as to cushion yourself in case of a 30 percent drop in the value of your portfolio. Another way to accomplish the same thing is to set up an Emergency Line that could tide you over. This is our preferred solution. We prefer Emergency Lines to Emergency Funds because, by borrowing rather than saving up for emergencies, you are siphoning off fewer of the assets you have available to achieve your Plan.

We suggest that you always have an Emergency Line in place and that you set it up when times are good. The old saying is true here: "When you don't need it, you won't have any trouble getting it, and when you do need it, don't even bother asking." With your Emergency Line in place think positive. Historically in the stock market what goes down comes back up and then goes even higher. If you plan for the lowest point on the Volatility curve, you will end up with a severely "overcapitalized" (too much money doing too little) life. Pitch your plan to average results, don't panic when stocks plummet, and don't lose your focus when returns head for the sky. Like Aristotle, go for the Golden Mean, moderation in all things.

There is a Risk that you won't get as much out of your assets as is possible. You've done your Plan-Ahead Budget and your Long-term Projection, and you find that you have a whole lot more Resource than you have Support Expenses and Business Investments. Your first conclusion is that you are even better off than if your Resources had only just covered your needs. Think again. This is an old-paradigm conclusion. The Life Business conclusion is that you are running the Risk of leaving opportunity for additional satisfaction on the table, including the satisfaction that comes from helping family, friends, and the broader society. If you were a business, it would be like having resources lying around that were not being leveraged to generate profits. In Life Business terms your additional Resources are not helping you achieve higher levels of satisfaction. Even worse, though you aren't getting the value from these resources, it still takes your energy and time to husband them. In working with some of our high Financial Net Worth clients, we have found that having more than enough Resources often presents a significant existential challenge. Sometimes the last barrier to becoming independent of your finances lies in overcoming having more than enough Resources, rather than less!

A final word on Risk. If a financial planner proposes to Allocate your funds on the basis of your answers to a risk profile questionnaire that includes a question such as, "What percent loss to your portfolio would cause you to lose sleep?" look up, put your papers away, politely say good-bye, and leave. Your sleep should have nothing to do with your money. If you know what you want to achieve, what funds you'll need to make it happen, and set your Allocations accordingly, you'll sleep just fine. If you lose sleep over the roller-coaster ride your portfolio might well take, you've lost your way in the Life Business process.

Clarifying Your Role in the Money-Management Process

You're the CEO of your Life Enterprise. Do you also want to be the CFO (chief financial officer) or would you just as soon delegate these responsibilities to a full-time professional and hold that agency accountable for meeting the Goals that you set? If you decide to keep the execution of your resource plan "in-house," there are two other important considerations. Which of your Management Team members should have this responsibility, and what is going to be his or her remit?

Jack is a Life Business participant who loves to dabble in the market—he has, not entirely incidentally, a "happy gambler" Internal Management Team member. Marie, his wife, is concerned that Jack's somewhat gung-ho approach to managing their financial portfolio may not be compatible with the achievement of their chosen Dreams. Through our work together Jack began to appreciate the difference between resourcing his and Marie's Life Business Plan and playing gotcha in the stock market.

Finance and speculation are two different things. One is not better or worse than the other—they are just two different things. You can't have as much fun testing your stock-picking and market-timing prowess if you need to think of individual or family cash-flow issues at the same time. Alternatively, it's kind of scary to see someone bet the farm when you were planning to live on it!

Room can be made for both. In Jack and Marie's case, they decided to set aside a sum of money each year for Jack to challenge himself in the market. At the same time, they developed a comprehensive mutual fund program designed to meet their Short-, Medium- and Long-term cash-flow needs (respecting both Allocation and Diversification considerations). In essence, Jack is now managing an exciting and legitimate New Venture in the context of his and Marie's larger enterprise. It's horses for courses. Jack is happier and more productive in running this smaller piece of the action than he had been when he felt financially responsible for the whole shooting match.

When it comes to executing your Life Business Plan resource Strategy, here are your choices: (1) Choose your own financial placements; (2) choose someone or a group who then chooses your financial placements; or (3) choose someone or a group who then chooses someone who chooses your financial placements. (Note that we use the word "placement" where the financial planning industry uses "investment" because in Life Business terminology an "investment" is a resource specifically dedicated to making a particular Life Business Project happen, not something you do to grow your money.)

Choosing Your Own Financial Placements

If you have a member of your Internal Management Team who has a Motivated Talent for the portfolio management process—for analyzing, executing, monitoring, and living with the tactical responsibility—then, by all means, let him or her have a go.

As in all choices consider the "opportunity costs." Spending your time and energy managing your portfolio means that you are not spending your time and energy doing something else. On the other hand, if portfolio management proves to be a Motivated Talent, then you will do it more efficiently than an activity that you are not motivated to do. Keep in mind that because you are good at something does not mean that it's a Motivated Talent. A Motivated Talent provides it's own energy. If you are employing a Motivated Talent, you will get enjoyment from doing the task. Even then the question still remains as to whether or not, bottom line, you get as much reward from exercising this Motivated Talent as you would another. If you manage your portfolio yourself, your expenses will be your trading costs through a discount broker, computer gizmos, software, and the cost of refreshments for late night vigils.

Delegating Your Financial Placements to Someone Else

This could be a stock picker or a mutual fund. They both do the same thing; that is, working from your description of your Goals, and an agreed Allocation and Diversification strategy, they try to get you what you've said you need, when you need it. This relationship gets worked out face to face with the individual stock picker and on the Internet or through a questionnaire with a mutual fund group. The difference these days between a professional individual stock picker and a mutual fund is around $100,000. Most individual stock pickers won't be interested in your account unless you have got at least $100,000 to put into play. Stock pickers go by different titles, but many stockbrokers, financial planners, and financial consultants fall into this category.

You have done your homework. Having gotten this far in the Life Business process, you know (1) what you want money for, (2) how much you want, (3) when you want it, and (4) how much you have now. The individual stock picker will be impressed, or if it's a mutual fund, it'll at least be a whole lot easier to fill out its complex questionnaires. Money managers dream of clients like you and rarely see them in real time. And despite some of the shenanigans they can get up to, most professionals really would like to be helpful if only their clients could give them an inkling of what real help might look like. Congratulations, you can.

Stock pickers should cost you something like 1 percent annually on assets invested, over and above trading charges. Mutual funds can cost you anywhere from 1.5 to 5 percent annually, but they pick up the trading costs. Some mutual funds have no up-front charges, others have a sales charge, and still others levy a charge when you sell. If you plan to keep a fund for more than 4 years, it's possible to pay nothing but annual charges.

Delegating Your Financial Placements to an Agency that Reassigns Them to Specialists

You are going higher up the food chain here. If you've got $200,000 to plunk down, you can get help that traditionally has been available only to individuals or corporations who want to place $1 to $5 million. Merrill Lynch, Prudential Bache, Edward Jones, and other large brokerage houses all have what they call *wrap accounts*. These contracts are called wrap accounts because you pay one fee, a percentage of the assets under management, and it covers all your costs. Basically these brokerages have contracted with a stable of investment advisers, each a specialist in a specific "investment" strategy. These groups of investment advisers have been chosen because of their track records. Their strategies range from Federal bond ladders to emerging economies and speculative growth and every stop in between.

Once you agree to the ground rules with the brokerage's agent (see our discussion above), these respected money managers give your account a degree of individual attention. Because of the rigorous selection process used by the brokerages, regardless of the returns you realize, you can reassure yourself that you've employed the best outside resource available to you. The primary problem with the wrap account is that each of the money managers manages in a style that best suits his or her skills. If one is a large cap growth manager, he or she usually stays totally invested in large cap growth stocks. Once you chose the manager and put down your $200,000, you'll get the particular manager's approach until you decide to cash out. When times are good for, say, large cap growth, you do well. When times are bad for large cap growth, your only choices are to stay, get out completely, or partially liquidate your account. Sure you'll be advised to diversify when you sign up, but after that, even if you have allocated across several wrap accounts with different strategies, there isn't anyone around taking an overview and suggesting when you should shift funds from one wrap to another. Still, if an 8 percent return floats your boat, you don't care of you ever earn a penny more, you really are tired of thinking about money, you want minimum hassle, and you like the feeling of having the benefit of a good deal of due diligence, this approach could work.

Expect to pay between 2 and 2.5 percent annually on up to the first $1 million placed. This approach has become quite popular, and as a result your Risks may be increasing. First of all, since most of the big money managers are now involved through the auspices of one brokerage or another, there is the danger that you end up getting nothing more than you might have achieved with a less costly mutual fund. Second, be aware of nonaffiliated financial planners who operate a similar approach but add on another 1 percent or so to cover their oversight of your account.

Monitoring Your Progress

Once you've established and started to carry out your Life Business Plan, you'll want to decide how best to monitor your progress. Depending on your needs, concerns, employment situation, and experience, what is monitored, how often it is monitored, and the level of detail will differ from one reader to another.

Harry has a lot of confidence in his ability to estimate how things are going. He feels that an annual review of expenses and revenues meets his needs. Harry carries out his annual review each spring when he is putting together his tax return.

Sandy finds sorting through a lot of account summaries and credit card statements confusing and overwhelming. She feels more confident that she knows how things are going if she gets ahold of her expense information "at the point of purchase." Sandy has modified her check register so that she can record all her expenditures (check, credit card, cash) when they occur. She also uses her modified check register to distinguish between Support and Business expenditures. She summarizes these data monthly and reviews her performance against her Plan-Ahead Budget at the same time.

As a self-employed consultant, Peter has variable income. He is most concerned about his cash-flow situation and whether or not he has realistically estimated his monthly liquidity needs. To keep a handle on his situation, Peter generates a monthly liquidity statement covering all his tax-deferred and taxable financial assets. This report includes both funds committed and receivable. Peter produces a second monthly report showing how his financial assets are currently "allocated" among value and growth, international and domestic, large and small capitalization stocks, as well as among stocks, bonds, and cash. Otherwise Peter reviews expenditures against Budget on a quarterly basis and refreshes his 10-Year Projection annually.

Peter and Sandy have their own incomes and line item commitments. They use a common credit card for shared expenses such as food, entertainment, and travel. This credit card was issued to Peter, and he writes the check to cover the monthly bill. Otherwise, Sandy contributes to the cost of utilities, pays the cell phone bill, and has the cost of Peter's health insurance deducted directly from her salary. In order to keep these cross-payments straight, Peter and Sandy produce a monthly "reconciliation" spreadsheet and exchange checks to reimburse whoever has come out on the short end.

You'll probably want to track at least (1) how much you spend against your Budget targets, (2) how much you earn against your income targets, (3) whether Projects set out in your Plan are achieved, delayed, or abandoned, and (4) the effect of Project performance on your sense of progress. You may find that you evolve a "looser" approach to monitoring as you become more confident in your Plan and feel more on top of how things are going. But even if it's only a gut check, don't forget to reflect on your progress.

For those of you who, like Sandy, feel you want a reliable and seamless way of tracking your expense data from when they happen to how they affect the performance of your budget and projection, we are developing a software package for handheld devices that will allow you to review your performance against Budget, having entered your expense data just once at the point of sale (see our Web site, www.lifebusiness.com for details).

Summary of Life Business Money Management

What it all boils down to is that you are going to have to retrain your personal financial consultant to respond to your own definition of your priorities and the kind of assistance that you will require. Whether or not you choose to work with a financial planner, keep the following summary of Life Business money management ideas in mind:

- Focus on improving your life's Net Worth, not your money's.
- Invest to realize your key Life Business Dreams after having committed the bare minimum needed to fund your Support Expenses.
- Continue to squeeze resources out of Support Expense, and Invest these found resources in the achievement of your Life Business ambitions.
- Budget your energy, time, and money annually to enable your Life Business Goals.
- Strive to meet your Budget—it's problematic to be over or under.
- Project your Budget over at least 10 years to establish a modeling environment in which you can experiment with the implications of nearly limitless choices.
- Strive to have a "0" in the last bottom right cell of your Projection—its problematic to be over or under.
- Understand that any combination of earning and saving and/or borrowing that gives you the cash flow that enables you to live your Life Business Dreams is just fine.
- Understand that your only real financial Risk is not having funds available when your Dreams require them.
- Understand that the right Allocation of your assets is determined by the funds you need and when you need them.

Conclusion

A recent article in *Money* magazine offered readers the opportunity of comparing their spending habits with those of other Americans.[4] Encouraging readers to think of their "finances much the way an analyst views a company's financial statement," the article quotes a financial planner as saying that "the key question is how much of your income is being transferred to your balance sheet—that is, into assets that will increase your [financial] wealth." At first reading this seems like Life Business–type advice and right on target. But, as in psychotherapist Albert Ellis's characterization of neurosis, this true statement is often followed by a false one. In this case, the implied and false statement is that your real wealth is your financial wealth. It is on this second and false premise that much of the financial services industry concentrates. Consciously or unconsciously many financial planners are still working to get you, their client, to focus on growing your money rather than your lives.

A business's balance sheet contains the value of all its physical plant and real estate, managerial and technical talent, market relationships and brand identities, products in the market and on the drawing board, as well as its net financial assets. Applying this idea to your own life, clients who invest their financial assets in the development of their own and their loved ones' current experience, skills, and happiness can be seen as increasing their own value and the value of the collective family enterprise. This is the way real Net Worth is built.

Notes

1. Jean Chatzky. "Are You Saving Too Much?" *Money*. November 15, 1999, p. 232.

2. Margaret Popper. "Low Savings? Big Deal." *Business Week*. May 20, 2002, p. 60.

3. Peter Coy. "A Smooth Financial Ride." *Business Week*. November 15, 1999, pp. 284–286.

4. Walter Updegrave, Rob Turner, Joan Caplin, "How Are You Doing?" *Money*, July, 1999, pp. 62–74.

Epilogue: Life Business in an Age of Abundance and Anxiety

I see the corporate ideal as a confederation of individuals . . .

—*John Harvey Jones, Chairperson, ICI, 1982*

In the late nineteenth century, the Supreme Court held that corporations were entitled to all the due process rights and privileges provided to individuals under the Fourteenth Amendment. Now early in the twenty-first century, the Life Business Program provides individuals with the conceptual and practical tools that the best corporations use to become productive and profitable enterprises. Life Business is a way of thinking whose time has come.

Indeed, the Life Business Program can be seen as the "owner's manual" that accompanies the American freedoms of "life, liberty, and the pursuit of happiness" proclaimed in our Declaration of Independence.

It gives you a way to:

- Review the past and to understand where your life satisfactions and dissatisfactions are coming from and what your real financial situation is (Step 1).
- Formulate the key themes in your life and to define them as Life Businesses—those important areas of Commitment that help structure and give meaning to your life (Step 2).
- Evaluate whether those Commitments are providing the satisfaction you want in life; and how you are using or misusing your inner resources to produce these results (Step 3).
- Identify the important dynamics and issues in the web of relationships that support and constrain your Life Enterprise as well as forecast the future Trends and Events that will impact your Life Businesses (Step 4).
- Create a detailed positive Vision of your preferred future (Step 5).
- Decide on Strategies for your Life Enterprise: which Life Businesses to wind down, to maintain, to grow, and to start (Step 6).

- Determine your Goals and develop heartfelt Projects that will achieve them (Step 7).
- Prioritize and sequence these Projects into Short-term, Medium-term, and Long-term Commitments (Step 8).
- Understand the financial dimensions of your Life Enterprise and free yourself from the outmoded ideas which constrain your financial choices (Step 9).
- Budget Commitments of time and money that will allow you to reach your Short-term Goals (Step 10).
- Project Commitments of time and money to Investment and Support expenditures for the Medium and Long term (Step 11).
- Match Life Business Investment and Support needs to revenue sources through a seven-level analysis; find your magic number(s) (Step 12).
- Prepare your Life Business Plan and advance it in relationship with the financial services industry (Step 13).

Invest in Your Life: Make the Choice, Face the Anxiety, Take Responsibility, and Use What You've Learned

Even the most helpful prescriptions come with warning labels about potential side effects. We have said over and over that Life Business is a methodology about discovering and realizing your Dreams. Life Business is also inevitably a program about exercising your freedom to choose how you will spend your energy, time, and money, and to what you will be committed.

We recently met a woman who had been through the Life Business Program some years before. She said bluntly and somewhat proudly, "Because of that program, I got a divorce and went to law school." What she did not say, but was obvious, was that neither of those choices were easy ones to make.

Unfortunately, choice is often accompanied by anxiety and a sense of loss, as well as optimism and a sense of clarity. To choose something is also to leave something else behind. To close a Life Business is to leave a bit of yourself behind, and perhaps to let a once valued part of your identity die. To start a new Life Business is to invest time, effort, and feeling, and to risk failure and frustration as well as to hope for success and greater satisfaction.

Psychologists tell us that in trying to do more of what we want, to be more of who we are, and to get more of what we Value, we are likely to run into inner resistances that will make us anxious. Often these resistances have to do with going beyond the emotional boundaries and rules that were set up for us early in life. These rules might involve the anxiety of succeeding in an area that our parents failed in, or in venturing into an area that is meaningful to us but would not have been valued by our parents, close relatives, or friends.

Such resistances might also include the anxiety attendant to giving up a Life Business that has limited but certain rewards for one that promises much greater rewards, but where the rewards are in fact more uncertain, or we irrationally believe them to be more uncertain. The fact is that daring to Dream and to Commit to realizing your Dreams is bound to make you nervous at some level. It is because of this that most people stick "with the things they have always done," and "get the results they have always gotten." Whole books have been written about "the Escape from Freedom."

By creating a specific Vision and a detailed Plan, you build a specific, step-by-step road map from your current state to your preferred Vision. Having this Plan in hand is bound to make the journey easier. Having people in our lives that understand and support where we are going, and can guide and encourage, is also a big help. Finally, we also draw confidence from the fact that the Life Business Program is drawn from the practices that have created successful businesses the world over.

It all comes down to your Internal Management Team. Do you have the discipline, creativity, courage, and ambition to live your life the way you really want to live it? There is no getting away from the fact that embarking on the Life Business Program is an adventure and a journey. Like all adventures and journeys there can be scary times, especially when we confront the inner fears that hold us back from our full potential. Yet this particular journey IS your life. You owe it to yourself to make the most of it.

Our Abundant and Anxious Times

We are now in the midst of the third great revolution in employment in the United States[1]. When this country was founded, most of us were employed in agriculture. Now only 2 percent of our jobs are agricultural. The industrial era replaced the agricultural one and has been in turn replaced by the information age. The proportion of Americans employed in manufacturing declines every year, and Americans are increasingly working in service jobs.

Global markets have increased competition. Despite rising overall prosperity, new, disruptive technologies have made business conditions more uncertain. Socialism as a system for organizing production has been discredited. Free markets and entrepreneurs are seen as the engines of growth and development the world over.

With these changes have come an end to lifetime employment with (and retirement from) one company and the growing knowledge that we can no longer depend on anyone but ourselves for our economic survival. Job security and income is more and more tied to what you know rather than what you do.

In his 1990 book *Trust Me*, William Morin, principal in the human resources consulting firm of Drake, Beam, Morin, was already advising employees: "Just as your company has a business plan that looks one, two, five years into the future, so you should look ahead by making a personal business plan of your own. After all you are a business that sells certain services to your employer. If you don't plan ahead, you may go out of business."[2]

Ten years later when the dot.com bubble burst, taking with it the "Great Bull Market," many Generation X'ers learned that they couldn't expect dot.coms, NASDAQ or IPO's to provide a substitute source of security. In the 2000 election, both parties fielded plans to privatize aspects of Social Security. The message is clear. In the future we will have both more choice and more responsibility. It is time to become CEOs of our own lives.

Life Business as a Support for Couples and Families

One of the consequences of this new economy and society is an increasing divorce rate signaling that managing spousal relationships is harder than ever. While this book has focused on the Life Business for individuals, it is also true that many couples have benefited from using the Program. Couples work—in Life Business terms— draws on the analogy of the corporate merger. Each individual is encouraged to develop his or her own Dreams and essential Projects, and then these two separate lives are "merged" via Projects and Businesses that are jointly owned and resourced. We encourage couples to merge their Dreams before they merge their finances. Where there is "Strategic" commitment, resources follow easily; when money is merged without strategic commitment, confusion, misunderstanding, and disagreement are often the result.

For each person in a couple then, there is both a realm of wholly owned Businesses (e.g., Sandy's Being & Becoming) in which the life partner is customer and/or supplier and also Life Businesses jointly owned and managed with their life partners (e.g., Harry's and Helen's Teen Bird and Sandy's and Peter's Roaming).

In successfully merged Life Enterprises, couples collaborate in deciding on the timing and amount of "Investment" in both individually owned and jointly owned Life Businesses (e.g., Harry gets bridge night out and time at the gym; Helen gets ladies night out and Yoga class; they put off their foreign travel this year to make possible college trips with the Teen Bird)

Most family psychologists agree that to build a healthy family, it is important for parents to be in charge, set norms of behavior, provide high-level expectations and support for children, and see and value each child individually. Couples who, through Life Business work, have learned to share a Vision, have negotiated their differences in that Vision and made a plan for achieving their Vision, are less likely to be pulled apart on a day to day basis by the demands of work and family Commitments, the manipulation of their children, or other marital stresses. In short, they are aligned with one another and well positioned to lead the family toward its valued Goals.

Life Business for Organizations

The Life Business Program was originally developed to support large organizations such as ICI, Royal Dutch Shell, Procter & Gamble, and British Petroleum in their attempt to adapt to changing economic conditions by helping their employees become more empowered, creative, and proactive.[3]

Individuals who have participated in the Life Business Program renew their individual commitments to organizations in ways that make sense within the total context of their lives. They thus bring more energy to the enterprise, or they decide that their future lies elsewhere and exit gracefully. Here are some examples:

- Mary didn't go for the big job in Atlanta, but instead stayed in Chicago to serve the bank in an entirely new role for which she had real enthusiasm.
- Jena conceived of an important new initiative which got her excited again about her corporate human resources role in a global pharmaceutical company.
- Carl, a first-line manager in a big tech company, found that he needed to put aside his conflicts with his boss and work on doing his job. Performing his job well and maintaining a good work record was more important for him now than winning.
- Phil, an economist, decided that he should stop working for his employer, a large contract research firm, and go independent so that he could realize his Dream of working internationally sooner rather than later.

In addition to clarifying their commitments to their organizations, participants in Life Business Programs understand Strategy, change, and growth at a deep level and can apply what they have learned to business problems. Here are some examples:

- At the end of one program the vice president for strategic planning of a Fortune 500 company said, "Now I finally understand the planning process."

- The head of environmental health and safety for a large chemical company found language and concepts he could use to reposition his entire effort to get greater buy-in from his manufacturing colleagues.
- During one of the early Life Business Programs a group of participants got together and redesigned both their company's career succession and career development processes

By introducing Life Business into their organizations, leaders have not only provided employees with a very tangible personal benefit, but they have created a management cadre and workforce that better understands the process of corporate growth and change and has a common language and experience which establishes the basis for joint problem solving.

Life Business for the Financial Services Industry

The personal financial services industry, including banks, securities firms, insurance companies, financial planners, trust attorneys, accountants, etc., is in full transformation from a fragmented system of services toward a one-stop financial shopping mall. In the rush to be in sync with the flow of the industry, all financial service organizations are claiming to provide ever-more customized services.

It is fair to say that never before have financial services organizations depended more on their professional staff, and never before have these professionals needed more support in the performance of their evolving roles. Yet, as we have seen, the financial services industry is burdened by concepts and frameworks that really do not make a lot of financial sense to a person who has really thought through his or her needs.

Members of the financial services industry need a framework that can genuinely support the market-driven demand to become more customer-focused. The Life Business Program is one such framework. Financial planners who have been through the Life Business Program:

- Have greater insight into the needs and concerns that customers bring to financial planners and investment advisers.
- Are better able to build more authentic, personal relationships with customers.
- Are better able to provide advice that is more responsive to a customer's needs and less influenced by outmoded or self-serving financial planning concepts.
- Are better able to generate new services and new delivery approaches.

While the Life Business model is a tool for the building of an effective organizational culture in general, for the financial services industry it can be the engine for linking the culture of the industry to the customer's key requirement: "Treat me like an individual."

Life Business in Communities: Leaving a Legacy

Conservatives and liberals both believe that the public sphere in our country needs more attention. There are glaring problems in the areas of housing, child care, economic development, health care, environment, and race. In the Life Business Program we have learned that it is not enough to put forward a Vision. You have to resource that Vision with effective Projects and stable Commitments of energy, time, and money.

There also seems to be a consensus for the moment that taxes are high enough and that our top priorities are defense and homeland security. If we do not wish to address these other domestic problems through government, then the only other answer is volunteerism and philanthropy through the work of individuals and nonprofits.

In Life Business terms, when people find that they can fund all their Dreams, take care of their extended family in a way that is consistent with their Values, and still have financial assets left over, then it is time to think of how to create a meaningful legacy for the communities and concerns they care about. Such an activity goes beyond the calculations of the "Charitable Remainder Trust." Though it may ultimately involve such vehicles, it is more the challenge to the individual to find a charitable purpose that connects deeply to his or her own sense of purpose, and, in a businesslike way, use his or her assets to advance that purpose.

This question of legacy is first and foremost a question of Values, a question of what one truly cares about. To answer this question honestly might involve some kind of personal quest designed in a Life Business Program that brings a person into contact with an important community problem. This encounter then translates into a desire to act and to give.

The same question arises for the person who, surveying his or her Life Enterprise, finds that, while their funds are all allocated to important Life Businesses, they still have time on their hands. They may also lack a feeling of connectedness to the community or human involvement. These individuals also have the opportunity to ask the legacy question. While they may not have vast dollars to contribute to some community need, they may have time and skills to contribute through a mentoring program or through a program like Habitat for Humanity or through their faith community. They can create a Life Business that involves giving to the community in a way that can return to them tremendous satisfaction and provide opportunities for personal development.

Envisioning the Life Business Process for a Community

The process described here is consistent with other well-documented community-building projects. As part of its community development and strategic planning process, the residents of 6 neighborhoods known as the "Washington Heights Community," with foundation support, embark on a Life Business empowerment process. Through a series of involving community workshops they produce:

> An Annual Report—which describes the history of their community, the community Businesses (e.g., education, child care, crime prevention) they are in, the current return on those Businesses, and the reasons for that return (e.g., business strengths and weaknesses).
> A Market Report—which details the critical internal and external relationships for their community Life Businesses, the messages they are getting, and the trends and events that could help or hurt their community enterprise in the future.
> A Strategic Plan—which sets out a positive Vision for their community, a Strategy for each of their community Businesses, including New Ventures they need to start and a detailed set of Short-, Medium-, and Long-term Projects.
> A Business Plan—which Budgets volunteer resources, institutional Commitments, and funding Investments (including new resources they seek) against these Projects and creates an on-going management process to see the Plan through.

Life Business, Responsibility, and Society

Life Business is a methodology for individuals, families, organizations, and communities to discover and realize their Dreams. It is essentially a democratic philosophy because it assumes that all people are entitled to have positive Dreams of the future and to organize themselves in the most effective way to realize them.

Life Business, then, combines freedom and responsibility—the freedom to dream the best Dream we are capable of for ourselves and the responsibility to follow through on that Dream using the best methods of planning and financing that are available.

By applying the same principles to the way we live in our families, organizations, and communities, we can be responsible in another way as well: taking care of what are the common Dreams of all rather than limiting ourselves to the Dreams of an individual. As Rabbi Hillel said 2000 years ago, "If I am not for myself, who will be for me? If I am for myself alone, what am I? And if not now, when?"

Life Business Meditation

You are the CEO of your life.
You are the business owner.
Your Life Business is yours to mind and no one else's.
You are the principle investor.
You are the attractor of investment.
You are the investment.
You are the return on that investment.
You are the present value.
You are the net worth.
You are the estate.
   And, finally,
Your life is the legacy.

Notes

1. See the discussion in recent work by Ted Halstead and Michael Lind, *The Radical Center: The Future of American Politics*. Doubleday, 2001.

2. William J. Morin. *Trust Me*. Drake Beam Morin, 1995, p. 35.

3. Jaap Leemhuis, John Eckblad. "Planning Doesn't Stop at the Top." *Training and Development Journal*. 1985, pp. 62–63; Dennis Bumstead, John Eckblad. "Meaning Business: Values in the Workplace." In David Clutterbeck (ed.) *Tomorrow's Working Patterns*. Gower, 1985; Dennis Bumstead, John Eckblad. "Developing Organizational Cultures." *Leadership and Organization Development Journal*, 5/4, 1984.

4. This process is consistent with a variety of well-documented community-building processes, including the ICA process, the Future Search, the Asset Based Development Approach, and the MDC's Vision to Action Model, yet adds the explicit link with business planning models, which should help in engaging the corporate community as well as the nonprofit and government agencies that are often the key players in such programs.

Your 12-Month Expenditure Analysis

The following expenditure analysis and your reflection on your expenditures will enable you to employ your financial resources successfully in support of your chosen Life Business Goals. Couples may want to do the following analysis either individually or as a team, depending on how they currently organize their finances. Do the analysis the way that feels most efficient.

Expense Analysis Procedure

In order for you to completely understand where your money is currently going, please review your check registers, bank statements, and credit card statements for the previous 12 months and record your expenses on the enclosed House-hold Expense Schedule and the Overall Expense Worksheet. Once you have entered your expenses, total them across categories and by month.

Table A-1   Household Expense Schedule

Months	1	2	3	4	5	6	7	8	9	10	11	12	Totals
Food													
Services (e.g., housecleaning etc.)													
Furnishings													
Equipment (e.g., appliances etc.)													
Clothes													
Transport													
Personal (e.g., toiletries etc.)													
Children													
Alimony													
Child support													
Leisure													
Entertainment													
Support of parents													

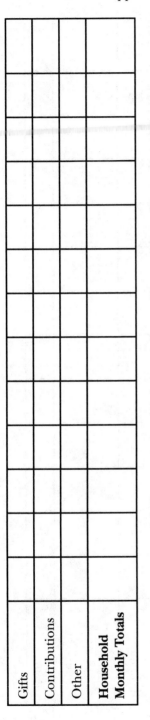

Gifts			
Contributions			
Other			
Household Monthly Totals			

Table A-2   Overall Expense Worksheet

Months	1	2	3	4	5	6	7	8	9	10	11	12	Totals
Rent/ mortgage													
Telephone													
Electricity/gas													
Water													
Installment 1													
Installment 2													
Education													
Real estate taxes													
Income taxes													
Insurance													
• Home													
• Life													
• Auto													

Appendix A: Your 12-Month Expenditure Analysis

Medical												
Dental												
Savings												
Enter Household Monthly Totals (from previous table)												
Other (itemize on separate sheet)												
Monthly Totals												

Reflections on Expense Analysis

1. When you look over what you have put down, what are your immediate thoughts or feelings?
2. Do any specific expenses seem surprisingly low or high? Which ones?

The Life Business Concept Quiz

Circle the letter of the response that most clearly states the Life Business definition of the following terms and concepts.

1. Your Net Worth is:
   a. The net dollar value of your financial assets less your financial liabilities.
   b. The cost of opening and operating an Internet account.
   c. The amount of money you need to put aside in order to ensure a long and rewarding retirement.
   d. Your bottom-line assessment of how well your life is going at any given moment considering your joys, your challenges, your sorrows, your concerns, your plans, your hopes, your values, your skills, your needs, and your relationships.

   Scoring:

   a. −5 points; the classic "things as they were" definition.
   b. & c. 0 points; congratulations, you haven't learned the classic definition of net worth, so you won't have to unlearn it.
   d. 10 points; you've got it! Now use it as a foundation for the rest of the quiz (and the rest of the book; indeed, the rest of your life!).

2. Cash flow is:
   a. What happens to the money you earn every month. At the end of the month the proper term is *cash flew.*
   b. The technical term for what corporations do to hide their debts and diddle away their employees' retirement funds.
   c. The sum total of money that you require on a daily basis to fund your Life Business Investments and meet your Support Expenses. This is a much more important concept to your personal and family well-being than Financial Net Worth.

d. The cash you have available to you after liquidating your stock, bond, and real estate portfolio.

e. A silly word not recognized by most computer spell-check programs.

Scoring:

a & e. 0 points; not entirely untrue, but entirely unimportant.

b. –5 points; try to rediscover your quiet spot—you appear to have a bad case of Enronitis.

c. 10 points; you are indeed financially independent if you've got the cash you need when you need it. It is, in fact, entirely possible to have a very high Financial Net Worth and be in financial trouble because you don't have the cash flow you require. This is called a "liquidity problem," and it can hurt like hell.

d. 5 points; this is true. But you can also guarantee the cash flow you need through the judicious use of OPM or other peoples' money—that is to say, by borrowing.

3. Financial Risk is:

a. That scary, undefined thing that, if you have too much of, will keep you from sleeping.

b. Not having the money you need when you need it.

c. The same thing as stock market volatility.

d. A concept that has triggered an enormous amount of hype, anxiety, and due-diligence activity.

Scoring:

a. 5 points; yeah, OK, but what is it?

b. 10 points; you'll experience no risk at all no matter how volatile stock and bond prices are if you always have the funds you need when you need tbem.

c. 0 points; so your funds are experiencing extreme volatility. (If you're still 7 or more years away from needing the money, funds placed in growth stocks today may well minimize the risk of there not being enough money to meet your needs when the time comes. Equity investments have nearly always outperformed less volatile, fixed income instruments over periods of 7 years or more.)

d. 5 points; a few points for paying attention and having a modicum of healthy cynicism.

4. The purpose of a Budget is to:
   a. Enable your dreams while taking into account current financial realities.
   b. Keep track of where my money went last year.
   c. Keep track of where my money is going this year.
   d. Establish targets and then keep track of where my money goes.

Scoring:

   a. 10 points; the elegant and essential statement. Budgets are designed to enable the goals and objectives we want to reach.
   b. & c. 5 points; we're being generous here. "Keeping track" is important, but it's only the beginning of the budgeting process.
   d. 7 points; this choice is only as powerful as response *a* when targets are driven by heartfelt goals and financial objectives that enable these goals.

5. Saving is:
   a. Your patriotic duty.
   b. The only way you can get enough money to retire.
   c. About rightsizing your expenditures.
   d. A matter of depriving yourself of things you really want today for things you really want tomorrow.

Scoring:

   a. –10 points; tell it to the Japanese whose high domestic savings rates were for years the envy of national planners and now are the lament of the world's economic observers and at the core of the so-called Asian crisis.
   b. –5 points; more hype, this time generated by the financial planning industry, as deenergizing and disempowering as saving for God and country.
   c. 10 points; this is it. Putting money aside for a rainy day is not saving (nor is it investing, unless of course you just love rainy days and have really exciting things you want to do when it rains.) Saving is wringing energy, time, and money resources out of line-item expenditures while continuing to achieve desired outcomes.
   d. 0 points; can be, but shouldn't be. Savings come from "rightcosting" what it is that you chose to do, not depriving yourself of what you want.

6. Investing is:
   a. Not putting money away for an undefined rainy day.
   b. Putting as much money as you can into your 401K pension (or similar) so that you'll be able to retire at 70 percent of the average of your last 3 salaried years.
   c. The same as saving.
   d. Putting energy, time, and money into increasing your personal and family Net Worth, as Life Business Net Worth is characterized in question 1 above.

Scoring:

   a. 5 points; for paying attention while we were discussing the idea of saving.
   b. –10 points; a particularly pernicious form of putting money away for a rainy day. Whose retirement? Change jobs, avocations, how you spend your time—what is retirement other than finding a more appropriate, more interesting, or more meaningful way of carrying on with your life? What is it you want to do? When do you want to do it? How much energy, time, or money is it going to take to do it? The answers to these questions form the specification we use to determine our investment requirements.
   c. –5 points; see scoring for question 5c.
   d. 10 points; saving provides funds to invest; investing puts your funds to use supporting the achievement of your Life Business projects. Achieved projects bring you closer to realizing your goals. Meeting your goals increases your Net Worth. Budgeting keeps your plans on target. Voilà, you've got a life.

7. Borrowing is:
   a. To be avoided by all means possible.
   b. Your patriotic responsibility.
   c. A legitimate money-management option.
   d. A good idea at any cost.

Scoring:

   a. –5 points; old think.
   b. –5 points; you may be confusing borrowing with the popular, though also incorrect, notion about saving.
   c. 10 points; borrowing is often the most cost-effective way to provide you and yours with the resources you require to fund your Life Business

Plan. In business accounting, funds borrowed appear on the asset side of the ledger.

d. −5 points; you're not alone here. The personal debt rate in the United States is staggering and usually not undertaken to achieve Life Business goals, or managed effectively using businesslike thinking.

8. Asset Allocation is:
   a. The hook of the popular song "Allocation, allocation, allocation."
   b. The be all and end all of personal and family financial planning.
   c. A financial planning concept that states that how you distribute your funds among stocks, bonds, and cash will have a bigger influence on how much return you achieve than which stocks you put your money into.
   d. One single set of percentages indicating how much of your money you should hold in stocks, bonds, and cash.

Scoring:

a. 0 points; you might be thinking of "Location, location, location."
b. −5 points; you might well have thought so from how financial planners have placed this idea front and center in their discussions with clients. The truth of the matter is that it demonstrates good "due diligence" to help clients find their appropriate levels of comfort with Market Volatility through employing Asset Allocation techniques.
c. 2 points; the classic definition.
d. −10 points; you need at least three different asset allocations to reflect your different cash-flow needs for the Short term (0–3 years), the Medium term (3–7 years), and the Long term (7+ years).
e. 10 points; a process whereby you allocate funds to stocks, bonds, and cash so as to take advantage of stock market volatility and reward in order to achieve the cash flow you need when you require it.

Score summary: Congratulations! You are an instant winner. A score of −40 and above suggests that you are getting a lot out of reading this book.

INDEX

About the Authors and
Life Business International

John Eckblad (johne@lifebusiness.com, jeckblad@mindspring.com) concentrates his work on developing effective families, organizations, communities through enhancing individual focus. John is the president of Life Business Development Corporation (est. 1978) and Life Business International (est. 1986) and has sat on the boards of two European corporations. John has been a presenter, session chair, and national conference designer for the American Society of Training Development (ASTD) and the Society of Manufacturing Engineers. He is a recipient of ASTD's Outstanding International HRD Practitioner Award.

John is a coauthor (with Wout de Leeuwerk and Mary Hebrank) of the management book *At the Heart of the Business* (Kluwer, 1986), which describes a comprehensive organizational and cultural change effort in Royal Dutch Shell in the Netherlands. He is the author/coauthor of several book chapters and numerous journal articles (in *Construction Economics, The GRTA Journal,* and *The Training and Development Journal,* among others).

John received his Ph.D. in organizational psychology from Case Western Reserve University in 1972 and taught organizational behavior for three years at the Ecole des Hautes Etudes Commerciales in Paris. For twenty years he worked in Europe, where he cofounded the consulting group People & Potential Ltd. and consulted with numerous international corporations including Procter & Gamble, Royal Dutch Shell, and ICI.

John has served as President of Orange County's Habitat for Humanity and was a member of the County's Affordable Housing Task Force. John and his wife Susan live in Chapel Hill, North Carolina. Together they have six children.

David Kiel (davidk@lifebusiness.com, dkiel@mindspring.com) has been involved with the Life Business™ concept as a workshop leader, program designer, marketer, and writer since 1991. He is an organizational consultant whose projects focus on strategic planning, organizational design, team building, leadership development, and conflict resolution.

He has consulted with managers and management teams in IBM, Glaxo-SmithKline, Westinghouse, and Nortel. A former professor of Public Administration and Public Health, he has also worked with numerous government and non profit organizations including the National Governor's Association, USEPA, the National Congress of Community Economic Development, UNC Health Care, and the Instrument Society of America.

His work in the last ten years has featured assistance to innovative economic development organizations like the NC Rural Center, the NC Indian Economic Development Initiative, and NHS of Chicago. David is currently involved in forming a new program for faculty leadership development for the Institute for the Arts and Humanities at UNC Chapel Hill.

David studied organizational behavior at Yale University and received his doctorate from the UNC School of Public Health in 1974. His articles have been published in *The Public Administration Review, The Training and Development Journal,* and *Environmental Quality Management.* David is a member of the NTL Institute for Applied Behavioral Science He lives in Chapel Hill, NC with his wife Amey Miller and their daughter Rachel.

Life Business International (www.lifebusiness.com)
212 E. Rosemary Street, Chapel Hill NC 27514

By agreement with the Life Business Development Corporation, Life Business International markets Life Business™ materials, develops new business opportunities and certifies and licenses trainers and consultants to present the Life Business™ Program worldwide.

™Life Business Development Corporation.